Voices of the Arab Spring

Voices of the Arab Spring

PERSONAL STORIES FROM THE
ARAB REVOLUTIONS

Asaad Alsaleh

Foreword by Peter Sluglett

COLUMBIA UNIVERSITY PRESS

NEW YORK

Columbia University Press
Publishers Since 1893
New York   Chichester, West Sussex
cup.columbia.edu

Copyright © 2015 Columbia University Press
All rights reserved

Library of Congress Cataloging-in-Publication Data

Alsaleh, Asaad.

Voices of the Arab Spring : personal stories of the Arab revolutions / Asaad Alsaleh.

pages cm

Includes bibliographical references.

ISBN 978-0-231-16318-7 (cloth : acid-free paper)—ISBN 978-0-231-16319-4 (paperback : acid-free paper)—ISBN 978-0-231-53858-9 (e-book)

1. Arab Spring, 2010– –Personal narratives.   2. Political activists—Arab countries—Biography.   3. Arab countries—Biography.   4. Protest movements—Arab countries—History—21st century.   5. Revolutions—Arab countries—History—21st century. 6. Political participation—Arab countries—History—21st century.   7. Social change—Arab countries—History—21st century.   8. Arab countries—Politics and government—21st century.   9. Arab countries—Social conditions—21st century.   I. Title.

DS63.12.A57 2015

909'.097492708312—dc23

2014019952

COVER IMAGE: © ALEX MAJOLI/MAGNUM PHOTOS
Cover Design: Martin Hinze

*For all the fallen heroes of the Arab Spring
who no longer can tell their own stories.*

CONTENTS

FOREWORD

UNDERSTANDING RECENT SOCIAL AND POLITICAL DEVELOPMENTS IN THE MIDDLE EAST AND NORTH AFRICA: A PERSONAL ODYSSEY

Peter Sluglett

For most of my adult lifetime, the news from the Middle East has been almost uniformly gloomy. Until quite recently, it seemed that the Arab world was unable to leave behind its postcolonial trauma. There were some exceptions: for a while in the 1950s and early 1960s, Arabs now in their sixties and seventies had a window of hope. Nasser and his Free Officer colleagues took Egypt out of British control and set it on a path that seemed to be moving toward the recovery of national dignity and independence, overthrowing the monarchy in July 1952 and nationalizing the Suez Canal in 1956. That same year, unable to bear the expense of maintaining control over all three of its North African possessions, France gave independence to two of them, Tunisia and Morocco. In July 1958 in Iraq, a military coup that became a revolution overthrew the monarchy and established a republic. In July 1962 a long and bloody colonial war in Algeria ended with the defeat of France and the independence of Algeria. These were indeed heady days, and I think that except for the hopes raised and so soon dashed for the Iranian revolution in 1979, nothing of such moment, and certainly nothing promoting such optimism, happened in the Middle East between the early 1960s and 2011.

Historians tend not to try to guess what may or may not happen in the future. As I sometimes say to tease my colleagues, we leave that sort of speculation to political scientists. That said, however, I am not very optimistic about what may happen in Syria, still less about the international community's being able to do anything especially positive there. Because of the way the United Nations is set up and a fairly widely held belief that states should not intervene in the internal affairs of other states, it is almost bound to fail the people of Syria in much the same way it failed the people of Sarajevo in the early 1990s.[1] Furthermore, there are few indications that Libya is emerging from the chaos that it inherited from Colonel Muammar al-Qaddafi. In Egypt, I imagine that the definition of an optimist is someone who thinks that Field Marshal Abdel Fattah el-Sisi will be or is an improvement on ex-president Hosni Mubarak.

Growing up in England in the 1950s and 1960s, I believed that the world was a dangerous place, the main issue being the ever present, if always somewhat distant and unreal, possibility of nuclear annihilation as the result of a planned or accidental confrontation between the United States and the Soviet Union. As I grew older, though, it became increasingly clear that this was not going to happen. Nonetheless, one of the principal manifestations of the Cold War was a series of proxy and regionally bounded wars fought by clients of the superpowers. These usually took the form of "quarrels in far away countries between people of whom we know nothing," to echo the assertion by British prime minister Neville Chamberlain on Hitler's takeover of the Sudetenland, part of Czechoslovakia, in 1938. Some of these "far away countries" were in the Middle East, although as Fred Halliday reminds us, the proxy wars in that part of the world generally had many fewer casualties than did those in many other Cold War conflicts: "For all its participation in a global process, and the inflaming of inter-state conflict, the Cold War itself had a limited impact on the Middle East; in many ways, and despite its proximity to the USSR, the Middle East was less affected than other parts of the Third World."[2]

Despite these relatively modest casualty figures, the Cold War had deep, lasting, and traumatic effects on the Middle East. Apart from prolonging the region's de facto colonial status, the United States' and the Soviet Union's constant struggle for influence polarized and/or anesthetized political life in most Middle Eastern countries, facilitating the rise of military or military-backed regimes and generally stunting or distorting the growth of indigenous political institutions. The superpowers' various clients also contributed generously to the region's destabilization by attempting, with some success, to involve their patrons in the local conflicts in which they were engaged.

It is often alleged that democracy has no "natural" roots in the Middle East, or in the Muslim world in general, and hence the growth of democratic institutions is impossible and should not be expected. But the Ottoman Empire had a constitution in 1876; Tunisia, in 1881; Egypt—sort of—in 1882; and Iran, in 1906.[3] Also, as is clear from events in the Arab world since 2011, it is absurd to pretend that Muslims or Arabs or any other people are inherently antithetical to democracy or incapable of embracing democratic institutions. On the contrary, Asaad Alsaleh believes that allowing individuals to express themselves in written narratives, collected here in *Voices of the Arab Spring*, will cause many readers to reassess the potential for social, political, and cultural change in the Arab world.

Only two countries, Turkey and Israel, have functioned continuously since the 1940s as more or less recognizable parliamentary democracies in which the rule of law has generally prevailed and the opposition has won parliamentary elections and then become the government. Even here, though, the record is not spotless, given the number of military interventions in Turkish politics and the fact that about one-third of Israelis have no say whatsoever in the most basic aspects of their governance. In addition, during the period between the two world wars and immediately after 1945, there were, albeit within limits, lively and contested parliamentary elections in Iran, Iraq, Syria, and, in some sense, Egypt.[4] There also was a spirited anticolonial and anti-imperialist movement led by local communists and leftists.

What these leftists were actually advocating, or what they did achieve in the limited arenas in which they were able to take charge, was quite modest and restrained: the creation of trade unions, the fundamentals of compensated land reform, the nationalization of leading industries, a free health and welfare program, and so on. In fact, with the exception of land reform, almost exactly the same goals were prominent on the platforms of almost all Western European social democratic parties.

Regardless of what they could or would have done had they ever come to power, in the 1960s and 1970s the communists and the Marxist left in the Middle East were increasingly persecuted and driven underground. This group included most of the leading intellectuals of the day and, perhaps most important, most of those who could not be bought and/or co-opted by the regimes that subsequently came to power. The influence of these courageous individuals on the cultural life of their countries and the region as a whole and on its political culture was, and has been, paramount and lasting.[5] For the most part, leftist or left-leaning regimes were replaced by more or less vicious forms of national socialist dictatorship or, in the case of Iran under the shah, by an autocracy that became increasingly less benevolent as the years passed. The CIA and British intelligence were behind the coup that overthrew Iran's prime minister, Mohammad Mosaddegh, and restored the shah in 1953. Perhaps less well known is that the CIA was behind the coup that overthrew 'Abd al-Karim Qasim in Iraq in February 1963. The CIA also had been in touch with members of the Ba'th party, probably including Saddam Hussein, on the grounds that the Ba'thists were both the "force of the future" and virulently anticommunist.

Perhaps the most unfortunate general consequence of this fear or hatred of local communists and leftists was that the *secular* opposition was driven underground almost everywhere in the Middle East. In such circumstances, participating in "politics" either became extraordinarily dangerous or degenerated into sycophancy. Opposition to, or criticism of, the regimes or the leader's policies became tantamount to treason and could be punished as such. As a result, any remaining opposition gravitated toward various religious organizations, since governments in Islamic countries could not close down mosques. This, then, was one of the major consequences of the Cold War in the Middle East. Even though the Soviet Union has collapsed and the Cold War has ended, the scars that this conflict left on the region will not go away quickly.

The fall of the Soviet Union did not, however, end either the regional conflicts or American support for authoritarian regimes, both republics and monarchies. The Israeli-Palestinian conflict continues; the Lebanese civil war ended in a temporary truce rather than a permanent settlement; and none of the region's governments have taken any significant steps toward democratization.

In 1971, Syria began moving toward what was thought to be economic liberalization, taking modest measures that were meant to encourage wealthy Syrians to repatriate capital from abroad; the terms became more generous after 1973 when foreign exchange controls were more or less abandoned. In the 1980s, the country adopted various structural adjustment plans and liberalized the agricultural economy, at least partly reversing the land reforms of the early 1960s, so that individuals could once again own large estates. In 1991, law 10 permitted Syrian and foreign investors to invest in virtually any field of the Syrian economy, and they were given a tax holiday for seven years.[6] Nonetheless, there was no political "opening" under either Hafez al-Assad or his son Bashar. Indeed, the much vaunted Damascus spring of 2001—the hope that Bashar's accession might bring about a more open and pluralistic society— rapidly turned into a Damascus winter,[7] and of course, far worse has happened since. Much the same is true of Morocco, when Mohammed VI succeeded King Hassan II in 1999. There was great excitement at the prospect that the new young leader would bring with him change and democracy, but it soon became clear that it was to be more or less business as usual.

Sunnis and Shiites have not always been enemies. In Iraq until the early 1960s, education and the expansion of state employment went a long way to close what was most visibly (though not always) a poverty gap between Sunnis and Shiites. And in the secularizing atmosphere of the 1930s and after 1945, intersectarian marriage between members of the rising middle classes was not uncommon. It was the seizure of power by the Ba'th Party, first in 1963 and then permanently after 1968, that made the pernicious, atavistic, and primordialist doctrine of pan-Arab nationalism a permanent part of state ideology. In its manifestation in Iraq, Ba'thist pan-Arabism became a Sunni phenomenon in that it identified Sunni Iraqis as "Arabs," and thus full members of the rest of the Arab world, whereas Shiite Arabs were regarded as foreigners, *'ajam*, Persians or of Persian origin. Not much of this really mattered until the Iranian revolution in 1979 and the war between Iran and Iraq that broke out in 1980. At this point, the Ba'thists began to portray the Iraqi Shiites as potentially pro-Iranian sympathizers or traitors and to perpetuate the myth that they were "really" Iranian. For example, men were offered financial inducements to divorce their Shiite wives, who then were deported to Iran.

Eventually, the danger that the Iranian revolution seemed to represent to Saddam Hussein and his government turned almost all Iraqi Shiites into potential enemies of the Iraqi regime and was a major reason for Iraq's war with Iran, which lasted for most of the 1980s. Sunni-Shiite hostility continued after the war. Iran's Republican Guard took terrible revenge after the American- and British-encouraged uprising/*intifada* against the regime in southern Iraq in 1991, which was followed by the forcible uprooting of much of the population of the southern marshes.[8] For much of the rest of the period until the American invasion, the Shiite opposition was sectarian rather than religious; that is, it was generally a reaction to discrimination against Shiites by the regime rather than a religious platform as such.

When the Americans invaded Iraq in 2003, they set up a largely pro-Iranian government in Baghdad (that is, composed mostly of people who had sat out the 1980s and 1990s either in London or in Teheran as guests of the Iranian regime), from which Sunnis—not all of whom had been well treated by Saddam Hussein and his circle—felt completely alienated. Although some de-Ba'thification was necessary, it should have been selective rather than wholesale, since not all Sunnis were implicated in the terrible crimes of the old regime. Moreover, Ba'th Party membership was obligatory for those holding a position above a certain level in any state organization, including seemingly innocuous institutions like hospitals and university departments.

Lebanon, as well, seems to be riven by what appears to be sectarian strife. Here the problems are somewhat more deeply rooted than those in Iraq, but the underlying causes are not dissimilar. V. P. Gagnon's book *The Myth of Ethnic War* (about the former Yugoslavia) is very helpful in explaining the phenomenon of sectarianism, particularly how people who have lived next door to one another for years, intermarried, collaborated politically, and so on, suddenly turn on one another. Violence of this sort almost always takes place during a hiatus or transition after the state has collapsed and a relatively ordered past has given way to a suddenly uncertain future.[9] Journalists and others often explain the conflicts in Iraq, Lebanon, or Yugoslavia as representing the unleashing of ancient ethnic hatreds that were never far below the surface. But in fact, ethnic or sectarian hatreds are not essentialist, permanent, or monolithic and, in most cases, are not primordial or spontaneous but almost always are refashioned, reorchestrated, and reinvented each time by those who want to use them, whether they are Saddam Hussein, Samir Geagea, or Slobodan Milošević.

Let me turn now to the events since the end of 2010. What were the reasons for the Arab Spring, and why did it begin at the end of 2010? Except for Saudi Arabia and northern Yemen, which were never colonized directly, most Arab states had emerged from colonial rule by the end of the 1950s (Bahrain and the United Arab Emirates as late as 1971). These postcolonial states were fairly weak, and their institutions (whether republican, monarchical, parliamentary, or military) had been established or reinvented more to serve the interests of the colonizers than those of the colonized. The weakness, or relative autonomy, of these states meant that they were extremely vulnerable to seizures of power by disaffected elements in the armed forces. Consequently, a series of military dictatorships were established through a number of coups d'état, especially at various times in Algeria, Egypt, Iraq, Libya, Syria, and Yemen. Some of these states have oil and/or natural gas, and some do not. In the oil-rich states of the Arabian peninsula and in Libya, because the indigenous populations are relatively small, the day-to-day functioning of the economy is dependent on migrant workers, most of whom are hired on fairly draconian, short-term contracts. For much of the second half of the twentieth century, unemployment or lack of opportunity in, say, Jordan or Egypt, was made bearable by the availability of relatively well paying work in Iraq or the Arabian peninsula. But when the price of oil plummeted in the 1990s, the number of these openings steadily declined. At almost exactly the same time, neoliberal policies and the "Washington consensus" meant that the poorer states in the region had to stop subsidizing basic foodstuffs and to dismantle, or greatly reduce, their welfare structures, which meant that while some of the rich got richer, most of the poor got poorer, and their social safety net gradually disappeared.

One feature common to many Arab regimes, both monarchies and dictatorships, until comparatively recently has been their generally close and cordial relationship with the United States. For this reason, the United States has found it difficult to criticize, for example, the Bahraini government's treatment of demonstrators against it because Bahrain is the headquarters of the U.S. Fifth Fleet. Similarly, the unrepresentative family-run regimes in Saudi Arabia and most of the Gulf states also have escaped criticism from the United States, with a few exceptions. Until it agreed to give up its weapons of mass destruction in 2003, Libya's relations with the West were fairly hostile; and Syria (with its long-standing relations with Iran and its support for Hezbollah) was regarded as a pariah by most Western countries well before 2011. In contrast, although the United States and Iraq fell out over Iraq's invasion of Kuwait in 1990, this rupture was preceded by more than a decade of cordial relations between the two states.

A country's closeness to the United States has had remarkably little effect on whether it was utterly dictatorial or partly democratic, that is, whether it upheld the rule of law and had a government that could be voted in or out by some form of universal suffrage. Jordan, Lebanon, and Morocco upheld such principles from time to time, but in general, democracy in the region has been conspicuous by its absence. This was the case in those states close to the United States (Bahrain, Egypt, Saudi Arabia) and in those much further from its good graces (Iraq, Libya, Syria). Why has some form of democracy so far eluded the Arab world? There are probably five main reasons.

First, the necessity of protecting the "free flow of oil" to the West has historically trumped other considerations, including what might be generously described as the more "humanitarian instincts" of the United States. Almost all Arab oil goes to the United States, Europe, and Japan, so whether the exporting states were either dictatorships or "family enterprises" mattered far less than their ability to ensure the delivery of oil and gas.

Second, during the Cold War, the United States' and the local regimes' obsession with the potential dangers of "communism" led the states themselves to drive the "democratic left" into exile, prison, or worse and promoted the notion that maintaining the status quo was the least risky course of action. Later, particularly after the attacks on September 11, 2001, dictators like Mubarak and the monarchs of the Arabian peninsula fine-tuned their discourse, claiming that while their regimes might be a little harsh, they were effective in stemming the tide of Islamic extremism. More recently, Egypt's Field Marshal Sisi and his supporters were making much the same argument.

Furthermore, the richer states were able to buy off the opposition through extensive welfare programs, the creation of public-sector jobs, and payments to their more politically aware citizens to keep quiet or stay abroad.

Third, the "postrevolutionary" states in the region have continued to be worried by the democratic left, largely because of the left's brave if futile insistence on some form of democratic accountability. In contrast, most Arab nationalism has been chauvinistic and promoted blind obedience to the leader. Long after the ideology lost any popular resonance, the leaders (or their sons) have remained implacably in power. As a result, without opposition from the left, the focus of such movements shifted to "Islam." Although Islamic political movements were harassed by the various states, the states could not completely eliminate opposition from that quarter because, again, Islamic states cannot shut down the mosques. Also, beginning with the siege of the Great Mosque in Mecca in 1979 and continuing with the assassination of President Anwar el-Sadat of Egypt in October 1981, some Islamic movements turned to violence, including suicide bombings and attacks against civilians, which, as the perpetrators intended, terrified both the regimes and their patrons.

Fourth, the monarchs and dictators have been quite successful in convincing both friend and foe that they are the only ones capable of stemming the tide of fiercely anti-Western Islamic movements, which surely would emerge in the event of any openings toward greater political liberalization. In fact, of course, "Islamic movements" are political organizations like any others, and they appeal to different constituencies, so to write them all off as dangerous extremism is, at best, highly misleading.

Fifth, second only to its concern about the free flow of oil has been the U.S. desire to defend what it takes to be Israel's interests, which often have not been entirely congruent with those of the United States.[10] The fact that the conservative Arab states have either treaties or "understandings" with Israel and that both the monarchies and the "revolutionary states" have almost completely lost interest in the Palestinians is perfectly fine for many of those concerned.

Now we might ask, Why now? Obviously, the revolution in communications technology has been a major factor, but there are others. The median age in Egypt is twenty-four; in Syria, twenty-two; in Tunisia, thirty. Unemployment is extremely high, even for young people with university degrees; the cost of living is constantly rising as a result of higher world food prices; social, educational, and health services are declining as a result of neoliberal economic policies and privatization; and some of the dictators and monarchs are old and/or ailing and are trying to pass the baton to their sons (Egypt, Libya).[11] There were earlier signs of significant dissatisfaction, including the Kifaya movement (*kifaya* means "enough" in the sense of "we have had enough"), which began in Cairo in 2005, and many Iranians joined the Green movement in 2009, which took the form of large demonstrations against the reelection of Mahmoud Ahmadinejad, which was widely, though perhaps inaccurately, believed to have been rigged. Some people claim that the origin of the current movements in the Middle East was the Iranian Revolution of 1979, but this seems a bit far-fetched.

In the spring of 2014, it is difficult to say where all this might be going, given that in all liberation movements, people generally agree more on what they do not want than on what they do want. In addition, many of the authoritarian regimes have been far more resilient than their subjects or outside observers had anticipated. In any case, democracy at least holds out the possibility of a better life than the citizens of this troubled region have long been obliged to endure. Of course, it will not be straightforward, and it will take time—far more time than the young people who spilled out onto the streets of Cairo and Tunis had hoped. According to Asaad Alsaleh,

> Although we cannot be certain about the immediate stability of the countries of the Arab Spring or even of the entire region, it is almost impossible to imagine that the future rulers will be facsimiles of Qaddafi or Mubarak. Indeed, I believe that the same people who contributed to this book would rise up again if any future leader turned into a new dictator.

The removal of the dictators will not, by itself, fix their countries' shattered economies, and in some places (the Gulf states, Bahrain, Saudi Arabia, and Syria), authoritarian regimes are still firmly in place. The military's overthrow of the elected government in Egypt—however maladroit and incompetent it may have been—can be described only as a setback. At first I thought that the magnitude of the support for change in Egypt would mean that there could be no turning back; now I am not so sure.

In *Voices of the Arab Spring*, Asaad Alsaleh has assembled a remarkable collection of testimonies of the events from late 2010 to mid-2011, which also recount the repression that preceded them. In a curious way, though, this book offers a message of hope, and perhaps cautious and realistic optimism is the best course of action for those of us observing from a distance.

NOTES

1. See Mark Mazower, *No Enchanted Palace: The End of Empire and the Ideological Origins of the United Nations* (Princeton, NJ: Princeton University

Press, 2009); and John J. Mearsheimer, "The False Promise of International Institutions," *International Security* 19, no. 3 (1994/1995): 5–49. Also see Noel Malcolm, *Bosnia: A Short History* (New York: New York University Press, 1996), 234–71.

2. Fred Halliday, "The Middle East, the Great Powers, and the Cold War," in Yezid Sayigh and Avi Shlaim, eds., *The Cold War and the Middle East* (Oxford: Clarendon Press, 1997), 16.

3. Matthieu Rey, "Un parlementarisme oriental? Eléments pour une histoire des assemblées au Moyen Orient des années 1850 aux années 1970," *Parlements: Revue d'histoire* 17 (2012): 162–76.

4. Matthieu Rey, "Le parlementarisme en Irak et en Syrie, entre 1946 et 1963: Un temps de pluralisme au Moyen-Orient," Ph.D. diss., École des hautes études en sciences sociales, 2013.

5. For a discussion of the activities of such individuals in Iraq, see Orit Bashkin, "Advice from the Past: 'Ali al-Wardi on Literature and Society," in Jordi Tejel, Peter Sluglett, Riccardo Bocco, and Hamid Bozarslan, eds., *Writing the Modern History of Iraq* (London: World Scientific Publishing, 2012), 13–24.

6. Bassam Haddad, *Business Networks in Syria: The Political Economy of Authoritarian Resilience* (Stanford, CA: Stanford University Press, 2012).

7. Alan George, *Syria: Neither Bread nor Freedom* (London: Zed Press, 2002).

8. See Hamid al-Bayati, "Destruction of the Southern Marshes," in Fran Hazelton, ed., *Iraq Since the Gulf War: Prospects for Democracy* (London: Zed Press, 1994), 141–46.

9. V. P. Gagnon, *The Myth of Ethnic War: Serbia and Croatia in the 1990s* (Ithaca, NY: Cornell University Press, 2004).

10. See John J. Mearsheimer and Stephen Walt, *The Israel Lobby and US Foreign Policy* (New York: Farrar, Straus & Giroux, 2007).

11. Roger Owen, *The Rise and Fall of Arab Presidents for Life* (Cambridge, MA: Harvard University Press, 2012).

ACKNOWLEDGMENTS

This book would have been impossible without the contributors, who come from five Arab countries with various revolutionary experiences. They kindly agreed to share their stories and viewpoints in writing, allowing me in the process to intervene numerous times for clarification and editing. Although some gave up, others patiently continued to work on producing this document, which contains their fresh memories of both exciting and anxious times. I am deeply grateful to them, for their belief in the value of such a project and for opening my eyes to the state of their countries and the grandeur of human resistance in face of oppression. They are the heroes of the book (one Yemeni participant was on the phone with me while explosions were taking place in his neighborhood). To them I would like to say: words of appreciation cannot express my admiration for all of you. Because of you, my quest for the book material has a happy ending!

While working on this book I have been fortunate to find many generous people who provided a great deal of encouragement and assistance. I would like to acknowledge everyone who contributed to the book by giving advice, providing personal contacts, and showing enthusiasm. I am sincerely grateful to my colleagues at the University of Utah's Middle East Center, particularly

Peter Sluglett, Peter von Sivers, and Hakan Yavuz. Their scholarship provided inspiration, and their guidance substantively enlightened my academic focus. June Marvel read all the stories and provided many intelligent corrections, and so did the university writing fellow, Sheena Mugavin. My friends Leonard Chiarelli and Raymond Hain gave invaluable time to discuss and read portions of the book.

My graduate students at the center have been also an inexhaustible source of inspiration as they engaged me in their intellectual interests and were always delighted to know about mine. Ben Smuin and Tatiana and Feras Klenk tried to connect me with potential contributors overseas, and no matter what the outcome was, they never stopped cheering for the project.

I would like to thank Maria Dobozy and Joseph Metz for their tireless support of my academic endeavors on this book and beyond. Gary Atwood and Christine Jones critically read a substantial portion of the book and made very helpful suggestions. I greatly benefited from the insights and guidance of my lifelong mentor, Joel Gordon, whose work as a scholar and director of the Middle East Center at the University of Arkansas has not prevented him from answering my calls for help. Special thanks go to Nadine Sinno, who always saw this project as a reality. My appreciation also goes to Anne Routon and her staff at Columbia University Press for seeing this book through to completion.

Voices of the Arab Spring

Introduction

The power of the people is greater than the people in power.
—Wael Ghonim, creator of one of the Facebook pages that
started the call for the Egyptian revolution

This book tells the personal stories of individuals who participated in the Arab Spring, written by the activists and participants themselves. These stories offer readers a deeper understanding of the motives, activities, and lessons learned from the revolutions that swept across the Arab world in late 2010 and toppled dictatorial regimes in Tunisia, Egypt, Libya, and Yemen. The forty-six narratives reveal the multifaceted dynamics that brought about dramatic and appalling changes in the history of the modern Arab world. Written mostly by young Arabs, these accounts give voices to the people who lived under regimes that long oppressed them and describe the social, political, and historical context of the Arab Spring. The participants' emotional, psychological, and cultural foundations and assumptions add a human element to concepts of narrative and social movements that reflect real-life experiences. Besides giving an account of the uprising, each writer explains his or her personal and collective reasons for wanting to start a revolution against the regime.

Voices of the Arab Spring is intended for an audience of general readers, scholars, and undergraduate and graduate students and is not meant to provide a comprehensive historical account of the events. Rather, it gives space to individual citizens from the Arab world who were willing to share their reasons for participating in the Arab Spring. And what they present here are not just accounts of their experiences but stories showing the psychological and inner workings—and, eventually, actions—of the marginalized Arab people.

THE ARAB SPRING

During the spring of 2011, revolts started to sweep through the Arab world, and in a few months, revolutionaries mobilized in the phenomenon that became known as the Arab Spring. It rolled through five different countries—Tunisia, Egypt, Libya, Yemen, and Syria—either toppling the government (as in Tunisia and Egypt) or ending in a bloody conflict (as in Libya, Yemen, and Syria). The Arab Spring began with the self-immolation of a fruit vendor in Tunisia. Its last instantiation was a revolution sparked by the imprisonment and torture of Syrian schoolchildren who, emulating the bravado of the people of the Arab Spring, had defaced the walls of their school with antiregime graffiti.

The organizing force behind this string of revolutions was primarily young Arabs who were technologically savvy, politically deprived, and unmoved by the antiquated rhetoric of their rulers masquerading as tribunes for the people. Intersecting with other layers of the population, including Islamists and the labor force, the youth became the leaders in organizing the protest, particularly in Tunisia and Egypt. They were educated and from middle-class families, looking for a better future than what the current order offered them. In Libya and Syria, former regime loyalists, military defectors, veteran dissenters, and tribal leaders also were instrumental in taking over the regime system. But in Yemen, reemerging elements of the old guard outmaneuvered the youth and took control after the revolution. Dictators, who for too long were used to monopolizing the media, found their own messages deconstructed on sites such as Facebook, Twitter, and YouTube, where dissenters could refute the dictators' tired propaganda and summon already antagonized people to act. As the personal accounts of revolutionaries in this volume reveal, these revolts were not random; rather, the Arab people started to resist when the security states slowly began to show their true face, targeting dissenters and buying loyalty through cronyism, nepotism, and brutality.

All the contributors to this book embrace the term, "Arab Spring," that has come to denote these events and their abiding spirit of renewal. Whether "spring" is more appropriate than "awakening," "uprisings," or "upheavals" is still being debated. Many of the contributors trace their decision to join the revolution to January 14, 2011, when Tunisia's President Zine el-Abidine Ben

Ali at last lost his grip on a quarter century of uncontested power and fled the country. Less than two weeks later, Egyptians joined the Arab Spring, forcing President Hosni Mubarak to flee the capital, resign, and ultimately face trial and imprisonment. On the same day, Yemenis launched uprisings against the rule of Ali Abdullah Saleh, who, as a result of a deal brokered by the United States and Saudi Arabia (which maintained the regime without him), eventually resigned. At much the same time, Colonel Muammar al-Qaddafi's brutal response to demonstrators drove the Libyan version of the Arab Spring to turn violent, eventually resulting in Qaddafi's own death. Finally, in Syria, the popular uprising against Bashar al-Assad is still unfolding, albeit with the regime greatly debilitated.[1]

The term Arab Spring was used for the first time, on January 6, 2011, by one of *Foreign Policy*'s most prominent contributors, Marc Lynch, in his article entitled "Obama's Arab Spring." Two weeks later the Egyptian opposition leader Mohamed ElBaradei used the term in an interview with the German magazine *Der Spiegel*. ElBaradei's concluding remarks set the term in its historical context: "Perhaps we are currently experiencing the first signs of an 'Arab Spring' [that is, similar to the Prague Spring of political liberalization in 1968]. Our neighbors are watching Egypt, which has always played a pioneering role [in the region]."[2] The term also had been used earlier, in April 2005, when the U.S. columnist and political commentator Charles Krauthammer employed it on two occasions to describe the Arab world after President George W. Bush announced his "freedom agenda."[3]

At one point, some of the most sensational news stories on the world's media outlets were about the Arab Spring. *Ash-Shabab al-Ghadib*, "angry youth," constituted the main component of these uprisings, reflecting the demography of the Arab world, 60 percent of whose population are under age thirty. Their dissatisfaction with the lack of jobs, stagnating salaries, and authoritarian governments and their desire for political change made them ready to embrace any move toward such a change. As the political scientist Jean-Pierre Filiu observed, anger is "the power for the younger," which is, for him, one of the lessons to be learned from the Arab Spring.[4] All the leaders overthrown by the Arab Spring tried to mitigate or channel, but never resolve, this anger. These leaders' tolerance for civil societies and opposition parties (although Libya had neither) coincided with their selectivity in allowing freedom of speech and expression. For example, while still living in Syria in 2005, the journalist and television host Ibrahim al-Jubayn wrote a daring critique of President Bashar al-Assad and the ruling party.[5] Addressing the president directly, he asked,

How can you tolerate seeing torn-out government buildings clad with rust and burned diesel or even seeing the backward architectural structure while you pass in front of it in your car? How can you tolerate that?! And for whose sake?! You are getting rid of the old guard and starting a new stage. But let's make no mistake: no change will be effective until it comes to replace the tediously boring slogan of the Ba'th party [*wahda, hurriya, ishtirakiya* (unity, liberty, socialism)].[6]

The political scientist Lisa Wedeen describes such spaces of freedom in Syria as "sites of licensed critique"[7] that exist alongside the regime's strict control and surveillance. The literary critic miriam cooke noted that such criticism created *tanaffus*, or breathing space, offering Syrians the "pleasurable release of pent-up pressure."[8] Ironically, because *tanaffus* was permitted in the first decade of Bashar al-Assad's rule, the uncontrolled demand for democratization became extremely dangerous after the Syrian revolution of 2011.

In the years leading up to the Arab Spring, uncensored (and uncensorable) access to news allowed young Arabs, for the first time, to view and compare their conditions with those of their leaders. So, while many young married Tunisians could not afford an apartment, they were able to see Ben Ali and his family members enjoying lavish parties, running several business enterprises, and living in luxurious palaces, news of which not only became the talk of the town but also the subject of unflattering diplomatic correspondence. As WikiLeaks revealed, Robert Godec, the U.S. ambassador to Tunisia from 2006 to 2009, wrote three cables warning of the gross and growing corruption by Ben Ali's family members as "the nexus of Tunisian corruption." Written in July 2009 and made public in the first week of December 2010, one of Ambassador Godec's documents provides an image similar to that revealed by the Tunisian contributors to this volume, except that his account was meant to be top secret. He stated,

Even average Tunisians are now keenly aware of it, and the chorus of complaints is rising. Tunisians intensely dislike, even hate, First Lady Leila Trabelsi and her family. In private, regime opponents mock her; even those close to the government express dismay at her reported behavior. Meanwhile, anger is growing at Tunisia's high unemployment and regional inequities. As a consequence, the risks to the regime's long-term stability are increasing.[9]

If the word "corruption" (*fasaad*) is closely associated with "destruction" (*ifsaad*), then these leaders already had destroyed their integrity through widespread favoritism, bribes, and abuse of influence. The stories in this book make clear that grand and petty corruption became the operational system, making these leaders insufferable to the people of their own countries. One of the popular slogans chanted by Tunisians was "No, no to the Trabelsis who looted the budget," whereas Egyptians chanted, "O Mubarak, O the one who made us poor, tell us what you did with our money." If the Arab Spring has shown us anything, it is that the loss of the ruler's integrity leads to the impossibility of ruling by means of charisma (as Egyptian president Gamal Abdel Nasser did between 1956 and 1970) and to the necessity of ruling by sheer brutality. This situation can lead only to the demise of the regime itself, as such inequities can be tolerated for only so long.

Besides living the last years of their lives off the backs of a population assumed to be comatose with fear, these aging despots were preparing their sons to succeed them. Never mind that their lifelong hold on and planned hereditary transfer of power only deepened the political and economic problems in their countries. Never mind that they violated the democracy framed by their constitutions. Their countries were ruled exclusively by the president and for the benefit of the president and his children. For example, Gamal Mubarak, a son of Hosni Mubarak, president of Egypt since 1981, enjoyed increasing attention in the Egyptian state-run media and was the most influential member of the ruling party. But after the Egyptian revolution removed the regime, Gamal was imprisoned on corruption charges and accused of using his influence to award illegal contracts to foreign companies.

In Libya, the sons of Muammar al-Qaddafi, especially the heir-apparent Saif al-Islam, were often in the news for their boundless influence in matters of state and their abuse of the country's wealth. Their lavish parties in European countries were featured in gossip columns all over the world. But to pave his way toward a grand entrance, Saif al-Islam worked to cultivate the image of a reformer. He even went so far as to respond facetiously to a U.S. congressional aide's question regarding Libya's efforts at expanding democracy, by saying, "More democracy would imply that we had some."[10] Saif al-Islam eventually joined his father and his brothers in their failed attempt to crush the revolt against their father, and he was eventually captured and now faces a war-crimes tribunal.

Ali Abdullah Saleh, the Yemeni president who filled the army and the government with family members and relatives, was likewise preparing his oldest son, Colonel Ahmed Saleh, to become "a serious contender for the office of president upon his father's death or retirement."[11] But Saleh backed away from having his son succeed him, because of the so-called Pink revolution, which started near the end of January 2011, and instead demanded reform rather than regime change. Only when this failed did the people of Yemen rise up to crush this planned succession from father to son and to call for Saleh's departure.

Of the nations in the Arab Spring, only in Syria did the president, Hafez al-Assad, manage to transfer power to his son Bashar al-Assad.[12] When the Syrian revolution began, Ali Ferzat, a prominent Syrian opposition activist and a world-renowned political cartoonist, drew a caricature of President Bashar al-Assad running to the airport with suitcase in hand while his own son (named after his grandfather Hafez) clasps his trouser and pleads, "I don't care. I want to be [the next Syrian] president." Afterward, Ferzat was attacked by Syrian security forces, who kidnapped him and broke his hands. After issuing the message "Do not defame your masters," he was thrown, bleeding, out of their car onto the side of the road.

Another often cited motivation for the uprisings is economic liberalization and privatization, in which the state "opens up" to foreign markets and investment with minimal political interference. The subsequent sale of public enterprises and utilities to opportunists associated with the regime allowed the public to witness firsthand the theft of "their" economy by the regime's cronies. In Tunisia, Egypt, and Syria, this metonymizing of cronyism and neoliberal economic policies became increasingly obvious in the years leading up to the Arab Spring. According to James Gelvin, income inequalities and the denial of both "the benefits targeted to the very poor and entry into the ranks of the very privileged" drove scores of middle-class, professional youth to join the Arab Spring, which also explains "the upsurge in labor activism . . . and the prominent role played by labor in the uprisings in such places as Tunisia and Egypt."[13] As the narratives of this book explain, these conditions suffered by various groups nurtured a culture of despair—an overall sense of hopelessness for a future of dignity, a theme taken up independently by revolutionaries in all five countries.

This was the despair apotheosized by the twenty-six-year-old Tunisian fruit vendor, Mohamed Bouazizi, who set himself on fire on December 17, 2010, in a rural town two hundred miles south of Tunis. Before this desperate act, a popular Arab uprising was not considered possible because of all the regimes' massive security presence. Bouazizi was not a political actor by choice, and he died before he could see his fellow Tunisians and, later, other Arab citizens, take to the streets. Even before Bouazizi, people like him, particularly in Tunisia and Algeria—disenfranchised, struggling to make ends meet—already had practiced self-immolation as an act of self-distancing. Although burning oneself is unacceptable in Arab and Muslim societies, the burning of documents symbolizing one's identity has been recognized as a phenomenon called *harragas*, an Arabic term meaning "those who burn" and referring to young people who burn their identity papers upon their (illegal) arrival in Europe. They burn their identities, so to speak, because they would rather live as illegal, undocumented immigrants than be deported to countries they see as unjust, corrupt, and repressive.

Before and during the Arab Spring, the frustrations of Arab youth with their social and political realities were communicated on the Internet. Communication is a necessity of any revolution, so it is not surprising that social media websites helped orchestrate this unprecedented moment in modern Arab history.[14] Social media also were important to mobilization in other revolutions before the Arab Spring, not the least of which was the 2009 Iranian Green revolution, whose protest movement faced the government-directed blocking of social media and other forms of communication. In the Arab Spring, the private and public spheres merged to create a revolutionary space oscillating between virtual reality—inciting, organizing, and subsequently documenting protests—and actual reality—using the streets and the squares, the long sit-ins, and the jarring intensity of demonstrations. Each reality contributes to the other. For instance, the Egyptian testimonies in this book frequently refer to the popular Facebook page "We all are Khaled Said," a revolutionary space where activists both organized demonstrations and later uploaded their footage, which in turn inspired followers to choose virtual or actual participation or both. Indeed, as the critic Douglas Kellner argues, "If revolution is to have a future in the contemporary era it must incorporate technopolitics as part of its strategy," because using technology for political goals "opens new terrains of political struggle for voices and groups excluded from the mainstream media and thus increases the potential for resistance and intervention by oppositional groups."[15]

Even though it has been more than three years since the Arab Spring began, the future of it and its major players is still unknown. There will be both many political possibilities as well as challenges to the transition from dictatorship to postrevolutionary democracy. Although we cannot be certain about the immediate stability of the countries of the Arab Spring or even of the entire region, it is almost impossible to imagine that the future rulers will be facsimiles of Qaddafi or Mubarak. Indeed, I believe that the same people who contributed to this book would rise up again if any future leader turned into a new dictator. The immediate outcome might well be an unstable, struggling, or partial democracy before these revolutions can achieve their ultimate goal of "overthrowing the regime."

THE VOICES OF THE ARAB SPRING

The idea for this book came to me in the spring of 2011 while I was preoccupied with the news of the Arab revolutions and decided to teach a course entitled Revolution and Literature in the fall semester. With my students, I wanted to explore past and modern revolutions and their role in modern world history, which often was to transform a country and its people from one set of power structures, ideologies, and cultural norms to another. While preparing material for the course, I noticed that although major revolutions like the American Revolution (1765–1783), the French Revolution (1789–1799), and the Bolshevik Revolution (March 1918–November 1918) have been well documented by historians, there were only a few first-person accounts written by ordinary people. One of these few, for the Bolshevik Revolution, is Isaac Babel's short story collection *Red Cavalry*, in which he recounts his own experiences as a journalist accompanying the Red Army during the war against Poland in 1920. For me to include some of the recent and current Arab revolutions in my course would be doubly difficult, not only because of the lack of history in 2011, but also because of the lack of personal accounts of these events. This disappointing situation thus persuaded me to collect personal narratives myself from those who had participated in the Arab Spring, particularly verified testimonies.

According to William Westerman, Archbishop Oscar Romero first defined testimony as the "voice of the voiceless,"[16] and Lynn Abrams maintains that this phrase is one of the intentions of oral history, in addition to giving "narrative to the story-less and power to the marginalized."[17] I know that perceptions of the Arab Spring have already started to change, with an obvious dwindling of enthusiasm. But the mostly optimistic testimonies in this book depict the feelings that emerged at the height of the Arab Spring. That is, these narratives describe two worlds: the one before the Arab Spring and the one during it, as told by the people who were defeated in the first and were victorious in the second.

My reasons for creating this collection also are personal. I grew up in a small town in eastern Syria and lived there for twenty-six years before moving to Kuwait for two years and then coming to the United States in early 2003. In Syria, I witnessed the grievances of many citizens in a country controlled by *mukhabarat*, security agents, blindly serving the regime. I was harassed by them for the first time in 2000, before I decided to leave the country. While teaching an English course at the University of Damascus (my first and last government job), I realized that a *mukhabarat* agent was waiting to interrogate me after my lecture. Because I did not have an office, he escorted me to a small kitchen where someone was making coffee and hot drinks for the faculty. He started by taking some personal information about me—as if he did not know! But then he asked simple and rather unintelligent questions like, Was your paternal grandfather a member of the Muslim Brotherhood or the Ba'th Party? I answered that my grandfather died when I was a child before I could know him. I imagined saying to the agent that my grandfather had not shared his political views with his family, but I cannot remember now if I said that to him or only thought it. When he finished and went away, without thanking me for my time but acting as though I had wasted his, I hoped that this useless investigation would be the last one. But then an unexpected visitor to my apartment turned out to be another agent asking me to come in for more security screening. The next meeting was at the security headquarters in Damascus, and I was requested—but was not forced when I refused—to report my activities to them. These investigations indicated that I was not yet cleared to work safely as a teacher, or perhaps the agents did not consider someone like me to be a responsible citizen. This meeting and other bureaucratic annoyances related to work subsequently prevented me from getting my salary for one semester of teaching at the University of Damascus. Apparently, teaching at the university level was not possible without a "security clearance," which needed to be in my file at the Human Resources Office before I could be reimbursed. But being followed on a few occasions was the most terrifying experience. After these interrogations, whenever I went to Syria, arriving from Kuwait or the United States, my family used to tell me that "they" had been asking about me. I still do not know what led to these interrogations. By Syrian standards, mine was a minor experience compared with those of many other Syrian academics and intellectuals who openly opposed the regime and whom the regime imprisoned and tortured.

Expanding on my own experience, then, my main concern in this book is to show why and how so many individuals from different walks of life and with very different kinds of experiences on both national and individual levels engaged in collective rebellion. As a scholar of literature, with an emphasis on autobiography, I always have been intrigued by human memory and its insights into events. The stories in this book are by individuals who participated in the Arab Spring, plus a few by foreigners who witnessed it. I invited people from Tunisia, Egypt, Libya, Yemen, and Syria who had either basic or established writing skills to describe how they participated and what they saw during the revolution. I tried to ensure a diversity of class and gender by also including antirevolutionary accounts or thoughts and sentiments deploring the revolutions. However, I found no one willing to write what could be considered a counterrevolutionary narrative. This does not mean that the uprisings were universally popular or that the regimes did not have supporters. Rather, such support, particularly in Syria, played an instrumental role in prolonging the regime's survival.

COLLECTING THE VOICES

In *Autobiographical Acts*, Elizabeth Bruss sets down several rules that make a text count as autobiography, and in collecting the stories here, I adhered to the first of these rules:

> (a) The author claims individual responsibility for the creation and arrangement of his texts. (b) The individual who is exemplified in the organization of the text is purported to share the identity of an individual. (c) The existence of this individual, independent of the text itself, is assumed to be susceptible to appropriate public verification procedures.[18]

I undertook the "verification procedures," however, in order to guarantee the individual identity of each participant writer. But I did not take a conservative approach while considering other rules or definitions of autobiography, a genre described by Michael Spinker as "a pervasive and unsettling feature in modern culture, the gradual metamorphosis of an individual with a distinct, personal identity into a sign, a cipher, an image no longer clearly and positively identifiable as 'this one person.'"[19] The subjects in this book thus are symbolic and beyond the individual, as they are Arab citizens remembering their involvement in a public political phenomenon. The Arab Spring arose on both social and personal—hence both collective and individual—levels, thanks to a collective memory that recounts a history of oppression preceding it. Autobiography in this sense "attends to the aspects of power inherent in acts of autobiographical inscription and recognizes . . . those whose identities, experiences, and histories remain marginal, invalidated, invisible."[20] As we now know, this history could not be publicly articulated sooner, given the difficulty of finding spaces where one might be able to speak, let alone act. Such spaces were necessary in order to put into perspective the experiences of living under a dictatorship, albeit with the possibility of change. In this sense, these texts function to justify the participants' actions and frame their actions in the lenses that the writers themselves used to make sense of their experiences. These texts follow Jerome Bruner's description of autobiographical accounts as conveying "what one thinks one did in what settings, in what ways, for what felt reasons."[21] In other words, these authors do not tell us only what happened but also what they think it meant.

As Karl Joachim Weintraub maintains, in writing memoirs and autobiographies, men and women "undertake the difficult task of presenting their ideas about themselves,"[22] and it was particularly hard for people to revisit the "old days" when they were unable to affirm their dignity and selfhood. This is why in their first drafts, most of the contributors tended to emphasize only the Arab Spring and their connection to it. They were less willing to go back to an uncelebrated past, which they remembered with anger. Although their first inclination was to underscore their participation in the revolts, I eventually convinced many of them to write more about what happened before they became active and what led to this decision. I wanted to emphasize the role of memory. In *Memory and Political Change*, literary critics Aleida Assmann and Linda Shortt argue that memory "deserves more attention as an actor of change and factor of social integration—or indeed disintegration—in periods of transition."[23] The historian Jay Winter endorses this idea by pointing out that activists and writers "have recounted narratives of suffering and injustice, and made telling the tale an act of moral significance. Listening to the tale has come to have moral purchase too. By framing the arts of remembrance, those who speak and those who hear perform the dignity that human rights regimes affirm."[24] Since I was the first "listener" to these tales, I tried to reach a critical understanding of the events that led to this moment in history from the people who participated in them. Unlike autobiographies, which imply an individual choice or a desire to write one's life story, these narratives were produced as a response to an invitation, although the writers still could choose to refuse to share their memories with us. Nevertheless, by agreeing to tell their stories, the participants realized their significance.

The participants engaged in converting memory into a social movement and thus establishing agency in their recollection of the past and their role in writing their version of its events. The memory of the old regime was perpetuated in both their minds and their writings, and this memory was the means that they used to end the regime and to construct a new, emancipated identity. The participants in the first wave of the Arab Spring have become potential producers of new political reality and social values. Their memory is shared and deeply rooted in the consciousness of those who defied the regime's official history, and as the Arab Spring loses steam, these narratives will help us capture its first surge, especially the moment of emergence, and not just the consequences.

I see the Arab Spring as a divide between two collective memories: one from the past—from which people harness their power waiting for a chance to create an alternative reality—and one from the revolts themselves—in which the Arab Spring overrides the past and wipes away its legacy. As a result, the Arab people's ensuing visibility resists the power of forgetfulness and oppression from which they were suffering and might suffer in the future, especially if the Arab Spring fades away as merely a historical moment rather than material for real change.

I asked the contributors to express their thoughts or opinions about their participation in the Arab uprisings in a narrative between fifteen hundred and three thousand words long. I wanted the narratives to be about the same length, and only a few of them went beyond this limit. Shorter contributions were excluded, as were those written by authors whose identities I could not properly verify. Several of the narratives also came by way of a Facebook page that I created in June 2011, and I also used Facebook to find those people who were active during the revolutions and then contacted them by phone. Another criterion was to include only original content and previously unpublished personal narratives. Finally, in my call for submissions, which was circulated in both Arabic and English, I asked the contributors to answer the following questions: What were your reasons for joining the revolution? How did you participate? What activities were you involved in, and how did you understand their significance? If you did not participate physically, how did you participate, and how effective were you?

Even though I approached hundreds of people from these countries and made contact with many, only a few—the forty-six in the book—ultimately agreed to contribute. In addition to the posted, published, Facebook, and Twitter-based circulations of my call for submissions, I called, met, and exchanged emails with more than three hundred people. Of those who agreed to write, I excluded five contributions because they were not original accounts, the writers did not follow through with the editing process, or there were copyright problems. I know that I have left out many Arab citizens, such as skeptics of the Arab Spring, hard-core regime supporters, and those whom I could not reach through my channels of communication. The stories I did include are the participants' version of the events that they wanted to present to a public audience that, rightly or wrongly, they assumed to be empathetic. I assume that those who did not want to participate probably feared that they would say something "unpopular," even though I made it clear that the book was open to all voices, including those opposing the revolutions altogether. The most visible aspect of these narratives is their empowering collective state of "oppositional consciousness," which implies, according to Jane J. Mansbridge, "ideas available in the culture that can be built upon to create legitimacy, a perception of injustice, righteous anger, solidarity, and the belief in the group's power."[25] This consciousness allowed these individuals to identify with and contribute to the revolutionary phenomenon. That is why some thought that their different opinions might not fit this new state of "legitimacy," and they most likely kept silent while the Arab Spring was at its peak.

The contributors allowed me to directly or indirectly confirm their personhood. I have met only a few of them in person. To recruit those who were active in the revolts but might not be familiar with the project, I used personal connections. For this reason, I made phone calls to many of the authors, which allowed me to explain the project to them before they started writing for the book. Some of these calls were heartbreaking, as my contacts sometimes revealed that they had lost relatives or friends in the demonstrations. In one case, we were disconnected during our conversation, probably because of a combination of the Yemeni regime's intervention and the poor quality of the infrastructure.

The participants in this book vary in class, level and type of political activism, role in the movement and in society, experiences, and location. Some are rich and others are unemployed. Some are well-established dissenters, protest organizers, or journalists. Others are rebel fighters, doctors, or nurses. Some accounts were written by teachers, others by students. Some were arrested and others were tortured. Finally, some were living abroad and returned to fight for what they saw as the freedom of their country.

Most of the contributors told me that they had never done anything like this before. Certainly, in the Arab world the culture of writing memoirs or about oneself is not as prevalent as in the West, and it uses different conventions. In the first drafts of most of these narratives, I noticed a tendency to focus more on description than on reflection, more on general social and political issues than on personal concerns, and sometimes with a sense of unintentional ideology or the use of a didactic approach to why one should have joined the revolution and why it was significant. Generally, cultural conventions in Arab societies associate autobiographical writing with a recognized self-worth, such as that of literary figures or well-established politicians, who accordingly are entitled to write about their life and share it with interested readers. With a social emphasis on *tawadhu'* (modesty), individuals are expected not only to be reserved in talking about their great personal achievements but also (and more preferably) not to mention them at all, lest they be seen as boastful.

Nothing demonstrates this cultural phenomenon of self-reservation from public exposure, even in times of revolt, more than a Syrian Facebook page entitled "Shufuni" (Look at me). This somewhat humorous and popular page tracks pictures of revolutionary figures, including popular activists and opposition leaders, and re-posts them with comments expressing the assumption that these people are being pictured for indulging in unwelcomed acts of showing off. That is why it was hard to obtain "heroic" stories from these individuals. Many were trying to be modest, shying away from the assumption that they had done something heroic. Often they insisted that they had played only a minor role. "I did not do anything special" was a common response I encountered, which I understood as "I did something special, but I don't feel comfortable claiming it as such." It was only through the process of editing that I could get the writers to elaborate, explain, or consider replacing a general narrative with a more specific anecdote and reflection. My goal was to break away from impulses to tell the story as it happened to the entire nation. That is why Sidonie Smith and Julia Watson, scholars of autobiography, rightly state that "remembering has a politics" in the context of who is authorized to remember what.[26] For example, in the story "It Is Just . . . the Beginning," written by the Egyptian Sara Hany, she wrote, "Whenever we found a banner with any photo of someone from Mubarak's corrupted regime, we tore it down. The one I remember the most was a huge portrait of the governor of Alexandria, Adel Labib, stretched across the facade of a building at least fifteen stories tall." I wrote back asking her to elaborate, to "tell us about how it was torn down." Did I receive more description of and reflection on this particular incident, its political significance, and why she remembered it? The answer, as we see in the story, is no, which shows that the writers often did not want to respond to someone mediating—maybe too much—between their stories and narration.

These uprisings were a great social and political opportunity for individuals to mobilize for the sake of expressing their collective identity. To a large extent, the emphasis remained on, or it was seen as necessary to stay focused on, the collective rather than the individual. They had a tendency to insist that this was a revolution by all the people, not a single person or a certain group of people. But I did not want the individual to be forgotten. Indeed, many of the writers thought that they should not emphasize their individual roles but instead provide an account of what happened to the entire country. They felt that a national, rather than a personal, narrative was more important. My main task, therefore, was tracing the elements of this collectiveness and having the contributors express their individuality within a collection of narratives, making the movement go from the streets to the pages of this book.

Owing to the arduous process of collecting and editing, some great stories did not make it through the process. The book went through several stages: connecting with many potential authors and explaining the purpose and significance of the book to them, getting promises that they would write their pieces according to the criteria that I had set, reminding them to do so before

the deadline, receiving short pieces that needed extensive editing and clarification, sending the authors my editing suggestions and waiting for their
replies—which forced me to extend the deadline more than three times—
and, finally, translating the texts from Arabic into English. Two of the Tunisian stories were translated from French. For many reasons, some contributors
could not keep up, and the effort and time already invested in their stories had
disappeared, which, much to my regret, prevented some outstanding pieces
from appearing in this collection.

Because most of the accounts were in Arabic, the translation process was
less difficult than the process of collecting the narratives themselves. Nonetheless, the translation of many narratives had its own challenges. Particularly
when dealing with so many writing styles (some of which were written using
colloquial speech in dialects with which I am not familiar), I had to make
some tough decisions. The translation process also forced me to look more
closely at the Arabic narratives, which led to another round of editing and
communicating. I had to identify what might be missing, could be added, or
was needed for a definitive story, and, in some cases, to go back to the author
for more elaboration. I was relieved that dialects were not used very often and
decided to translate the meaning into English while preserving, to some extent, the informal style of the origin. If the narratives sounded "chatty," I did
not try to make them compact or concise, as I wanted them to express the
character of the writer. Finally, part of the shift to English was making the gender of the author clear. Many Arabic names in English are not necessarily gender specific, so I added gender to the contributor's occupation, location, and
age (which, in a few instances, was not provided).

My intervention in the original texts was minimal and always done after
consulting with the writers. My main desire was to produce the best narratives
possible in regard to details, reflections, and clarity. Adding or cutting was not
easy for some writers, and following up, encouraging, and even begging them
was not easy for me. On a few occasions, some writers asked me to suggest
what to eliminate. In all cases, I had them approve the final text before I translated it. Some of those who knew English saw my first draft of their translation
as well.

While negotiating the first drafts with the authors, I did not suggest certain
topics to be covered, but I sometimes did ask them to refocus on different aspects of the events if the stories covered the same event. Most of the authors
showed me one or more drafts of their narratives, and I suggested how to add
reflection, elaborate, and conclude their writing. I also wanted the events
recounted in an engaging and easy-to-follow manner, and the authors were
very patient in helping achieve this goal. From a "global" point of view, I

hoped that all the stories would reflect diverse identities, with fresh voices speaking about all the dimensions of the Arab Spring. Having a full and not biased representation became the key criterion of my selection.

This book is organized into five sections, each containing ten stories representing five regions of the Arab world (Tunisia, Egypt, Libya, Yemen, and Syria—in that order). Space prevented me from including countries, like Bahrain, that did not have a fully organized revolution. Each of the five sections begins with a short political and chronological explanation of the stories that follow. In these introductions, I focus on the major events that took place during the Arab Spring and up to July 2014. My hope is that by allowing individuals to have their voices heard through written narratives, they might force us to rethink certain of our ideas about social, political, cultural change in the Arab world.

NOTES

1. With the exception of Yemen, which was never colonized, these are postcolonial states. Egypt was ruled by Britain before gaining nominal independence in 1922, and the final British evacuation took place in 1965 under Gamal Abdel Nasser. Tunisia was colonized by France until 1957, when Habib Bourguiba became the first president of the state. Libya gained its independence from Italy in 1951 and was ruled by King Idris until Qaddafi's 1969 coup. Syria's independence from France in 1946 ushered in a variety of unstable governments until 1970, when the rule of al-Assad's family began.

2. See Joshua Keating, "Who First Used the Term Arab Spring?" *Foreign Policy*, November 4, 2011, available at http://blog.foreignpolicy.com/posts/2011/11/04/who_first_used_the_term_arab_spring (accessed December 15, 2012).

3. See Charles Krauthammer, "Syria and the New Axis of Evil," *Washington Post*, April 4, 2005, A-27; and Charles Krauthammer, "An Arab Spring?" *Hoover Digest*, no. 2 (2005), available at http://www.hoover.org/publications/hoover-digest/article/7361 (accessed December 15, 2012).

4. Jean-Pierre Filiu, *The Arab Revolution: Ten Lessons from the Democratic Uprising* (Oxford: Oxford University Press, 2011), 31.

5. Al-Jubayn was among the first journalists to flee Syria, and he created a TV program, *Road to Damascus*, which features the most vocal opposition leaders in exile.

6. Ibrahim al-Jubayn, "From the Syrian Ibrahim al-Jubayn to the Syrian Bashar al-Assad," *Alhewar*, May 17, 2005, available at http://www.ahewar.org/debat/show.art.asp?aid=41089 (accessed March 10, 2012).

7. Lisa Wedeen, *Ambiguities of Domination: Politics, Rhetoric, and Symbols in Contemporary Syria* (Chicago: University of Chicago Press, 1999), 90.

8. miriam cooke, *Dissident Syria: Making Oppositional Arts Official* (Durham, NC: Duke University Press, 2007), 72.

9. Ian Black, "WikiLeaks Cables: Tunisia Blocks Site Reporting 'Hatred' of First Lady," *Guardian*, December 2010, available at http://www.guardian.co.uk /world/2010/dec/07/wikileaks-tunisia-first-lady (accessed December 15, 2012).

10. Alison Pargeter, *Libya: The Rise and Fall of Qaddafi* (New Haven, CT: Yale University Press, 2012), 201.

11. W. Andrew Terrill, *The Conflicts in Yemen and U.S. National Security* (Carlisle, PA: Strategic Studies Institute, U.S. Army War College, 2011), 26.

12. Bashar al-Assad's presidency began with the notorious act of lowering the constitution-imposed age for the Syrian president from forty to his own age of thirty-four. He was seen as an educated reformer, but for many inside and outside Syria, hopes dwindled as he became increasingly intolerant of any civil society organizations or democratic forums, or what is called the Damascus spring, which started with his assumption of power, only to be repressed in 2001.

13. James Gelvin, *The Arab Uprisings: What Everyone Needs to Know* (New York: Oxford University Press, 2012), 18–19.

14. In this regard, I believe that the stories will correct one of the other commonly held beliefs, that the Arab Spring was merely a Facebook revolution. Reading these stories, one can see that participation in a revolution is not the outcome of a particular type of technology. Rather, there need to be certain circumstances affecting the individual directly, as being denied political participation or economic opportunities, or indirectly, as showing solidarity with an imagined community of citizens being targeted by (and in need of help against) an actively repressive regime. Certainly Facebook was used primarily to disseminate information and to organize opposition events, and its role was just as important as the one played by, say, Al Jazeera, with its round-the-clock coverage of the revolutions, which allowed greater awareness of what was happening.

15. Douglas Kellner, "Globalization, Technopolitics and Revolution," in John Foran, ed., *Future of Revolutions: Rethinking Radical Change in the Age of Globalization* (London: Zed Press, 2003), 181.

16. William Westerman, "Central American Refugee Testimonies and Performed Life Histories in the Sanctuary Movement," in Robert Perks and Alistair Thomson, eds., *The Oral History Reader* (London: Routledge, 1998), 229.

17. Lynn Abrams, *Oral History Theory* (London: Routledge, 2010), 154.

18. Elizabeth W. Bruss, *Autobiographical Acts: The Changing Situation of a Literary Genre* (Baltimore: Johns Hopkins University Press, 1976), 10.

19. See Aleida Assmann and Linda Shortt, "Fictions of the Self: The End of Autobiography," in James Olney, ed., *Autobiography: Essays Theoretical and Critical* (Princeton, NJ: Princeton University Press, 1980), 322.

20. Jane J. Mansbridge and Aldon D. Morris, *Oppositional Consciousness: The Subjective Roots of Social Protest* (Chicago: University of Chicago Press, 2001), 3.

21. Jerome Bruner, *Acts of Meaning* (Cambridge, MA: Harvard University Press, 1990), 119.

22. See Karl Joachim Weintraub, *The Value of the Individual: Self and Circumstances in Autobiography* (Chicago: University of Chicago Press, 1978), xiv.

23. Aleida Assmann and Linda Shortt, eds., *Memory and Political Change* (New York: Palgrave Macmillan, 2012), 29.

24. Ibid., x–xi.

25. Jane J. Mansbridge and Aldon D. Morris, *Oppositional Consciousness: The Subjective Roots of Social Protest* (Chicago: University of Chicago Press, 2001), 7.

26. Sidonie Smith and Julia Watson, *Reading Autobiography: A Guide for Interpreting Life Narratives*, 2nd ed. (Minneapolis: University of Minnesota Press, 2011), 24.

1. *Tunisia*

The events of the Arab Spring started in Tunisia on December 17, 2010. A twenty-six-year-old Tunisian, Mohamed Bouazizi, set himself on fire in front of a municipal building in Sidi Bouzid, a rural town two hundred miles south of Tunis, the capital. His act was understood by many as a protest against the confiscation of his cart, which he used to sell fruits and vegetables, and the dismissal of his complaint. While the specific circumstances are unknown— how much humiliation and frustration he felt because of official harassment, before acting so desperately—many understood and felt his grievance and even identified with it. There also was speculation that a policewoman slapped him, although she denied doing so.

This young man's death sparked an immediate response against the entire regime represented by President Zine el-Abidine Ben Ali, who came to power in 1987. Ben Ali's rule started with a bloodless coup when, as prime minister, he forced the removal of Habib Bourguiba, alleging that he no longer was mentally fit and forcing him into internal exile until his death in 2000. Bourguiba had been crucial to obtaining Tunisia's independence from France and often is credited for modernizing the country. He became its first president in 1957.

In solidarity with Mohamed Bouazizi, hundreds of youths began to protest, particularly in Sidi Bouzid. During the three days after December 17,
the number of clashes between citizens and the security forces grew. In addition to protesting the treatment of Bouazizi, who remained in a coma until he
died on January 4, 2011, the protesters' demands were centered on the high rate
of unemployment and marginalization, as well as the corruption associated
with Ben Ali's family and in-laws, the Trabelsis. These peaceful protests
ended in the arrest of dozens of young men and the destruction of some public
facilities. The spread of uprisings to other regions and cities in Tunisia
prompted the regime to take action, particularly after the constant coverage of
the protests by Al Jazeera and other international media, including videos and
pictures of the demonstrations widely circulated on social media. Ben Ali's
visit to the dying Bouazizi had no effect on public opinion.

On December 27, Ben Ali delivered a televised address announcing that he
would punish "rioters" and create more jobs, which is the pattern adopted by
many other leaders in responding to political unrest. Despite claiming that
the events were created by "a minority of extremists and mercenaries who resort to violence and disorder," he initiated reforms, including a reshuffle of
the government. Again, like most dictators, he denied that this was a popular
uprising. Instead, on January 9, Ben Ali sent snipers to the western towns of
Thala and Kasserine, where they killed more than ten Tunisians.

On January 13, as the demonstrations in the capital grew larger, the chief of
staff of the Tunisian armed forces, Rachid Ammar, refused Ben Ali's orders to
use the army against the protesters, marking the first of several defections.
The next day, Ben Ali fled to Saudi Arabia with his family. This was an unprecedented event in the Arab world: a united people could topple their dictator.
The prime minister of Tunisia, Mohamed Ghannouchi, a long-standing official in the regime, assumed the duties of the president but soon was dismissed
by the Tunisian people who demanded, and got, free elections in October
2011, which were won by the Islamist Ennahda Party. On Monday, December
12, Tunisia's new assembly elected as president Moncef Marzouki, a former
doctor and human rights activist. In the following year and a half, tensions
between Salafi groups and antigovernment liberals played out in Tunisia's
media and political debates. Islamic extremists in Tunisia became an increasing threat to the moderate Islamist ruling party. In February 2013, the secular
opposition leader, Chokri Belaid, was assassinated by two suspected Islamic
radicals, and the prime minister, Hamadi Jebali, called the killing a crime
against "the principles of the revolution and the values of tolerance and acceptance of the other." In addition to minor clashes between the government
and some hard-line Islamists, political debates regarding the efficiency of the

new government and its ability to maintain the secular nature of the state continue.

The events in Tunisia were watched by the entire world, and other Arab dictators were watching even more intently. On January 14, 2011, the day after Ben Ali's departure, the Libyan leader, Muammar al-Qaddafi, appeared on Libyan television to speak about the revolution in neighboring Tunisia. In his speech, Qaddafi expressed sadness for the events that had developed against Ben Ali, empathized with the Tunisian people, and praised himself and his regime as models for "leading people's revolutions" across the world. But by the end of February 2011, Qaddafi also was struggling with an uprising against his own rule, and Libya's neighbor to the east, Egypt, already was in revolt.

TUNISIAN REVOLUTION:
GAINING OUR FREEDOM AND DIGNITY

Abes Hamid

Judge, male, 36, Monastir

On December 17, 2010, the Tunisian people's revolution began after flames engulfed the body of Mohammed Bouazizi, the young man who could not take any more of the injustice that President Ben Ali had sown throughout the country during the twenty-three years of his rule. Ben Ali was a dictator whose authoritarian regime was enforced with the help of a gang, which is his wife's family. They transformed the country into private property, which they plundered and whose institutions they exploited for personal gain. Their wealth reached unimaginable amounts; it was obtained under the guise of electoral legitimacy and the complicity of Western leaders, who promoted the image of a bright and shining regime, despite knowing how false and ugly this image was.

We Tunisians realized that this regime violated all human rights, carried out torture and repression, and encouraged corruption that spread throughout all the state institutions, including the judicial system and the security forces. The latter became aggressive and was the striking hand of Ben Ali, whose regime oppressed all who stood against it or defended human rights and freedoms. We lost hope in reform and believed that any solution short of overthrowing the entire system would be futile, and we resolved that the regime should be toppled at any cost.

More than anybody else, I was personally familiar with these abuses through my work as a judge in Tunisia. Like most of my colleagues, I had been clinging to the principles of impartiality and independence, seeking to fulfill my duties perfectly. Yet I found myself working in a jurisdiction that was not independent and, in fact, was under the influence of the executive branch of the government—through laws that purportedly organized the profession but were in effect transforming the judiciary into merely an administrative body directed by the executive authority. Thus the judicial system was not operating as it was supposed to. Ben Ali's regime took advantage of the system to suppress freedom and silence the voice of every freedom-seeking individual. The judiciary was forced to protect the authority of the "royal" family—the president's in-laws and his entourage—through unfair mandates, which were subject to instructions from the regime. Even though this scenario involved (only) a small minority of judges, who sold their conscience to gain favors and promotions from the people in power, it contributed to the corruption of the entire system. Nevertheless, most of the judges wanted to work with autonomy and neutrality, but some of them paid a high price.

History must record the bravery of Judge al-Mokhtar Yahyaui, who sent a letter to Ben Ali decrying the situation of the Tunisian judiciary and the rampant corruption in its departments. As a result, he faced his death. Also historic was the strife of the Tunisian Judges Association and its unfailing efforts to defend the independence of the judicial system. The association suffered a blow to its legitimacy, and its members were punished with arbitrary work transfers (to other areas), salary deductions, and denials of promotion. Such honest judges as Mr. Ahmed al-Rahmouni, president of the Juridical Committee of the Tunisian Judges Association, and other members of the Executive Office and the Administrative Committee faced some of these consequences. Despite having been subjected to sanctions, these judges did not give up their struggle to defend the association's independence. They kept fighting as if waiting for January 14, 2011. This date will not be erased from the memory of the Tunisian people or from history.

The events of this momentous day started with a public meeting at Mohammed Ali Square in Tunis at nine o'clock in the morning. This massive march headed toward Habib Bourguiba Avenue. There, other marchers joined in from all other places and began to sweep all the streets. We—men and women, elders and children, illiterate and educated people, judges, lawyers, doctors, and artists—all stood together, a single body, and moved directly to the headquarters of the Ministry of Interior. This place was the center of terrorism and laboratory-tested methods of torture, the cruelest and most ferocious types of torture, carried out against detainees in dark cells. Those who had been in this place and were later released often wished they had died rather than live with the psychological and physical pain that turned them into bodies without souls. In our demonstration, we blocked all the roads leading to the ministry, and our voices rose loud and strong: "Leave, Ben Ali," forming a historic, epic melody played in front of shocked personnel and security force guards.

Peaceful as we were, we had no weapons except our throats, which did not fail us in loudly voicing our demands. Our cell-phone cameras and laptops were connected to the Internet so that video clips of the event would be circulated throughout the social media networks. Many websites showed the demonstration, even though the regime used spyware called "Ammar 404" to block the networks used to transfer vast amounts of pictures and clips. The spyware failed, and these images, showing the successive, rapid pace of events, were viewed by the entire world. Indeed, the January 14 marches were the culmination of a series of bloody confrontations that took place in the country's inland areas, where those most affected by Ben Ali's regime live marginalized and destitute. Families in these areas lost their sons for the sake of the freedom and dignity of the Tunisian people. They wrote, with their own blood, a new history of the country. I believe that it is our duty to perpetuate their memory by describing their martyrdom.

It all started in the city of Riqaab in Sidi Bouzid State where, since December 18, 2010, demonstrators had marched in support of the people of Sidi Bouzid. Clashes erupted between the security forces and demonstrators, reaching a peak on January 9, 2011. Security forces released tear gas, which infuriated the masses in the streets. Then, around 11:00 a.m., the security forces began to fire indiscriminately into the crowds to disperse the demonstrators. Their bullets struck Rauf al-Kaddosa, who was martyred while being transported to the hospital, leaving behind a one-year-old child. As his funeral procession was passing in front of a mosque in the city center, the security forces started shooting again to disperse the pedestrians, killing three—first Muhammad Jabli, then Muadth al-Khulaifi, and last Nizar al-Salimi—for a total of five martyrs killed that day.

On January 8, the city of Tala in al-Kassrain State erupted in demonstrations demanding an end to the security forces' siege of Sidi Bouzid State, but they quickly turned into a demand for the overthrow of Ben Ali's regime in the wake of the bloodshed by security forces. A young man, whose name was Marwan al-Jamali, participated in the demonstrations. He held a diploma in shipping but was unemployed, along with the rest of the region's youth who held university degrees but no jobs. In the demonstrations Marwan called out, "We want employment, O gang of thieves" and "Jobs, freedom, dignity, and patriotism." As his group reached the front of an elementary school, some security agents began shooting, with live ammunition, the protesters on Habib Bourguiba Avenue. Marwan looked for shelter to avoid the bullets, but he was hit and unable to move. One bullet hit him in the chest, passing through his lungs and left kidney. His friends went to him and took him to one of the neighborhoods. Monia Alaourwi, a well-known activist, followed them and drove Marwan to the hospital, but he died before reaching it. Marwan was a martyr, and that is why women did not show sadness but instead expressed their joy as they bid farewell to a young man who gave his own blood to the land and the proud city of Tala.

The city of al-Meknasi, in Sidi Bouzid State, was under siege on December 21, 2010, by countless security forces, but this did not prevent its residents from joining the demonstrations to demand better living standards and more jobs. They went to the main street, Habib Bourguiba Avenue, where security officers started shooting to disperse them. Forty-four-year-old Shawki Ben Hussein was shot and died on the way to hospital. Three days later, when a meeting was organized at the General Union of Tunisian Workers in Zaqzouq area, the union members joined the more than two thousand demonstrators. Confrontations broke out between the security forces and the demonstrators, resulting in the martyrdom of Mohammed al-Amari, who was killed with a bullet to the chest. He was twenty-five years old. The next day his funeral procession went to the cemetery accompanied by heavy security forces. Snipers on the rooftops in the city of al-Kassrain took their first victim, nineteen-year-old al-Habib al-Hussein, who was shot on the way home. Two days later, on January 10, 2011, Sheikh Ahmed Ben al-Azhar al-Jabari (sixty-five years old) also was shot by a stray bullet, which hit him in the chest. Over three days, more than fifty martyrs fell in al-Kassrain, the highest number of martyrs in a single Tunisian city who were sacrificed for the sake of freeing our homeland.

These events were bloody and painful, but they toppled a dictator and gave new life to the Tunisian people. They now feel the taste of freedom and inhale clean air infused with the scent of jasmine, which wafted through Arab countries, paving the way for the fall of other dictatorships. On January 18, 2011, the Juridical Committee of Tunisian Judges Association regained its headquarters, and the judges joined in supporting the revolution, raising the slogan, "Revolution is not complete without an independent judiciary." Indeed, I feel today that the coming days in Tunisia will not be worse than the past, whether or not the revolution is successful, and whether the entire regime falls or does not fall. All I know is that I am free and that my words are free as well.

THE DEATH OF MY COUSIN AND
THE BIRTH OF A NEW TUNISIA

Ahlem Yazidi

Student of linguistics and literature, female, Cherifet

It would be impossible for me to fully describe, to accurately put into words, what happened in Tunisia and what I witnessed personally, on the fateful days of January 11, 12, and 13, 2011. It would be impossible, even if I were given unlimited time to do the task. And it would be unfair to summarize it in a few lines, because the uprisings I witnessed undoubtedly changed not only the history of the Arab nations but also the way the world perceived them. I personally consider the Tunisian revolution as an *intifada*, the justified uprising of an oppressed and heroic people, willing to sacrifice everything for the pursuit of freedom and dignity, the two sacred words that the entire Arab world aspires to yet are denied. Now the Arab nations and our Arab sisters and brothers have come to respect us for our strong will and determination, having seen the power of our popular revolution. Our determination was not overcome by the bullets of the deceitful policemen or the bombs of the army that, in the last moments, sided with the people.

For a long time, my people were a symbol of moral corruption and depravity in the eyes of the rest of the Arab world. We were judged as having abandoned our Arab and Muslim identity while embracing Western European culture, even without being aware of it. These great Tunisian people, my people—of whom I am indeed proud when I am both inside the country and abroad—taught not only Arabs but the whole world a lesson that might be unique in history. My nation demonstrated to the whole world that the greatness of a nation resides not just in economic, political, or demographic power but also in its strong will. As our great poet Abul-Qasim al-Shabbi said: "If the people want, one day, to live [in freedom], then fate will answer their call."[1] Thus I say that if people want their freedom and dignity, presidents and leaders must surrender. This verse was adopted and chanted by the Egyptian masses demonstrating in Tahrir Square in their confrontation with the now deposed president Hosni Mubarak and his accomplices. It was echoed again across the rest of the Arab world from Libya to Yemen and to Syria.

Indeed, Tunisians erupted like a volcano after twenty-three years of seething and frustration, borne of twenty-three years of injustice, oppression, tyranny, spying, and police rule. The former president Ben Ali ruled the country with an iron fist. He maintained a tight grip over the three branches of power, to say nothing of the media, which were under his full control. During his rule, Tunisia had a shameful record, hiring one policeman for every three citizens. Moreover, an outbreak of the rampant corruption, marked by bribery and favoritism, went hand in hand with a punitive rise in unemployment. People's money was stolen. Tunisia itself was a "precious treasure," over which the ex-president's wife and her brothers vied for the biggest share. During Ben Ali's rule, civil, political, and religious freedoms were eliminated. His opponents were arrested and tortured, especially members of the Islamic movements, who often were labeled as "prisoners of conscience." The former regime, adopting a policy of intimidation, threatened the educated class, particularly lawyers and students, who nonetheless always sought to express their disapproval and rejection of the president's repressive policies: the media blackouts and cover-ups, the poor education policy, and the overall absence of effective, viable economic solutions.

Tunisians were not happy with Ben Ali, as he was a tough and cunning dictator, particularly because of his strategy to stifle any resistance against him. In 2009, my city, Soliman, played a special part in the story of their struggle against the former government. At the entrance to Soliman, which is situated in northeastern Tunisia, with a population of around thirty thousand, the antiterrorist police fired on citizens from my city, claiming that they were terrorists or members of the al-Qaeda organization. They targeted Tunisian citizens under the pretext that they were allegedly plotting a terrorist attack against Western interests in Tunisia. During those fateful days, I felt it was my duty to do something, no matter what or how, to protect my fellow Tunisians. Yet it was not easy for me, as a woman, to be openly active in the dissent movements because of restrictive (and, I believe, outdated) customs and traditions. My mother would repeatedly say to me that only men could handle these situations. Naturally, I don't share her opinion, having reached a level of education and awareness of the imperative to be an active citizen, capable of defending myself and my country. How could patriotism be reserved for men alone? In which culture or tradition should submission to a ruthless dictatorship be allowed to exist?

Thinking back to what happened during the days of the revolution of 2011, I should say that I had not been expecting it, nor had I been ready for it. All I wanted to do when it started was to join the crowds in the streets of the capital, to shout and cheer and to express my anger for the deteriorating and dire situation that my country faced. I have consistently participated in demonstrations and protests organized by the students of my university or those of other, neighboring universities, either to advocate for the Palestinian cause or to condemn the hostility against Iraq. But when I joined the demonstrations, I found myself, along with other peaceful demonstrators, surrounded and besieged by riot police. We were hit with nightsticks and batons, sprayed with boiling water, and mercilessly tear-gassed. I was shocked by the sheer might of the military arsenal let loose by the government against a peaceful student protest. But we were determined in opposing not only the government and its policies but particularly the corrupt ruling family itself.

During the last week of January, I tried many times to go to the capital, Tunis, but my family did their best to prevent me. My mother expressed her disapproval, threatening me with her anger if I went to the protests without her consent. On the appointed day, I just could not stop; ignoring her threats, I went to the place where the demonstrations were taking place. I went there because I could not prevent myself from participating in our self-rule, not Ben Ali's. I saw it as my duty and the duty of every Tunisian citizen to stand up for the right of self-determination for our beloved country. I feel that the outside world cannot imagine how much we Tunisians love our country. Despite the hardships that we have gone through, every Tunisian has stood ready to sacrifice his life, and the lives of those dearest to him, for precious Tunisia, as the poet said: "My country even when it is unjust, is still beloved to me. My family, though they can be avaricious, they still are generous."[2] I was extremely surprised by the bravery of my people. Even the Arab nations and many in the rest of the world admired our fearlessness and courage.

On January 13, I went to the streets because I felt that it was the right moment. It was the moment I had been waiting for, for such a long time; it was "now or never." I had to act as a committed Tunisian citizen, choosing to be either a true Tunisian or not. I left the village of Cherifet, where I grew up. Cherifet is close to the city of Soliman, where the demonstrations against the regime began. We were accustomed to a sense of stability, so I did not expect that something would go wrong. I could not fathom that a Tunisian Arab and Muslim would be capable of murdering his Tunisian countrymen. It was inconceivable for me that a Tunisian like me would consider me an enemy, because in our consciousness as Tunisians it is commonly known that the enemy is an alien, someone from the outside. At that time I felt like the world had turned upside down, because every government backer turned out to be the enemy of every Tunisian citizen. The police and the National Guard considered us their targets, as if we were not their brothers and sisters!

When I reached the capital, I was stunned and scared because of the large number of soldiers posted on every street, especially in the public squares. The military presence was strong in Barcelona Square and also in the main street called Habib Bourguiba Avenue. This was ominously accompanied by a complete withdrawal of the policemen who usually handle security issues. I heard people whispering and insisting on the need to go back home out of fear of what might happen next. I was no longer afraid. Deep in my heart I saw my life to be no more valuable than the lives of my fellow Tunisians now filling the streets, which was my answer to my mother when she tried to dissuade me from joining the masses.

I asked the taxi driver about the suspicious withdrawal of the police, and he told me that it was done on purpose. We thought that the regime forces would react aggressively, even violently, this time. I gathered from him that patience from both sides was wearing thin after the events of the last two nights. He advised me to find a shelter or go back home, because rioting would soon start, ultimately spreading throughout Tunisia. He added that the unrest would be coming to my town, Soliman, and that I should be very careful because he had been given inside information saying that the government was going to use whatever means necessary, no matter how ruthless, to quell the demonstrations. I did not give much importance to what he said, and I continued roaming in the capital. It was eerily calm and quiet—the proverbial calm before the storm.

I tried to stay in the capital that day, January 13, but an undercover policeman, or perhaps a government supporter, threatened me, and I felt the need to go back home. Upon my return to Soliman, I was surprised by the huge gathering of young people, high school and university students. Most of them came from nearby villages much like my hometown, Cherifet. This huge gathering thronged the main streets of Soliman; they stood like an army ready to face the enemy. As I walked, I was mesmerized by this epic scene. I was told by one of the demonstrators that they were preparing for a peaceful protest in the main street of the town known as Bab Bhar, where they would speak out against the president and his corrupt government. The last two days had seen the horror of violence, and the endurance of demonstrators was being pushed to the limit.

Meanwhile, I met my eighteen-year-old cousin Wael, a high school student, who asked me not to participate in this protest, as he feared it would be more violent than the other demonstrations. I tried to assure him that things would be all right, advising him to be careful and to avoid confrontation with police. His answer was to laugh, saying, "I am a man, do not worry about me." As I headed toward home, I opted instead to rush into an Internet cafe to watch the latest developments of the unprecedented events. Because of a media blackout, the TV channels were not covering the ongoing protests and violence. I browsed many sites, hunting for worthwhile news, but nothing came up. Finally, I had to settle on Facebook because I found some posted videos that had been excerpted and broadcast by the news outlets.

The Internet, especially the social networks, made it possible for activists to organize and mobilize with surprising speed. The activists were calling for general mobilization, a show of strength and defiance. Our banner was the Tunisian flag, but one with a black band and splatters of symbolic blood, which stood for the sacrificial blood of the nation's newest martyrs. As I sat there, my eyes wearily followed the vivid photos and video footage from the heart of the conflict. The scenes became more and more atrocious and bloody. Almost instantaneously, my colleagues and I were able to share images not only with one another but also with websites of the biggest world media outlets. We added our own eyewitness comments and links to many videos, some showing unspeakable violence and brutality. To my shock and horror, I saw of a video of a bunch of policemen assaulting one of the protesters on Habib Bourguiba Avenue. They were attacking him in front of the Interior Ministry, the place that ought to symbolize protection, not brutality, by the police. Disguised in plain clothes, other policemen were dragging a protester by his leg, much like dragging an animal to slaughter. At this point, I had had enough of Facebook and the violence itself, wishing that it all would end.

Once I was back home, I heard that the clashes were escalating. I began to hear gunshots coming from different directions. Stepping onto the porch, I became aware of the first martyr in our neighborhood. He was a sixteen-year-old orphan named Omar Bouallag. I was shocked when I heard this news and utterly unprepared for what followed. Word of a second martyr left me devastated, for this was my dearest cousin, Wael Agrebi. I could not believe it! I ran out to the street, barefoot, crying and screaming. My dad stopped me and assured me that he was only shot in his leg and injured. Deep inside, I didn't believe him. My suspicion was confirmed by the sight of Wael lying motionless on the ground, with a bullet in his chest. The terrible scene is one that I will never forget. At that moment, I felt as if my country had become another Palestine. Our countrymen were killing our brothers and sisters, which had been inconceivable for me and for every Tunisian. I am crying as I recall and write about this incident.

Later that week, another cousin, Samy, told me that his participation in the mass demonstrations on January 13, 2011, was a statement of opposition and defiance directed at the corrupt state and its supporters. It was what any truly free Tunisian citizen would proudly do out of love for his country. The death of my cousin did not stop us from continuing the peaceful fight for our cause. I am beyond words when I try to express my deep sadness at the loss of my cousin. He was like my little brother; more than this, he was my friend and my student. In spite of his tragic death, I am proud of him and of his courage. I believe it is a great honor that a member of my family sacrificed his life for the sake of our beloved homeland, so we can have a better life with dignity and freedom.

Every time I remember Wael, the innocent young man, I feel like I could have done more for our cause. At least this is what I feel because what I did is insignificant compared with the courage of my countrymen and the martyrs who sacrificed their lives. Many times I wished I could compensate for my failure to protect my own country. Today, I am writing these words as a humble attempt to atone for this shortcoming and to pay tribute to the martyrs of my village, Cherifet, in Soliman, including my lovely cousin.

I hope I have succeeded in communicating a faithful and realistic image that reflects my perception of the revolution of a people who suffered much from injustice at the hands of Ben Ali's regime. We were under psychological pressure caused by a dictator and by our brothers and sisters in the Arab world who initially did not understand our revolution. They often believed the media propaganda, which distorted the bright image of Tunisian culture and civilization, especially that of women. They accused us of losing our identity and religion. We also were mistreated by the international community, which overlooked the atrocities committed by the Ben Ali regime, like arbitrary arrests, tortures, and killings, claiming that they do not interfere in the internal affairs of sovereign states. Well, we did our best for the sake of Tunisia and for the principles of freedom, dignity, and democracy.

TUNISIANS BREAKING THE SILENCE

Marwen Jemili

Graduate student, male, Bizerte

As a Tunisian I think it is very important to convey the situation of the Tunisian people before January 14 when the president cowardly left the country. January 13 has been disregarded because there were not a lot of demonstrations, but I believe both days were really exceptional.

During the few days before January 14 I was extremely nervous—I felt the country was collapsing because of the instability. I remember people were saying on Facebook that they heard shooting outside or that somebody was shot during a demonstration. I questioned their honesty sometimes, and I thought that they just wanted to disseminate absurd ideas that would result in chaos.

At the beginning, all I cared about was safety and security. When I gathered with my family to watch the news, we saw propaganda and perpetual lies. No Tunisian television channel mentioned the fact that some people were killed during the demonstrations. On the national news, we heard that "unrecognized" or "veiled" persons were destroying public property, and they labeled them as "veiled" in order to instill fear among Tunisians. Those who set fire in certain stores were ordinary people, and in some cases they were fanatics and extremists. I am absolutely against riots, but I do understand that these people had tried all means and that burning or destroying public property was their last shot at awakening the "silent majority" of the country.

I was among the majority of Tunisians who favored silence, and that was for a reason. The regime of the ousted president Ben Ali was ruthless and terrorized anyone taking part in any kind of protests. One would not only be tortured but also "evaporated." The regime was very similar to the totalitarian regime of Big Brother in Orwell's 1984. I remember in a course on George Orwell that I took at the University of Manouba in Tunis, that nobody felt comfortable or able to express himself during the discussions. We were afraid of one another and of the teacher, and we were afraid that we might mention something related to the regime and that someone would report it. When I used the Internet to read what critics and thinkers were saying about Ben Ali, I was always afraid, even though I used a proxy to open YouTube, which was censored during his regime. Ben Ali had recruited many brilliant computer engineers from across the country, whose task was to spy on people using the network.

Ironically, for many foreigners, Tunisia seemed to be a peaceful and calm country where everybody was free and liberated from ignorance, but actually it was the opposite. Obviously, we Tunisians are not ignorant but are among the best-educated Arabs, but we really regret that we wasted twenty-three years of our lives with Ben Ali. The country would have declined if there had not been a revolution. Our situation was quite miserable—people were controlled, manipulated, and oppressed. Nobody could speak up because he would have been killed by the president's militias. The dictator Ben Ali also recruited people to pray in the mosques and report those who went to prayers regularly. The regime's deeds led to his demise, and I am going to describe the dawn of the Tunisian revolution and how January 13, 2011, was marked by a huge protest.

On that date, I had planned to meet some of my classmates in a café to work together on a project. This café is located in the most famous place in the capital city, Habib Bourguiba Avenue. It is adjacent to the Municipal Theater of Tunis. I am from Bizerte, which is sixty kilometers north of Tunis.

I went to the capital city by train, on which most of the passengers were as usual: sad, anxious, and silent. I was afraid that the situation in Tunis was going to be dangerous, especially if some of the protesters confronted the police. I met my friends at about 10:30 a.m., and we all started talking about the miserable situation in the country. We were not talking out loud, of course, because Ben Ali's loyalists were scattered everywhere, especially in cafés and bars.

Back then, we thought that Bouazizi's suicide would not change the country for the better. We thought this way in the beginning because we had not seen anything except chaos. We were so desperate because we knew how tyrannical the previous government had been, although later it turned out that no matter how tough a regime is, the people are able to bring about its end. Anyhow, while we were discussing our opinions and hopes, we heard a group of a dozen people or so shouting out loud, but the slogans weren't clear, since it was in Tunis's noisy downtown. The splendid chanting voices did not last long. I think the cops arrested them, and of course, there must have been all kinds of torture in the Ministry of the Interior, which was about two hundred meters away from where we were. That day was really special, since I have never in my life witnessed such unrest.

While we were still chatting in the café, some of my friends received calls from their families telling them to come home because the situation outside was not safe anymore. I was scared, and at the time I became sure there would be a change, although nothing was clear. I could not figure out where the country was headed. At about 4:00 p.m., we left the café and everybody returned home. I went to Barcelona Station where I usually catch the train to go back to Bizerte.

While I sat next to the window on the train, a man who looked very familiar sat next to me, with an old man in front of us. The man next to me was in his forties, and he worked in railroad administration. Right away he started talking about politics, which was so unusual, especially between complete strangers. We were allowed to talk only about foreign politics because Ben Ali saw himself as a semidivine figure in the country. The man next to me said, "Oh!! May God help us in this (hard) time," I smiled slightly, and to show a sense of astonishment, I asked: "What happened?" He told me that he works in the financial branch of the railroad administration and on that morning went to Jendouba (in the northwest part of the country) to calculate how much the broken windows of a train would cost. I asked him, "Who broke the window?" He replied, "Poor people. Sick and tired of the autocratic regime, they resorted to throwing rocks and stones. They were saying slogans like 'Bread and water only, but we will not accept Ben Ali anymore,'" meaning that they were ready to sacrifice and Ben Ali has to step down. He told me that there were many people cursing the president and his wife for stealing their land and farms. I did not want to comment on the man's remarks (cautious, as usual), so I just listened. For a moment I thought that if the people reached that level, we would be capable of getting our voices heard, which would force the president to leave. The slogans those people were chanting were direct and honest, and it was really a reflection of what Tunisians wanted.

While I was still on the train, my father called me to say that the situation was really serious downtown and that I should come home right away without hanging out with my friends. He told me that there would be no school the next day for safety reasons. I remember he told me that Ben Ali was going to make a speech in the evening about the latest events. My father expected him to announce that he would resign that night or stop supporting up his wife's brothers. My father's expectations made me think that the situation was easy, which raised my optimism about the future of my country.

The train arrived at six o'clock sharp. I went to have a look at the main streets, just out of curiosity, and I wish I hadn't done that. The situation was really disorderly; it was chaos. I saw broken supermarket windows, glass all over the streets, and a burned-out car. For a second I thought I was in Iraq or Afghanistan; I have never seen such things in my life and I never imagined that they could happen in my dear Tunisia. When I asked the people who live there what happened, they told me that groups of strangers came and destroyed as many things as possible. Even now I don't understand people who would destroy their own country. At the top of the list is Ben Ali, whom many people trusted while he repaid us with evil and oppression. Not to mention his wife and her brothers who divided Tunisia as if it were their own farm. They ruined the country by stealing public land and taking over international projects.

Now Tunisia is healing: real democracy is being established, and all citizens have just one dream left: to bring Ben Ali, his wife, and the snipers—whom Ben Ali ordered to kill dozens of innocent Tunisians—to justice. We have faith in God and justice, and we will never stop claiming our rights.

REVOLUTION FROM THE OUTSIDE

Noureddine Cherif

Graduate student, male, 24, Tunis

I left Tunis on August 10, 2010, to go to the United States as a Fulbright student. During winter break, I hung out with my fellow Fulbrighters having fun, traveling from one city to another, exploring the East Coast from New York to Miami while my home country was burning. The Tunisian revolution started in December 2010 when Mohamed Bouazizi set himself on fire. I felt ashamed that I was out of the country. While my fellow Tunisian Fulbrighters and I were on our trip, we heard that Sidi Bouzid was on fire, but I did not think for a second that there would be any serious change. I did not have access to the Internet, but once I got on Facebook, I was shocked. I thought the regime would soon suppress the people's protests and things would get back to normal within days. I was wrong. I was completely wrong.

I returned to Allegheny College in Pennsylvania at the beginning of January, and that's when my story starts. I was connected to my computer twenty-four hours a day, as I did not want to miss any detail, and I was completely stressed out. I wanted to participate and I wanted to go back home, but I never did. I had a contract with Fulbright and I had to teach because the spring semester would be starting soon. I stayed and I still regret staying.

I tried to do what many people (albeit not the majority) in Tunisia did: stay connected on Facebook and share links on my wall so everybody could see. I had been sharing videos, posts— everything I could find opposing the regime. One of the benefits of Facebook is the ability to get the word out. People could locate the oppressors and those who were attacking houses and share the information with others. Everybody was connected, and everybody's mission was sent via inbox messages to all their lists with important information and details that others needed to know. This method of communication also helped check information. For example, if I had a friend living in a given city, I could verify some piece of information with him or her, and then I could tell everyone whether it was right or wrong. This was a way to help spread the word, and I believe that social networking helped pioneer the revolution.

The first two weeks of January were the longest weeks ever. Rumors swirled everywhere. Some people were saying that Ben Ali had left; others said that change would occur soon, but I never had the chance to get the exact details.

I have to say that the "intox" (brainwashing) can easily find its way to people, especially the Tunisians. This was psychologically painful, as people were living in fear. They would hear all kinds of stories, telling them, for example, that a group of people in a particular area had been attacked and now the attackers were moving to another location. This made people live in fear, and they never had the chance to go out and check because there was a curfew during that time. The problem was that everyone was telling a different story, but the question was which story to believe. This is when the reliability of social networking was questioned. It is true that it helped spread the word, but at the same time, people had been told inaccurate stories, and a lot of mistaken information found its way to millions. This is why I tried to verify information with individuals who were experiencing the events firsthand.

The night before January 14, I was in my room waiting for the news to come. Ben Ali delivered a speech. His infamous speech . . . I have never seen him so unconfident and disorganized. I knew that the end was near. It was the night that divided Tunisians into two groups: those who supported Ben Ali and those who thought that he had to leave. That is to say, some people were convinced by his speech and believed that he needed another chance to make change happen. But it was too late because people would not accept any more promises: they had been oppressed for twenty-three years.

The fourteenth of January, the change . . . I had received some information from my family and friends that a big demonstration would take place on Habib Bourguiba Avenue in Tunis. Masses of people went to downtown Tunis. What a feeling! There were innumerable people yet one goal: to get rid of the dictator. This was the best moment in the Tunisian revolution, showing the solidarity of the Tunisians . . . people gathered in front of the Ministry of the Interior, and in one voice they shouted the famous demand: "Dégage!" (Get out!). This showed the world that Tunisians were not satisfied with this dictator and a change had to be made immediately.

As a Tunisian who left the country for only a few months, I know that toppling Ben Ali did not change the entire regime. He left, but his cronies remained. This resulted in a mess. The country was in total chaos. Rumors were everywhere that people supporting Ben Ali were attacking citizens in their homes. What a feeling! I was scared to death; I was worried and stressed while away from my homeland for the first time. My family lives in Cité ibn Khaldoun, one of the famous neighborhoods in the capital city of Tunis; I was afraid that they were in danger. I stayed connected twenty-four hours a day. I tried to call them every single hour to make sure that the "anonymous" people who were believed to be sent out by the "old" ruling party did not come to my house. I had been getting information from my mother and brother via Skype, and the posts on my friends' Facebook walls presented a clear picture of what exactly was going on.

What was impressive was that people in every neighborhood of the city formed groups at all the entries to protect their families and neighbors from the regime forces that were trying to terrorize citizens. This is what was said on TV. But fortunately nothing happened, at least where I lived. Hannibal television was later accused of spreading this kind of inaccurate information in order to terrorize people.

The period after the revolution was characterized by rumors and political instability. The situation was chaotic. I helped spread the word, trying to let people know about the revolution, its causes, and its "expected" future by posting on my Facebook page and by being a keynote speaker on different occasions. I think that it was a good way to present what was going on in this other part of the world, given that the Egyptian revolution had started during that time. I was interviewed by the *Meadville Tribune*, the local newspaper of Meadville, Pennsylvania. I delivered speeches at Allegheny College on several occasions, explaining the situation to my colleagues and the students. I believe that the revolution was all about media and that it was really important to make the world know what was going on in my home country.

Social networking was not always beneficial. Since the night between January 13 and 14, Facebook showed divisions of people into two major groups: those who did not believe in the change promised by the former president Ben Ali and those who said that Ben Ali had to stay in power. This resulted in virtual fights between people who were supposed to be "friends"! My brother and one of my best friends fought that night because they had different political views that emerged during the revolution. I cannot say that this was caused by their immaturity, but I would say that people were stressed enough by what was going on and it was very hard to communicate effectively and "peacefully" through written comments. Comments always lack tone and intonation, so they always are interpreted differently, depending on the mood of the reader. That was one limitation of social networking observed during the momentous events in Tunisia. Moreover, politicians found their way to Facebook after the revolution. Several parties were rich enough to pay the admins (the page owners) of some popular pages in order to spread information that fit their agendas. This unethical and damaging move resulted in total virtual chaos that had quite an impact on people's lives.

A lot of Facebook pages also were sold to political parties. Pages that were considered to be sports pages, for instance, became political pages. This resulted in a total misuse of Facebook. People were also manipulated by posts on Facebook. Many pictures were used in order to reorient political and even social views of the Tunisian people. Politicians' speeches were edited in order to fit certain circumstances. The huge number of posts, videos, pictures, and recordings that were uploaded every day made the whole political image unclear, and people got even more confused. This helped raise tensions, mainly because we Tunisians were not able to figure out what to believe and what to ignore. I think that this was not the social network's fault but the fault of those who, unlike myself, were posting without checking the source of the information they wanted to circulate.

Now after eleven months of revolution, I feel that Tunisians have changed. Was it a revolution? I doubt it. People became selfish. Every politician tried to serve his own interests. The parties are fighting not for the development of the country but for getting power. Tunisians started attacking one another. The country is splintering. Some are saying, "If you did not elect the Islamic party, you are therefore not a Muslim." People are being manipulated by money and by ambiguous language, which characterizes the speeches by Ennahda, the main Islamic party in Tunisia. This is the first experience that Tunisians have with democracy, and I think that "the Tunisians are having an overdose of democracy." More than a hundred parties were formed, which made it very hard for people to choose. A lot of different stories are told to people, and of course, the most financially powerful parties, such as the Islamic party, were the ones to reach the majority of people—especially those who are believed to be uneducated and those who are part of the "forgotten class."

I hope that these feelings of hatred arising between citizens of the same country will not result in a civil war. I hope that Tunisia will remain a land of peace and modernity where all people from different religions and origins have been able to coexist together for ages. If Tunisia loses its diversity, it will lose its charm. . . . But I am optimistic, and I hope that my country will move to a better stage of stability and harmony within the next few months.

Social networking was a pioneer of the Tunisian revolution, but even though it had inherent advantages, it also had some limitations. It was a medium used to spread information about events in the country, but it also spread mistaken information and provoked hatred among people with different points of view. The Tunisian revolution was the start of the Arab Spring, and as with any revolution, it will be called successful only after a few years. I hope that Tunisia will be safe and sound and that it will become a model of democracy that other Arabic countries can follow.

THE TORMENTS OF THE REVOLUTION

Marwa Hermassi

Student, female, 26, Mourouj

Before telling my story, I would like to say that my testimony is not a sufficient representation of the years and years of sacrifices and activism by many young people of my generation and the generations before. Even if some of my friends and family liked the militant side of my personality, I think I did not give to my country what many gave, what I should have given. I have always been interested in the political and social situation in my country. I think the reason was my father. He had many troubles in Bourguiba's era as an opponent and in Ben Ali's era as a unionist. But he always tried to protect me, hiding facts from me about what was happening in the country. So it was not easy to know what was happening exactly in Gafsa in 2008 when the workers of the mining area there rebelled: a few videos had been uploaded to Facebook but were quickly removed by the Internet police (what we used to call them). Tunisians were not really using the Internet that much at the time, and the media ignored Gafsa.

In April 2010, many blogs and websites were shut down. Things were different then. Tunisians were active on the Internet, and they started to notice that "Error 404 not found" was the message resulting from censorship. The ATI (Tunisian Agency of Internet) was randomly closing websites, blogs, and Facebook and Twitter profiles based on the use of certain words against the government. Some profiles were even hacked. The ATI kept closing blogs and websites, and it started to annoy people. Then the idea of a demonstration came up. We had chosen May 22, 2010, to demonstrate in front of the Ministry of Telecommunication. Everything had been organized on Facebook and Twitter. But the day before the demonstration, two of the organizers were arrested, kept in police custody, and told to cancel the event. It was not a surprise to anyone; we had a backup plan.

We decided not to go to the ministry; instead, everyone would just wear a white T-shirt. Some wrote on theirs "Sayeb Salah" (Leave Salah), a Tunisian expression that means "Leave me alone." The police reaction was brutal. They insulted us, molested us, and arrested some of us just because we were wearing white and having a cup of coffee on Habib Bourguiba Avenue. Since then, things have changed for me. I have met new people on the Internet, and I no longer am afraid. The closing down of blogs encouraged new people to start their own blogs to talk about everything. People used Facebook and Twitter to talk, to discuss, to share, to tell the truth, to show facts. The Internet became our weapon.

At the same time, the social situation in the country was getting worse: unemployment, poverty, rising prices. Even the families considered wealthy (like mine) could not make it to the end of the month. Yet still, because I lived with my family in Tunis, the capital, our situation was better than others. I could always find a little job during vacation or part-time jobs along with my studies to help cover family expenses. But the rest of my family in Kasserine (where we are from) struggled a lot. Each summer when I visited my grandparents and uncles there, horrible stories—of murder, suicide, illegal immigration, and robbery—made me realize how awful their situation was and the total indifference of the rest of the country to their condition. Kasserine is one of those regions in Tunisia known after the revolution as "the forgotten ones." Gafsa, Sidi Bouzid, Kasserine, Tozeur, Kebili . . . was where everything started.

For many years, most Tunisians were struggling every day to survive while the president's family (especially his wife's family), their friends, and their clan and anyone having close contact with the presidential family or their entourage were getting richer. Here was the situation: poor people getting poorer, rich people getting richer, no jobs, and not even the possibility of expressing ourselves or criticizing government policy or the president's wife or family. People were fed up with the social injustice. Bouazizi was not the first one who immolated himself, but he was the first one everybody heard about at a time when people could no longer be silent. The country was waiting and ready for a Bouazizi to set himself on fire.

On December 17, when I first posted the video from Sidi Bouzid after Bouazizi burned himself, showing the crowd on the site and people talking about poverty and unemployment, I never imagined the crowds would grow. But I guess everyone recognized himself in that young man, and that is how they mobilized themselves against the regime. During that period, I had just found a job to help with family expenses while finishing my studies. I remember we needed that job so much that I preferred missing some classes to accommodate the training for the job, because if I missed one day, I could get fired. So when Bouazizi burned himself, independently of how or why, I understood him; I could imagine his situation. And there I was, working all day and surfing the net all night looking for news in the country, talking with people about the situation, explaining that young man's act. . . . I cannot remember how many sleepless nights I had. And he was not the only one struggling to live a decent life.

People started to gather each day, in different places, each telling his story, talking about his suffering, shouting slogans against Ben Ali and the Trabelsi family (his wife's family): "Work is a right, you thieves!" The situation got worse when the first martyrs died in Kasserine, on January 8 and 9. I could not believe that some people were still talking about the soccer match that day and not even mentioning the unknown number of young people who had died in their country. I guess some were still afraid and others thought it would be the same as Gafsa in 2008, but it was not. On Monday, January 10, 2011, events accelerated: more demonstrations throughout the country, more arrests, more people talking about it, and more videos on the Internet showing the unrest. The more the government censored them, the more videos there were and the more people were encouraged to demonstrate. Some protesters started attacking police stations. No more fear. The army came to some cities and was welcomed by the people. It protected the people, and we feared fighting between the army and the police of Ben Ali.

Some of my friends started advising me to stop posting videos and antigovernment information because people had been arrested. But I did not stop because I thought (and still think) what I was doing was nothing compared with those who were outside and being killed. If the risk was a policeman knocking on our door, then it was really worth it.

On January 13, Ben Ali gave his last speech. I was so happy, I even cried, and everybody was saying "We did it!" He was finally giving the speech we had been waiting for since the beginning, but it was too late; nothing could repair what had happened that month and those years before. The next day, Ben Ali ran away. The days that followed his departure were both tough and wonderful. Tunisians were working together, hand in hand, to protect one another and their private property and to help the police and the army catch outlaws and Ben Ali's militia. Those days were synonyms of confusion, insecurity, happiness, hope, strength, and an unknown future, which is still unknown; yet we made it till now.

After Ben Ali left, we had three presidents, four governments, daily demonstrations and sit-ins of all kinds, violence, more unemployed people, an insecure climate, multiple curfews, and total doubt in everyone: police, government, any political personality, even the army at some point. It was obvious that we needed a new constitution. The main idea was a national assembly that would write it, and we wanted to elect this assembly. The first date was fixed, July 24, 2011. A panel of experts and some of the country's political parties created the High Committee to Protect the Revolution, or Instance supérieure pour la réalisation des objectifs de la révolution (ISROR), to prepare for the elections and the voting process. Then the date was changed because it was too soon and we were not prepared enough. Finally, it was set for October 23. Another authority was elected by the ISROR to prepare the elections.

I decided to seriously participate in helping make these elections successful, so I joined an observers' network. We had to be at the poll before 6:30 a.m., so I was at my poll in Mourouj near Tunis where I live, at 5:45 a.m. The night before, I barely slept, and as expected, some people were already waiting for the opening at 7:00 a.m. On that day, I saw a great Tunisian people. It was hot and so sunny, and yet they were there, standing for hours, determined to vote, to make a change! We finished counting at 3:00 a.m.

Independent of the result and all that has been said, the day was a wonderful experience for me and a tremendous success. It made me believe more and more in Tunisians. People from different political parties or associations were working together. We all left with respect, confidence, and, above all, faith in the belief that we took part in writing history. We had ensured the smooth conduct of the elections; we did a good job. For me, the revolution resulted in these elections, carried out by a united people who put aside their differences and looked forward to a great future for the country.

Today we have a new government, and the security situation is much better. However, the real problems, the revolution's raisons d'être, are still here: unemployment and poverty. Even though freedom of expression is way better now, we still have a lot to learn. This is why I cannot say that the revolution has succeeded or failed. The revolution is still going on. The basic goals have not been realized yet. People need jobs, money, a decent life, justice, freedom. People want to live, not just survive. This revolution needs time. Some have said that there was external intervention, but I am not sure. I strongly believe that regardless of the political abuses of the past, these people, at a historical moment, decided to take their destiny in hand and make real change. This revolution, before being political, was for social justice.

TUNISIA'S HARD TIMES AND ITS BEST TIMES

Yesmina Khedhir

English teacher, female, 25, Tunis

More than one year has passed since the outbreak of the Tunisian revolution. Tunisia, the country that started what we now call the "Arab Spring," actually marked a shift in the history of the Arab world. As a Tunisian citizen, both a witness and a participant, I really want to record my experience so that readers know more about what happened. Officially, the Tunisian revolution started in December 2010, but in fact, the seeds for the people's revolt were there before that. Tunisian people lived for more than twenty years under the control of a president who governed with an iron fist. Corruption, exploitation, a high cost of living, and the absence of any kind of freedom of expression were at the root of the outbreak. When people took to the street to express their anger and dissatisfaction after the self-immolation of Mohamed Bouazizi, their single demand was "dignity."

Like all Tunisians, I lived the Tunisian revolution moment by moment, either in the street or at home in front of my computer screen. Luckily, I was in the capital, Tunis, when the revolution began (my parents' house is in another city very far from the capital). I was living with my two sisters, my brother, and two other girls in the same house. When the revolution started, the parents of the two other girls came to live with us, together with their brother and their cousin. I am revealing these details because we spent around ten days living in hunger. Due to the lack of security, the curfew, and the unrest, all the stores were either closed or had run out of supplies. People were buying large quantities of food at once to protect themselves against an unknown future. Together we sat watching the news on television all day. Al Jazeera and Facebook were our main sources of information about what was taking place in my country.

Sometimes I could get out and see the events. My sister worked as a journalist for a German channel, so I went with her a couple of times to film the protests in the street. When she felt that the situation was becoming more and more unsafe and insecure, she did not want to take me with her anymore. I begged to go with her, but she totally refused. I quarreled with my younger brother over who should accompany her, but she said no to both of us. We lived fairly far from the city center where the demonstration took place. We could not join the protesters because of the difficulty of transportation, the enforcement of the curfew, and the fact that my sister and my friends' parents did not allow us to go out. (The exception was to go to the bakery to get some bread, where we used to line up in a very long queue for two hours to get one or two baguettes to feed nine people.)

During those days, we often skipped our breakfast because we could not find milk and bread. We had a very tiny lunch and sometimes no dinner. Although they were the most difficult days of my life, each time I think back on them, I feel incredibly proud. I also remember the nights when we used to sleep to the continuous echo of gunfire, waking up in the morning with the news that a police station had been burned or hearing that the police had arrested an armed gang that was trying to burn a big supermarket. There were so many other stories!

My house was actually next to the biggest military barrack in Bouchoucha, a neighborhood a little way from the city center where the protests were taking place. From my balcony I could see many military cars going in and out of the barracks, dozens of them every day. I was very worried about my sister, and I called her every now and then to make sure that she was all right and to get more news from her. Meanwhile, I was glued to my computer all day watching and sharing terrible videos of the police killing people, posting Facebook status updates, and expressing my anger against the oppressive regime. We were depressed and scared about what our future would be. After 5:00 p.m., for a week before Ben Ali's flight, the street and all the roads were empty of people and cars because of the curfew—except for the police cars. The ex-president had decided that there would be no school during those days because of the unrest, but actually it was just his way of avoiding more popular uprisings against him. I had to comply, angrily, and stopped going to the institute where I used to teach.

My mother and father were very worried about us. They called us several times every day just to make sure that we were at home and safe. All of us were very worried about my journalist sister and were always waiting for her to come home before the curfew. Sometimes she would spend the night in her friend's office to work on her reports with other journalists. Life during those days almost stopped: no school and not enough food, and people did not go to work because of the difficulty of public transportation. We went through hard times. During the day, protesters were resisting the regime's police force. At night, armed gangs were stealing things and burning public buildings, hospitals, and supermarkets. They were doing exactly what the regime wanted: frightening people and making them believe that the protesters were terrorists and that we should calm down to regain our security. But after the death of many innocent people, nothing could stop those Tunisians, whose growing outrage could be appeased only by Ben Ali's resignation.

On January 11, 2011, I received two sad calls. The first one was my mother telling me that my cousin's brother-in-law had been killed by a sniper in Sidi Bouzid, the same city where Mohamed Bouazizi was from. My cousin's brother-in-law was a religious man about thirty years old. He had a beard, and he was going home when he got shot. He was not with the protesters, but obviously the sniper thought that a bearded person was a target, even if he was a nonthreatening human being. It was a heartbreaking experience to know that he had been shot and bled to death. But all I could do was to call his brother (my cousin's husband) to express my sympathy and to wish that God would bless his soul.

The other sad call I got was from an unknown number. The zone code indicated that it was from the city, Sfax, in the south-central region of Tunisia, where my other younger brother studied and lived with my aunt. I had been calling my brother all that day, but he did not answer my calls. I felt that something bad happened to him. When I got the call, I heard an angry voice asking me, "Are you Yesmina Khedhir?" I said, "Yes, who is calling?" The man did not answer. Then, he asked me another question: "Do you have a brother named Najeh?" At that moment, I could not hold the phone anymore; I was too scared. I nevertheless answered him, "Yes, is he OK? Who is this?" The man hung up without saying another word. I was shivering when I tried to call back my brother to check on him. After a while—around ten minutes that I felt was ten hours—my brother picked up his phone and answered me by saying that he had been arrested with other protesters and that they all had been beaten, including a very old man. He said that they insulted them and that his leg was swollen because they all had been whipped. They were kept in detention for the entire day. The only reason they released him was because his identification card showed that he was only seventeen years old.

I started crying when he told me that his leg was badly hurt and that he could not walk back home. Our dilemma intensified because of other factors: he did not recognize the place where they took him; it was already 4.30 p.m. when they released him; the curfew would start in thirty minutes; and he did not have any money left. He told me that the person who called me was from the police station, and the reason for his call was that he suspected that my brother had stolen the phone from someone else. I recharged my brother's phone from my own account, and fortunately, he called my cousin and described the place to pick him up. Even though I knew that my cousin had dropped him off at my aunt's house, I could not breathe properly until I called her and made sure that my brother was safely at their home and that his swollen leg was properly treated.

My sad experiences during the Tunisian revolution did not prevent me from laughing when I heard Ben Ali's last speech on January 13. He sounded pathetic and weak, asking people to give him another chance to correct his faults and promising them a better future. After he delivered his speech, some of my friends on Facebook started to sympathize with him and believed his rhetoric. I remember I wrote on my profile, "It would be a great betrayal for the blood of the hundreds of martyrs to forgive that killer." A friend of mine had a car, and we made plans to join the protesters on Habib Bourguiba Avenue (the street where the Interior Ministry was) the following day. She came around 11:00 a.m., and despite my sister's and brother's insistence that I stay at home, I went with my friend in her car. Unfortunately, we could not reach the protesters because the police were everywhere and had blocked all the streets leading to our destination. My friend wanted to go back home because she was afraid that they would destroy her car. That same evening, we heard on the national channel that the president had fled to Saudi Arabia, leaving the country in a situation of total chaos and disorder. The streets were still dangerous, and the militias of the toppled regime were still there, frightening and killing more people and burning public property.

Yet the demonstrations went on because the former prime minister appointed himself as the new president. The Tunisians, of course, would not trust a man who had worked for years in Ben Ali's regime. I used to go frequently with my friends to Kasbah Square in downtown Tunis to protest against the new government and share food with the protesters who came from faraway cities to say no, "Degagé!" to the new president, the former prime minister.

My sister asked me to help a German journalist who wanted to interview some politicians, but everyone who had worked under Ben Ali refused to cooperate. So I helped him with translation when he finally could get some political and religious prisoners to talk to him. They told us about all the torture and humiliation they suffered at the Interior Ministry, just because they expressed their discontent with the situation or criticized the president.

Now, when all those images come to my mind, I feel sad about the blood spilled of more than three hundred people and for the injuries to more than seven hundred people. I feel sad for a country that lost much of its wealth because of a dictator surrounded by a bunch of thieves. But I still feel proud that I am Tunisian, that my people were the spark that illuminated the road for other Arab nations to democracy and freedom. Now the Arab world is witnessing radical changes that will shape its future. I do not know how optimistic we should be about our own future, but in my opinion, a nation that uprooted twenty-three years of dictatorship in just one month would never mistake its path. Indeed, the social and political experience in Tunisia, Egypt, Libya, Yemen, and Syria has taught us that the power of the people is mightier than any dictatorship. I would like to conclude with the verses that we learned from our great poet Abul-Qasim al-Shabbi:

If the people want, one day, to live [in freedom], then fate will answer their call.
Night must then fade away
And their chains must break.

THE SMELL OF JASMINE: THE TUNISIAN REVOLUTION FROM THE OUTSIDE

Nada Maalmi

Student, female, 21, Marsa

January 14, 2012, one year after Ben Ali fled the country. What is left? While browsing on Facebook, I noticed a picture shared by a current opposition personality. It was a screenshot of live streaming on the national television channel: Alwatanyia 1. This was the official ceremony to commemorate the Tunisian revolution. I asked myself, "What does the January 14 revolution remind me of? How do I relate to it after one year?" Young people, men and women, intellectuals, uneducated, and unemployed citizens together all took to the streets to protest against repression, unemployment, and corruption. But there are two pictures that embody the revolution, at least for me: the great number of people demonstrating in Habib Bourguiba Avenue, with some young men holding a Tunisian female on their shoulders. She is wearing a *chachia* (a traditional Tunisian hat), and she is demanding, with amazing energy, that Ben Ali go. I also still vividly remember the other picture, which I saw on the front page of the French newspaper *Libération*, of a Tunisian woman wearing a green scarf and holding a sign that reads "Ben Ali dégage!" (Ben Ali, get out!).

I am not trying to reduce the whole revolution to a symbol or an achievement made only by women, but it remains one of their accomplishments, reflecting women's significant political and social roles in our modern society. Tunisian woman played this role in the revolution because they are politically active and progressive. They have secured an influential position in society, not the one that is being promoted by Salafi, or conservative, discourses, which say that they should stay at home, look after their children, and satisfy their husbands. Now in Tunisia, Salafi groups are active in universities and in the public sphere, and the government turns a blind eye (or in one way or another supports them).

In my mind, the images of men commemorating the revolution are tired and old, among which is that of the Gulf delegation; this and other images make me fear for the future of our revolution. There also are shocking images, to me anyway, of men from the Gulf—including those from Qatar—who are in line to make sure they benefit from our revolution. Did those people make the revolution? Did they at least support it? Obviously not. The majority of Tunisians are suspicious of the Qataris' interference in the reconstruction of the country. There were a series of investment agreements in electricity and banking, but we usually joke that less Qatari money was invested in Tunisia than the money stolen by Sakhr el-Materi and Nesrine Ben Ali, the influential family members of Ben Ali who fled with him to Qatar. We also are uncomfortable because the first country that Rashid al-Ghannouchi (founder of the Ennahda movement and party) visited after the elections was Qatar. One part of Tunisian society believes that Qatar is giving money to Ennahda, which is unfair to the other parties. That is why, they assume, Ennahda is so powerful and well organized, because it is supported financially by the Gulf states including Qatar.

This latter scenario troubles me as I reflect on our revolution and see who wants to claim credit for it, including, strangely, those from the outside. That is why I sometimes wonder, Where is the energy that allowed a people to topple an oppressive government? Are they still in the streets demonstrating again and again or sitting behind their computers sharing information and circulating their critique and disappointment, as I usually do? Maybe to be revolutionary is always to be suspicious, critical, and provoking, particularly when the government that came after Ali does not represent the majority of Tunisians.

It is needless to emphasize the facts about the revolution, as some of them have become legendary. But it is crucial to pay tribute to Mohamed Bouazizi and so many other martyrs who sacrificed their lives for freedom and dignity. It also is necessary to pay tribute to those who bravely faced dangerous situations as the target of bullets, beatings, humiliation, and so many other tools that the regime used to make people submissive. Was Hamadi Jebali, the current prime minister of Tunisia and the secretary-general of the Ennahda movement, along with his movement's major members, part of the thousands of protesters who exposed their lives to danger a year ago? No.

Were all the demonstrators and opponents motivated by the same feelings as Mohamed Bouazizi was? Yes and no. The economic situation was obviously tough for everybody. Middle-class citizens were struggling to make ends meet. Nevertheless, Tunisian society enjoyed some comforts and a good standard of living, which indirectly enabled it to turn a blind eye to corruption, such as the elections—whose results were 99 percent in favor of the regime—and some malfunctioning of the government. People could easily enjoy or afford apartments, PCs, cars, Internet, alcohol, and parties. Some individual freedoms, such as consuming alcohol, wearing short skirts, and having private parties made Tunisians feel free in their daily lives. But does that mean that they supported Ben Ali only for these individual freedoms? For some of them, the answer is yes, particularly those who used to take advantage of the regime par-ty's benefits. The answer for others is no, particularly those who had intellec-tual objections to the regime. Though personal freedoms were allowed, not much space was given for intellectual liberties. The main discourse in the Tunisian media was controlled by and favored the regime.

We could blame lots of things on the former government, but we should acknowledge that even though intellectual freedom was controlled, the Tuni-sian educational system was good, but job opportunities were declining. Mo-hamed Bouazizi himself could not find a job. Tunisians arrived at a situation in which lots of young graduates faced a stagnating employment market. We can see that the new government, particularly Ennahda, is now focusing on education, because it is known that an educated population is hard to control. In fact, the educational level of our people helped overthrow Ben Ali, because if all Tunisians were illiterate, with no ability to analyze, no revolution could have taken place.

Some of those intellectuals fled to Europe, where they wrote and criticized the government. But this contribution may not be seen as directly linked to the revolution. In this regard, some would dispute my legitimacy to comment on the Tunisian revolution, since I was living abroad when it took place. No, I was not in Tunisia when the grassroots demonstrators filled the streets, and I do not claim to be a revolutionary, as some people did after Ben Ali was toppled, but it may be interesting to look at how this (my) part of the population lived and felt about the revolution. I find myself representing this portion of the Tunisian population. I belong to the group of those living abroad whose ac-tion was limited to a couple of demonstrations and to cyberdissidence. I re-member the month of January 2011, the toughest month in my student life. Like most of the students in France, I had exams in January, and the period before exams was usually spent preparing for them. Nevertheless, it was diffi-cult to study with all the shaking up going on in Tunisia. Instead of focusing on our studies, we followed all the events—and there were a lot of them, both interesting and unprecedented. Surprisingly, and for the record, French tele-vision did not cover the events immediately.

December looked pretty calm on French screens. That is when Al Jazeera became more visible in its coverage of the events as they were unfolding. With the censorship of Tunisian television and the lack of information from the Western media, Al Jazeera became the only official source of information besides Facebook, which was the informal source of information and the space for dissidence (and manipulation). The French media paid more attention to the Tunisian uprising after Michèle Alliot-Marie, then France's foreign minis-ter, was shown in a session of the French parliament offering to lend France's "savoir faire" to help fix the "security" issues in Tunisia. A dramatic controversy erupted, and therefore the French government had to choose whom to support: the unwanted president Ben Ali or the demonstrators seeking freedom and dignity. It is obvious that before this development, the French government could neither officially support the dictator nor endorse the demonstrators, because of considerations related to the benefits and advantageous commercial relationships that were established with Ben Ali's regime. At the time, I felt that the West was hesitant to support the Tunisian revolution because its support was useless and would damage some of their strategic positions. They never thought that our people would force him to leave.

I was living in Nantes, where Tunisian students organized a demonstration to support Tunisians living in Tunisia and to show encouragement for their actions and bravery. For logistical reasons—such as having it on the weekend rather than on a weekday so that more people could attend (on Saturday morning, many Arab people go to the local market) and making sure that the local authorities knew about it—we planned the demonstration for January 15, 2011, and when it took place, some non-Tunisians participated. There was a Tunisian association with which we had some difficulties organizing the demonstration, but eventually they came on the fifteenth. Because Ben Ali had fled the day before, everybody was taken by surprise, and the earlier designed banners and slogans of some demonstrators no longer applied. The speeches focused on Ben Ali and his wrongdoings instead of starting to think about the rebuilding process, which was wrong. The moment Ben Ali left, all we Tunisians had to start thinking about how to rebuild our country. It is worthless mourning the past, but what will be useful to Tunisia is critical, in order to not let any other force take over the revolution. We need to focus on rebuilding a country in crisis, in which unemployment is record breaking and corruption is everywhere. We need to restructure and reform institutions (and minds) for the people who have never had "transparency" and "democracy" in their vocabulary. For some, reconstruction is synonymous with regression, democracy with theocracy, and liberty with a unilateral policy (or the deviation of the Tunisian identity). This is wrong.

I also mentioned cyberdissidence, and I should state that Facebook played a remarkable role in this revolution. I think that the videos and photos shared through social networking supported the revolution in two ways. First, it showed Tunisian individuals that they were not alone—that other people cared about their revolution and supported it. These postings included people criticizing the government and its policies. Other people were sharing thoughts and comments about what was occurring during the revolution. The impression of unity given by this virtual space strengthened the unity in the streets.

Then the emotion of these violent and bloody videos and pictures ignited re-pressed feelings and actions. Nevertheless, it was not by hitting "like" that the revolution was made. I guess some of the Tunisians living abroad tried to play a role in controlling what was shared on Facebook by asking users to reveal their sources, to add the date and the place, and to explain the context. We Tunisians living aboard accepted a huge amount of the news and videos shared as true, yet we quickly felt the need to check their authenticity. Since we could not be there, we focused our energy on sharing and checking information to participate in our revolution, even from a distance.

A year after the revolution, almost three months after the elections, we still are waiting for the constitution (or at least the impression that the government is working on it instead of committing itself to restricting individual free-doms). Indeed, waiting is not sufficient, I thought, and that is why I went to vote. It seems like an old story is being replayed. The revolution is still on. The game is not over.

NOTES

1. Celebrating the will of the people, Abul-Qasim al-Shabbi (1909–1934) composed *The Will to Life*, in which he recited the popular verse.

2. This is the modern alternative wording of a popular Arabic verse that dates back to 1212.

2. *Egypt*

Thawrat 25 Yanayir, or the January 25 Revolution, is what many Egyptians call the popular uprisings to overthrow Mubarak's regime in 2011. This term filled the pages of the most widely circulating newspaper, *al-Ahram*, on January 25, 2012. On a full page with the headline "25 January: First Year of Revolution," the newspaper states that the revolution was launched "so that the Egyptian person regains his or her dignity, Egypt's democracy will be born, social justice will prevail, and jobs and opportunities will be available for all Egyptians, particularly the youth," but it also says that after all the sacrifices of Egyptian lives, the revolution needed "the execution of its demands, most of which remain only as slogans."[1] In the same way that Tunisians identified with Mohamed Bouazizi, Egyptians identified with yet another victim of state violence, Khaled Said, the twenty-eight-year-old Egyptian man who was tortured to death by Mubarak's police in June 2010.

On Tuesday, January 25, 2011, Egyptians headed to Tahrir Square in downtown Cairo to participate in a demonstration called for in a number of places, including the Facebook page "We are all Khaled Said." Two images of Khaled were posted on this page, one with a radiant and healthy face and the other, taken after his death, with a deformed face. The page devoted to him encouraged many Egyptian youths to resist the regime. Many of the Egyptian contributors in this book refer to this Facebook page as their guide to participating in the Tahrir Square sit-in and defying the state security officers and Mubarak's changing tactics before he surrendered to their will. The page was created by an Egyptian computer engineer, Wail Ghonim, born in 1980 and working as the head of marketing for Google in the Middle East. Ghonim later explained that the purpose of his page was "to mobilize public support for the cause," adding that his "ultimate aspiration" was that people would take "activism onto the street."[2] Egyptians saw what happened to Khaled Said as a brutal act that could happen to any one of them, so they united to prevent such a fate, and the result was a revolution inspired by the one in Tunisia.

On January 28, 2011, which was a Friday, dubbed by the increasing number of antigovernment Egyptians as "Friday of Anger," the eighty-two-year-old Hosni Mubarak gave his first of three televised speeches to pacify the angry crowds.[3] He reminded his people of what he had accomplished, emphasizing the allegedly positive "interaction between the forces of society" that he had created. He also warned against a breakdown of order, blaming people for getting involved in looting, chaos, and fires. Then the next day, in response to the popular demand that he resign from power, Mubarak appointed Omar Suleiman, the former chief of Egyptian intelligence, as vice president. This position had been vacant since Mubarak became president in 1981 following the assassination of Anwar el-Sadat. The police forces began gradually disappearing from the restive areas, and people formed their own security committees to protect their neighborhoods. Although the Egyptian army was deployed in many areas, it did not attack the protesters, thereby gaining popularity. Some angry crowds, however, stormed and burned down a few police stations, whose police officers were notorious for their brutality against detainees or protesters in the streets.

Mubarak appeared again on February 1, 2011, acknowledging that the demonstrations were legitimate but had turned into "sorrowful confrontations" encouraged by political powers seeking to escalate the unrest and trying to undermine the security of the homeland. He also announced that a new government would be formed and that presidential elections would be held in September 2011. Nonetheless, the next day, some of the regime's political figures and businessmen planned a raid on Tahrir Square by using *baltagyia*, thugs, most of whom were criminals who had been released and ordered to crack down on the protesters. These thugs stormed into the square on horses and camels, using sticks, knives, and swords before they were overpowered by the crowds. On Friday, February 4, Egyptians called their biggest day of protest the "Friday of Departure" when more than one million protesters in

Tahrir Square and thousands of protesters in different areas of Egypt demanded that Mubarak leave.

Mohamed Hussein Tantawi, then Egypt's defense minister, visited the square twice to check on the troops deployed there. During the revolution, he became the head of Egypt's Supreme Council of the Armed Forces (SCAF), a position that officially belonged to the president. Just like the military itself, Tantawi emerged as a protector of the people rather than the force that would blindly stand by the regime. The first statement by SCAF was on Thursday, February 10, and it emphasized that the council was meeting around the clock to follow the events in Egypt. What seemed to be his last move to show that he was still in power, Mubarak gave his last speech on the same day, which was his third since the onset of the protests, authorizing Vice President Omar Suleiman to assume all the duties of the president. Dissatisfied, activists planned Friday, February 11, to be the day when protesters would march to the government headquarters and even the presidential palace to force Mubarak to resign. On the same Friday, after eighteen days of protests, Suleiman announced that the president had stepped down and handed over power to the military. Ian Black, the Middle East correspondent of the UK-based newspaper the *Guardian*, described this event as "the unforgettable 'Berlin Wall' moment in the Arab world"[4] and rightly pointed out the inspiration it provided "for other manifestations of people power from Wall Street to Tel Aviv."[5] On this momentous day, SCAF issued its second statement, pledging to end the state of emergency, which had been enforced since Mubarak became president in 1981. SCAF also promised to prepare for free presidential elections and called for the return of normal life. After that Friday, and for more than a year, the military has been completely in charge of Egypt. The ailing Mubarak was tried, convicted, and sentenced to life imprisonment. He appealed his life sentence and, as of summer 2013, will be retried.

Parliamentary elections were held in January 2012, and the Muslim Brotherhood's Freedom and Justice Party (FJP) won 235 of the 498 seats in the People's Assembly, followed by another Islamic party, the Nour Party, with 121 seats. On April 26, the Supreme Presidential Electoral Commission announced the final list of thirteen nominees for the presidency, in a vote that would determine Egypt's first democratically elected president. In a survey conducted in Egypt between August and September 2011, 70.6 percent of those interviewed believe that chaos was the mostly feared scenario; 17.5 percent feared the rule of Islamists; and 8.6 percent were concerned about the dominance of the military. On June 30, 2012, Mohamed Morsi, an American-trained engineer and the FJP's candidate, was elected president. But many Egyptians were dissatisfied with Morsi's performance, especially those who believed he was transforming Egypt into a Muslim Brotherhood state, an accusation that he repeatedly denied. Anti-Morsi demonstrations were common during his year-long rule and peaked in June 2013, when opposition figures and a protest campaign named Tamarrud, "Rebellion," called for his resignation. An organized uprising of an estimated ten million protesters took place on June 30, 2013, and Tahrir Square became once again the scene for another call for regime change. Morsi's supporters also took to the streets to defend what he himself called, many times in his last speech on July 2, "legitimacy," insisting that he had no plans to step down. Amid widespread protests from both sides, the army delivered an ultimatum to both the government and the opposition to end the conflict, warning that it would intervene and impose a "road map" if "the will of the people" were ignored. The next day, the head of Egypt's armed forces, General Abdel Fattah el-Sisi, announced on state television the removal of Morsi, the suspension of the controversial constitution, and a transitional period with the head of the Supreme Constitutional Court, Adly Mansour, sworn in as the acting president of Egypt on July 4, 2012. Morsi's last announcement came via his Twitter account, denouncing what he called a military coup and asking people to reject it. During this period, clashes led to the deaths of more than fifteen people. Then on July 8, more than fifty-one people were killed as the military and police reportedly fired at protesters holding a vigil at the Republican Guard headquarters, where Morsi was thought to be held. Political polarization and tension in Egypt were leading to the possibility of internal armed conflict.

At the time this book went to press, Mr. Sisi (he resigned from the military before announcing that he would run for president) was vowing that he would not seek reconciliation with the Muslim Brotherhood. Moreover, since taking temporary control of the government, Sisi's police have been accused of assaulting Morsi's supporters and have thrown into prison a large number of Sisi's political opponents, including journalists and academics, hundreds of whom have been sentenced to death. Nonetheless, Sisi is certain to win the election and become the new president of Egypt.

THE MOMENT THE BARRIER OF
FEAR BROKE DOWN

Adel Abdel Ghafar

Activist, male, 32, Cairo

The place is Tahrir Square, in front of the American University in Cairo. The date is January 25, 2011. The time is approximately 4:00 p.m. The acrid stench of tear gas surrounds me. The sounds of bullets, screams, and sirens are deafening. A squad of Central Security riot police charge toward us, shields raised and batons drawn. Several protesters have fallen to the ground and are being brutally beaten by the riot police. I run, with a group of others, trying to scramble away from the carnage and escape the riot police. As I am running, I see a dying protester, his skull cracked open, his brains slowly pouring out.

Suddenly, a man next to me stops and shouts: "Do not run! Egyptians, when will you stop running away? Turn around and let's face them once and for all!" He grabs my shirt, and I stop. I grab the shirt of the person next to me, and he stops. Slowly, our entire group comes to a halt. The riot police continue to run toward us; they are dangerously close. The front row of Central Security police seem menacing in their riot gear as the officers behind them lob tear gas canisters at us. We stand still.

Place: My home, Cairo.

Date and time: January 25, around 8:00 a.m.

It started like any other day. It was a national holiday in Egypt, Police Day, to commemorate the Egyptian police officers who died at the hands of British forces during their occupation of Egypt. Like thousands of other Egyptians, I had joined the "We are all Khaled Said" Facebook page, set up in mid-2010 after the police murdered a young man in cold blood in Alexandria. It disgusted me that police brutality had taken this young man's life and how the regime of Egyptian President Hosni Mubarak had so blatantly tried to cover up his death. Protests against the police were being planned via social media platforms to coincide with the Police Day.

Several months earlier, the Mubarak regime had falsified the results of the legislative elections, winning approximately 90 percent of the seats in parliament. This parliamentary round was key to the regime, as it would rubber-stamp the expected rise to power of Gamal Mubarak, the son of and long-awaited heir to Hosni Mubarak's presidency. The key year for the "hereditary project," a term coined by the media to describe the transition of power from father to son, was expected to be 2011. The project was spearheaded by a group of Egyptian business oligarchs, ministers, and Mubarak's own family to pass power to Gamal under the pretext of democracy.

Personally, this so-called hereditary project has always infuriated me. I viewed it as an insult to Egypt, its people, and its history. The Assad family in Syria had completed their hereditary project; was this going to happen in Egypt, too? Disbelief mixed with anger as I watched Mubarak's regime advance the project bit by bit over the years, cementing it in Egyptian politics and economy.

For several years, the World Bank and the International Monetary Fund (IMF) spoke glowingly of the "economic reforms" led by Gamal Mubarak and his team of technocrat ministers. That team had implemented a neoliberal economic agenda of privatization, opening up the economy and eliminating trade barriers. In 2007, Egypt recorded a spectacular 7 percent GDP growth rate and was labeled by the IMF as a "top economic reformer." The IMF report for that year concluded, "Egypt's economy had another year of impressive performance supported by sustained reforms, prudent macroeconomic management, and a favorable external environment."

All this hid a dark reality: nothing trickled down to the average Egyptian. Even according to the World Bank, about 40 percent of Egypt's eighty million people live below or close to the poverty line, surviving on about two U.S. dollars a day. As a long-time resident of Cairo, I saw the disparity in wealth grow year after year. In the final years of the Mubarak regime, this disparity was obscene. The wealthy had begun to desert the old city of Cairo and move to luxurious, Hollywood-style, gated communities in the desert, with lush golf courses and artificial lakes. Old Cairo, with its pollution, traffic, and broken services, was being left to the poor.

Slowly but surely, Egyptians began to fight back. In the few years preceding 2011, Egyptian civil society and social movements had been reinvigorated, despite being stifled by the oppressive regime. A turning point was the opposition to the Iraq war in 2003 by the Egyptian people and several political groups. In 2004, the Kefaya (Enough!) movement was formed against the rule of Mubarak and the possible succession of his son Gamal, and it had brought Egyptians, albeit in limited numbers, out into the street. A resurgent Islamist current had seen the Muslim Brotherhood win approximately one-third of the seats in the 2005 parliamentary elections. Agitation against worsening work conditions as a result of the privatization program had resulted in several unprecedented strikes, most notably the one in the industrial city of el-Mahalla el-Kubra on April 6, 2008, creating a workers' solidarity movement of the same name. A grassroots campaign supporting Dr. Mohamed ElBaradei's candidacy grew in popularity in 2010, despite the regime's efforts to contain the emergence of any potential opposition leaders.

Socioeconomic turmoil and interpolitical tensions slowly bubbled under the surface in Mubarak's Egypt. With a mixture of fascination and envy, I watched the Tunisian revolution erupt and President Ben Ali flee the country in January 2011. I wondered, could this ever happen in Egypt? Is there a future that doesn't include the Mubaraks being in charge?

I contemplated these questions as I headed out to the planned demonstration. I met up with my friends, Arwa and Nadia, at one of the protest's designated meeting points in the Cairo suburb of Shubra. Upon arriving, we found dozens of Central Security trucks filled with riot police. The commanding officers were walking around, smoking and joking with one another, with the usual bravado characteristic of the Egyptian police. This was their day, and they would continue to crush any resistance to the regime. They had no idea how the day would end, and neither did we. I had been involved in prodemocracy protests since 2005, and the general rule was that the Central Security usually outnumbered the protesters ten to one, and today would be no different.

As we waited, not many protesters joined us. I found out later on that the Shubra location was a decoy to distract the police from the real meeting point in Tahrir Square. A friend called me. "Come to downtown Cairo near the High Court," he told me, adding, "The numbers are getting bigger!" We then headed to the court, where we found a large number of state security officers and riot police had cornered a few hundred protesters. But something seemed different; a mood of defiance was growing. Hundreds of protesters continued to pour in. The police made a human barrier consisting of several rows of riot police to keep us confined to the area, but bit by bit people challenged it. The police, probably for the first time in their lives, began to look intimidated. We pushed against that barrier, and finally it broke.

For the first time in our lives, we were in an uncontrolled demonstration roaming the streets of downtown Cairo. As we walked the streets, we chanted, "Egyptians! Join us!" Bystanders, both bemused and excited, watched us pass. There was no love lost between Egyptians and the regime, but Hosni Mubarak had consistently crushed all attempts at opposition while placating other segments of society. People were afraid of both the regime and the consequences of joining a demonstration.

Then something incredible happened: the bystanders, who had initially watched us with curiosity, began to join us. What began as a protest of a few hundred had become a demonstration of several thousand. Torn between fear and excitement, I slowly realized that this was not just any other day. Some people began to climb signposts and tear down pictures of Mubarak. We headed straight for Tahrir Square as the chants grew louder and the crowds swelled. Approaching Tahrir from the north through Talaat Harb Street, we saw a squad of riot police forming a line to stop us from entering the square. They fired rubber bullets and lobbed tear gas canisters at us. We momentarily dispersed, struggling to see through the smoke and gagging from the tear gas. Tear gas is one of the most horrible things that you can inhale; it makes you tear profusely and unable to breathe, coughing uncontrollably, eyeballs bulging. Despite all this, we were able to regroup and enter the square. Our group had now grown to around twenty thousand people.

The scene in Tahrir Square was surreal. Riot police threw tear gas canisters, violently beat people, and sporadically arrested protesters. It was open season on the Egyptian people, courtesy of Mubarak. But something curious was happening; people were fighting back. More and more protesters poured into the square from other directions. Several thousand people comfortably held the middle of the square. Makeshift barricades were set up. Riot police amassed on Qasr al-Ayiny Street south of the square, and we headed toward them. The protesters threw rocks at the riot police, and the riot police threw rocks back. We had made it to the front and stared down the policemen, who were beating any protesters they could get their hands on. All of a sudden, a siren and microphones blared out loud commands to the riot police. The order had been given to the police to charge the protesters and get rid of them once and for all.

Place: Tahrir Square, in front of the American University in Cairo.

Time: January 25, around 4:00 p.m.

It was that man—whose loud shouts implored, "Do not run! Egyptians, how long will you continue to run?" "Turn around and let's face them"—who had a calming effect on me, even though the riot police were charging at us. I look to the people next to me, all young Egyptians, facing down tyranny. I feel a sense of pride to be making what could be our last stand against a brutal regime. The riot police were getting closer and were finally upon us. No one ran. We stood still, preparing to face our destiny.

I am reminded of Kapuściński's book *Shah of Shahs*, in which he describes protesters in the 1979 Iranian revolution as follows:

> The policeman shouts, but the man doesn't run. He just stands there; looking at the policeman . . . he doesn't budge. He glances around and sees the same look on other faces. Nobody runs, though the policeman has gone on shouting. At last he stops. There is a moment of silence. We don't know whether the policeman and the man on the edge of the crowd

already realize what has happened. The man has stopped being afraid—
and this is precisely the beginning of the revolution.[6]

Kapuściński made the astute observation that is relevant to Egypt: Revolutions are not hatched in smoke-filled rooms or by activists armed with Twitter
and Facebook accounts; rather, revolutions are made by everyday people who
are no longer afraid. That is the profound change that happened in Egypt on
January 25. Egyptians, who had bowed down to their pharaohs for seven thousand years, simply said, no more.

As the riot police approached us with their armor and batons raised high,
they noticed that we were not moving, something they had never seen before.
The line of soldiers started to slow down until they abruptly stopped a few
meters in front of us. For a moment, both crowds stared at each other, polar
opposites on an urban battlefield. That moment will be etched in my memory
forever; time almost seemed to stand still.

Then the most incredible thing happened. The riot police turned back
and started running for their lives. We chased them, captured a few, hit them,
and took away their weapons and helmets. They ran back to their lines, psychologically broken. Although they would still fight us in the coming days, we
all knew that something profound had just taken place. There was a raised
collective consciousness among us. A realization. An epiphany. Simply that
we will no longer be afraid. We drew strength, courage, and resolve from one
another, from our numbers, and from our conviction. Our small group right
there reached that conclusion, just as other Egyptians had reached it across
the country that day. And in that moment, the Mubarak regime had lost its
most significant weapon: fear. Eighteen days later, the tyrant stepped down.

I was born in 1979, and in 1981 Mubarak became president. In my lifetime,
I have known no other president. His picture adorned offices, classrooms, mu-
rals, and posters across the country. It was accepted that Mubarak is Egypt and
Egypt is Mubarak. This all changed in eighteen days in 2011. I went through a
life-changing experience on January 25, and it was incredible to share it with
thousands of my countrymen. I am proud that we inspired millions more to
join us in the days until Mubarak left. But the Egyptian revolution continues.
We took down the head of the regime; the body remains. Every day there is a
struggle against a different, smaller Mubarak: in offices, in universities, in
government departments, in schools, in factories, and on farms. Seven thousand years of pharaohs' rule will not be erased easily, but they will nonetheless be erased. On January 25, 2011, an ancient country and its people were
reborn.

FUNNY BEGINNINGS AND HAPPY ENDINGS

Mona Prince

Novelist and university professor, female, 41, Suez

After the Tunisians toppled their president, I called my family and friends to offer congratulations on the Tunisian revolution as if it were our own. Of course we wondered, "Would the Egyptian people revolt?" But we concluded, "Not during our lifetimes." Few Egyptians resorted to self-immolation, following the example of Tunisia's Mohamed Bouazizi, the trigger of the Tunisian revolution. Even though a very small number of injuries were caused by first-degree burns, they led to a barrage of jokes by Egyptians. For example, "A call to all Egyptians! Do not set yourself on fire, because if the revolution begins, there will be no more Egyptians left." Obviously, though, everyone who tried to immolate himself was labeled as insane, mentally unstable, or someone looking for fame and, certainly, a condemned sinner.

But there was a frenzy of sarcasm shared over the Internet about self-immolation in Egypt. Some of the comments mocked people associated with the regime. For example, a joke about the trader Ahmad Ezz went like this: "To solve the problem of people burning themselves, increase the price of gasoline."

Boutros Boutros-Ghali, finance minister: "We will impose new taxes on the family of each person who burns himself with gasoline." Environment minister: "The burning of citizens is the reason for the black clouds in Cairo." Labor minister: "The burning of citizens provides new jobs for young people to work as fire fighters." Ahmed Aboul Gheit, foreign minister: "Citizens lighting themselves on fire is an internal matter, and every Egyptian citizen is free to set himself or herself on fire." Barack Obama, U.S. president: "America wants to deploy its military forces to Egypt to protect foreigners and minorities from the smoke of burning Egyptians." Hamas: "The reason for what is happening to Egyptians, burning themselves, is that they feel guilty for participating in the siege of Gaza." Ehud Barak, Israeli defense minister: "The act of Egyptians burning themselves threatens peace and security in the Middle East."

As an Egyptian citizen, I am not impoverished, and I do not belong to any political party or particular intellectual school. I believe in freedom of expression, but I do not think that demonstrations that end with arrests and beatings are the solution. I have no proposals to change reality and do not see the horizon of the future as better or worse.

These thoughts came to me as I finished grading the exam papers of my students, who usually frustrate me with both their shallow answers and the deterioration of their intellectual and linguistic capabilities. But these students (as one of the university deans told me) must not remain at university for more than four years, and thus they must pass and graduate—the implication being that I should let them pass their exams no matter what. So I had to read through their answers and try to find a useful phrase to justify giving them a passing grade. This troubled my conscience because I knew very well that if I had read those answers carefully, no one would have passed.

Looking at the clock on Tuesday, January 25, 2011, I realized that it was one o'clock, almost one hour before the demonstrations were supposed to start, as stated on the Facebook page "We are all Khaled Said." I wore heavy clothing that would not hinder my movements and put on athletic shoes suitable for running in case I needed them. "Mama, I'm going down to join the demonstration in Shubra," referring to the district of northern Cairo. "Is Shubra also demonstrating? I thought demonstrations were at the Lawyers Association and Journalists Association neighborhoods?" she replied.

"Demonstrations today are supposed to be all over Egypt. The demonstrations in the center of the capital usually have about fifty or sixty participants, and they last for two or three hours before the Central Security agents disperse them by beating or arresting some of the protesters. I'll go and see what happens in Shubra."

"Don't be late," she told me.

"OK. I'll be gone for only about an hour because I still need to finish grading exam papers."

I had never been to Shubra Duran before, so I contacted my Christian friend who lives there and asked him how to get there. He gave me directions but advised me not to go. I got angry and insisted that I would anyway. I took a bus that left from my neighborhood and headed to Shubra. On the way, I saw a lot of vehicles belonging to security agents at Ramses Square. When I told the driver to drop me off at the next station, Shubra, the same request was made by a veiled girl sitting behind me. I turned around and saw a young woman who might have been a university student. I asked her if she were going to the demonstration.

"Yes, I am."

"How did you know about it?"

"I saw it on Facebook. There was an 'event' posted."

"An 'event'! But this is not a "Mohammad Munir—the famous singer—party"; it's a demonstration!"

"Of course, I know that."

We smiled at each other, and I asked her: "Do you belong to a particular party?" Her answer was that she did not.

The veiled girl and I both went down together and walked to Shubra Road, which is a very wide street. There was no sign of any demonstration. A small number of military officers could be seen on a few corners in the area. One of them looked at his watch; it was quarter to two in the afternoon. A lady in her forties was near us, and she went to one officer and started to talk to him. We could hear a few words about demonstrations, dignity, and high prices. It was clear that she was involved in the demonstration. When we asked her later if she had come to demonstrate, the military officers who heard us started laughing.

At two o'clock, the first group of demonstrators appeared, and the security personnel seemed confused. The protesters succeeded in joining together, and the number grew to hundreds of people shouting: "We either have a life that is deluxe (that is, high-quality) or we will get in the box" (the security vehicle). The military officers started to get impatient as more demonstrators showed up. The Christian demonstrators came, even though the night before, three major churches had advised people not to participate. The security agents were putting up cordons to separate the demonstrators but still allowing anyone wanting to join the demonstration to get inside the cordon. One young officer saw me carrying my camera and taking pictures of anti-Mubarak slogans. With a sarcastic tone he asked me if I wanted to get in while sexually harassing me by touching my arm. I looked at him with contempt and asked him loudly: "Are you touching me?" He took off his hand immediately.

Violence began at four o'clock as the security agents started to attack and detain people. I took some quick out-of-focus pictures. One of the security agents saw me and hit me so hard that the camera fell from my hands one meter away. I cannot say that I reacted by pushing him away, because he had a huge body, but I may have had my arm waving in front of him as a failed attempt to keep him away from me for a few seconds. I jumped quickly and picked up my camera, but another person, or perhaps the same huge man, hit me again and this time the camera fell more violently than the first time. One of them picked it up and gave it to their boss, a man in his thirties wearing civilian clothes with sunglasses. "Give me the camera, please!" I demanded.

"I will not."

I put my hand in his pants pocket and tried to take the camera, but he clutched my hand firmly and I moved it away.

"What gives you the right to take my camera?" I asked.

One of the *baltajya*, or thugs, intervened and told me that the man was a security officer.

"So what? I am a university professor," I replied, adding, "Should I believe anyone who claims to be working for the security authorities?"

He then gave me the camera and told me that his wife also was a university professor. I thanked him and showed a faint smile. At this point, I realized that the clashes had resumed between demonstrators, Central Security agents, and the state security informant. They went back and forth throwing bricks at each other, and the protesters chanted, "Peaceful, peaceful." I finally decided that I had had enough Shubra demonstrations for the day and took the subway to Tahrir Square.

In the evening, Egyptians decided collectively to have a sit-in in Tahrir Square. I saw one person climb a traffic signal column in the middle of the square while another man handed him a microphone so that the man could loudly recite the demonstrators' demands. As I remember them now, they were as follows:

1. President Mohamed Hosni Mubarak and Gamal Mubarak publicly announce that they will not nominate themselves for the 2011 elections.
2. Dissolve the current Egyptian parliament.
3. Abolish the Emergency Law.
4. Release all political prisoners.
5. Amend the constitution.

Even though I was not part of the revolution of July 1952, I thought the demands were practically the same. The difference was that our statement was broadcast primitively with a microphone connected to the traffic light, which was flashing only the green light. In contrast, this statement was read by a person in the heart of the Tahrir Square, with applause, cheers, and chants of the Egyptian national anthem.

Then suddenly we started chanting what Tunisians before us had demanded: "The people want the fall of the regime." We had moved from simple, achievable demands to demanding the fall of the regime! I felt that the matter was becoming more serious and critical. I was confused. I had conflicting feelings of joy and pride but also puzzlement and shock. "So what?" I said to myself. "Do we have anything to lose? And spontaneously I started repeating the words with them as loud as I could, with all my emotion: "The people want the fall of the regime."

THE EGYPTIAN REVOLUTION:
A PERSONAL ACCOUNT

Jordan Fitzgerald Smith

American student, female, 29, Cairo

As my roommate and I watched the revolution unfold in the streets of Cairo and Alexandria on January 28, 2011, I said, "We had better get out of this café *now* and get some groceries. This doesn't look good at all!" This was perhaps the most intense day for me, as an American woman living in Alexandria, Egypt, during the Egyptian revolution, which had begun three days earlier. In 2009, I had come to Egypt in order to teach English and to learn Arabic, and with the hope of helping bridge the gap between the Egyptian and American cultures.

Before January 28, we had been warned not to leave our houses because there would be demonstrations all along the waterfront and in the main square in Alexandria. We did not live near any of those places, so we went out cautiously when necessary. Before January 28, the revolution did not seem as if it were going to amount to anything. There had been protests since January 25, 2011, and it was clear that the Egyptian people wanted President Hosni Mubarak to leave, but it seemed impossible in a country that one man had been ruling for thirty years.

On the morning of January 28, my roommate, Sherry, another American, and I had an important meeting scheduled at a café in downtown Alexandria (far from the protests). The first strange thing we noticed was that we had no cell-phone service. We were not alarmed—it is not uncommon for the networks to malfunction. However, the Internet also was down and that was a bit disconcerting. Nevertheless, we figured it would not last long. At first, we wondered if we should cancel our plans, but we decided to proceed with them anyway. We found ourselves intensely watching the television screen at the café. It was 11:00 a.m., and, from what we could see, there were (only) a few people in the streets of Cairo. We relaxed and even joked that this was not going to be a real revolution. Surprisingly, we were wrong. Two hours later, around 1:00 p.m., everything changed dramatically. It was as if someone had flipped a switch. We suddenly found a completely different scene in Tahrir Square in Cairo and Ramleh Station in Alexandria. The army tanks rolled through the streets, and hundreds of people came out to fight for their rights.

We watched tear gas being fired on people, and it became very clear that this situation was going to go from bad to worse very quickly.

Sherry and I left the café and headed for the "safest" grocery store, a place we could reach without having to drive through mass protests, in order to stock up on provisions for the weeks to come. What we saw as we went to the grocery store and after we left is something I will never forget. Fortunately, we found a taxi, and even though he took us the safest way he could, we still were not without some fearful moments. Police stations were being burned down all around us! People surrounded us with signs shouting and setting fires in the streets. This was not the peaceful Alexandria that I had known for the two years I had been living here. I felt like I had been dropped into a war zone.

After leaving the grocery store, it was practically impossible to find another taxi for our trip back to our place. It was 4:00 p.m., and people were scrambling to get home. The trams were packed with people and were stopped by protesters crossing the streets in huge numbers. Since we had around twenty bags of groceries, we really needed to find a taxi. Everyone advised us to take the tram because there were no other types of transportation available. About thirty minutes later, a taxi finally appeared and was traveling in the opposite direction. We begged him and paid him extra money so that he would take us home. By the grace of God, we arrived home safely. The streets were on fire, and we could see thousands of people protesting along the Alexandria waterfront. When we arrived home, Sherry's ten-year-old daughter, Amira, was inside the house, terrified. Thankfully she did not have to see the things that we saw that day.

The following day, January 29, was equally intense. At least the phones were turned back on at 11:00 a.m. I contacted my family in the United States to let them know that we were all right. It was nice that there was an open line of communication between our friends in Egypt. Our Egyptian friends called us throughout the day to check on us and even offered to go out and buy anything we needed.

We learned many things that day. The momentum behind the revolution was increasing, and the police were removed from the streets and replaced by the Egyptian military. A curfew was put into place to limit activity in the evenings. Since the police had been removed, looters began to break into apartments and stores all over the city. Two of my Egyptian friends' buildings had already been broken into before sundown. We were also warned that foreigners (that is, Americans, British, etc.) were primary targets of looting because thieves figured we had more money. That news made me feel completely vulnerable. I do not think I had ever been that worried about the safety of the country where I lived since the attacks of September 11, 2001, on the United States. It was completely impossible to sleep that night. We barricaded our front door with our sofas and locked our door in three different places. We lived on the third floor of our building on a fairly busy street, but our building was the nicest one on the street and also had glass doors. This made me feel very uneasy.

Since the police had been removed, the Egyptian people decided to defend their own streets. Of course my roommate and I were awake all night trying to figure out why there were men with sticks in the streets patrolling the area. We were unsure whether they were the "good guys" or the bad ones. Many fights broke out that night in front of our eyes. We heard the shots of machine guns being fired on the street that ran parallel to ours. So much screaming and shouting was coming from everywhere. It was as if people were running for their lives, and as we looked from our balcony, I wondered if we'd be running for ours as well. Unable to sleep, I kept a broom beside me in my bedroom and I lay awake, listening for anything strange. Suddenly I heard an extremely loud sound coming from our balcony doors in the living room. I was sure that someone had broken into our apartment. Apparently my roommate heard the loud noise as well and came out to help me. After realizing that nobody was in the house except for us, we were relieved and began to walk back to our rooms for more sleeplessness. Then we heard a huge fight break out in the street below us. We were terrified we would be seen, so we got down on our hands and knees and crawled out to peek over the balcony. The scene below was of people with sticks chasing a man down the street. Suddenly, a sweet voice above us said, "Do not be afraid . . ." I have never been so embarrassed in my entire life. We looked up toward the balcony next to us, and we found our neighbor looking at us as if to say, "Why are you on the ground? Nothing is going to happen to you up here!" That is when we learned that the men with sticks were there to protect us. I realized at that moment that we were completely safe.

The revolution was such an intense experience, but it proved that the spirit of the Egyptian people is strong and it showed that people *can* truly set aside their differences and fight for the same cause if they have the desire to do so. People were not concerned with what religion or social background or job or status a person had—instead, people of all religions, races, social backgrounds, and families became one during the Egyptian revolution of 2011. There was one common goal: to fight for the people's rights and to remove a dictator who had overstayed his welcome since 1981. Freedom and democracy were the important focus of the revolution, and people fought for eighteen days to earn their freedom. This is what I saw while living through the revolution and what

I found while discussing it with people afterward. The way in which people helped one another during this time was truly admirable, and I hope to see this oneness of purpose spread all over the world. Indeed, I have never been more proud to have lived through something so potentially dangerous.

IT IS JUST . . . THE BEGINNING

Sara Hany

Visual artist, female, 25, Alexandria

Egypt is not Tunisia and Tunisia is not Egypt. That was what almost everyone said after the Tunisian uprising. No one thought that the tide of the Arab Spring would come to Egypt as well.

A few days before January 25 when my friends and I heard the announcement of the revolution, we reacted sarcastically. Not because we liked the regime but because we thought, "How can you organize a revolution and give it a date?! A revolution just bursts out with no date. Giving it a date will make the police and the regime ready to crush it." We were certain that no one would go out in the street and that it would be nothing but a tempest in a teacup.

Which day was that, the twenty-fifth? That day I called my friends. They all shared my doubts, so we went out into the streets. We began to receive calls from other friends telling us that thousands of people were in the streets and demonstrations were everywhere. I remember a friend of mine saying, "It seems we missed something big." My parents called me to urge me to get back home because things seemed very unsafe. On my way back, I saw demonstrations heading to the corniche in Alexandria. My thoughts were still unclear about why.

Watching television and the Internet—which had not been banned yet—with the news and the famous photo of Tahrir Square with millions of people occupying it, I felt very happy that my doubts had turned out to be wrong. I posted the photo on Facebook and commented, "The day the Egyptians said NO." A Spanish friend of mine wrote, "Go . . . Go . . . Go. . . ." I thought to myself, "This is big. . . . It's happening and the world is watching." At home, we always had disapproved of Mubarak and his regime. My mother always wondered what had happened to the beautiful Egypt she was brought up in.

Why had things always gone from bad to worse? I thought this was our chance to change those ugly times.

The protests began early on the morning of January 28. My parents tried to keep me from going. They were too scared to approve, and my dad locked the door of the house. At that point, I had to cross the first obstacle and get out of the house, so I lied, saying that I was just going downstairs to watch the protests when they got close to our house. I went down and headed to el-Raml station where the protesters had gathered at the el-Kaed Ibrahim mosque.

A street away from the meeting area on Champollion Street, we saw smoke coming from el-Raml station. A girl was shouting that they had locked people inside the mosque before the prayers finished to prevent them from protesting and that her mum was locked in there. A man came running with a rubber bullet in his head, and blood was everywhere. Through the everyday bustle of people coming and going at el-Raml station, some hurried to defend the people in the mosque. We could hear the ringing of bullets getting closer and closer. The police shot rubber bullets, lead bullets, cartouche bullets, and tear gas. It felt too surreal. They began randomly shooting at us. The shooting receded over a distance because of a gas station where the crowds chanted, "The people want the fall of the regime."

People ran in all directions, attacking the police with stones—which for me was a painful reminder of Palestine—and the tear gas filled our lungs. I do not know how long the battle lasted. I had no sense of time or place. People started to open their houses for the wounded and demonstrators suffocating from the tear gas. People threw vinegar and onions from their balconies to us, a tip from the Tunisian revolution that we, Egyptians, learned through Facebook. Freedom, justice, and true democracy were common values that tied us together and made us realize that we were fighting the same enemy and shared the same goal.

Afterward, we started marching on the corniche to spread our demands throughout Alexandria. We marched with the police chasing us, and between every couple of districts, there would be a police checkpoint where demonstrators were attacked. At some checkpoints, the policeman in command refused to attack us as we chanted out loud: "Selmeya, selmeya" (peaceful, peaceful). The more I walked, the more I felt courage running through my veins. I felt emboldened as I had never felt before. People threw fruit, water, and juice from their balconies while we were marching. Whenever we found a banner with any photo of someone from Mubarak's corrupted regime, we tore it down. The one I remember the most was a huge portrait of the governor of Alexandria, Adel Labib, stretched across the facade of a building at least fifteen stories tall.

During the march, there were thousands of people. We were men, women, Muslims, Christians, atheists, veiled women, unveiled women, children, public figures, homeless people, students, and foreigners married to Egyptians supporting the cause. The usual verbal and physical harassment of women ceased to exist. National television reported that revolutionaries were burning police stations and releasing thugs and criminals from jails. I did not believe that those brave revolutionaries, who almost died in the demonstrations, would do this, especially since burning police stations would make us no different from those who were trying to quash the revolts. Since the outbreak of the revolution on January 25, national television was either ignoring the protests or spreading lies. Other news channels started reporting what was later called the "camels' battle," which took place in Cairo at Tahrir Square. The twenty-eighth was by far the most intense, violent day of the revolution: many lost their eyes because of rubber bullets; others were severely wounded; and hundreds lost their lives. The bloodshed that day gave us the strength to go on because each of us believed that one day those martyrs would ask us if we avenged their murders.

On the same day of "the black twenty-eighth," thugs and prisoners were released from prisons to distract us and scare protesters all over Egypt, which was no doubt a conspiracy by the regime. Citizens formed civil committees to protect homes and property during the curfew imposed by the army. All these actions by the regime did not weaken the resolve of the people to bring it down. On the walls around Alexandria, you could see graffiti saying, "Protesting in the day; protecting our homes at night till the regime is gone."

We marched daily in Alexandria and gathered to discuss the situation. I used to go to the protests in the morning and get back before the curfew started. It was strange to see a city as lively as Alexandria totally lifeless at the curfew. The joyful sounds of the city, known as the bride of the Mediterranean, were replaced by the sounds of gunfire and army tanks with their scary sounds. They were firing artillery in the air and roaming the streets. At night, my dad and our neighbors spent all night protecting our street from thugs and criminals; it became a regular occurrence to hear the sound of shooting at night and to hear of people getting shot or killed.

The whole country was at a standstill. No one went to work, and as a result, the fear of food shortages haunted us. The supermarkets opened for less than three hours a day for people to buy food. People started to run out of money because withdrawing money from banks was impossible. The banks were closed, and the banks had emptied all the ATM machines because thugs were stealing from them. People were frustrated and terrified. Watching the regime's response to the protests and every speech Mubarak gave only increased people's hatred of his regime. In one of his speeches, Mubarak promised that he would leave office in September, but many were confused and frustrated because we were leading very insecure and uncertain lives at that point. Most people believed that the regime was playing one of its tricks in order to stay in power, so we continued with our demands.

A few days before February 11, there was a march announced to take place on the eleventh on the corniche with the longest Egyptian flag in Alexandria, starting from the Bibliotheca Alexandrina. I grabbed my camera and went. There was so much hope that day and so much determination among the people. The protesters decided we would go to protest at all the presidential palaces in Egypt to force Mubarak to step down.

Later that day, I had a terrible headache, as the sun was very strong. I told my friends I would go home for a brief rest and would come back to the streets later. While at home washing my face, I heard my mum scream, followed by hysterical claps and screams from my dad. I ran from the bathroom to the living room and asked, "What? What? He died? He died?!" I was hoping Mubarak was dead and that everything would be over then. My parents gleefully told me, "He stepped down. He stepped down." Endless screams were heard everywhere. I had never before seen my parents that enthusiastic, joyful, and spontaneously expressing their extreme happiness. My mother kept laughing, jumping in the air, and singing on the balcony, and my dad kept saying, "Unbelievable. Unbelievable."

I went down to the street where all of Alexandria was celebrating; everyone was greeting everyone: "Mabrouk le Masr. Mabrouk le Masr." There were fireworks and people singing and dancing. It was an unforgettable night of extremely joyous feelings, tears and smiles, and laughter and hope. I had my camera with me and people posed and waved in front of the lens, each trying to prove himself happier or more patriotic than the other. I bought a big flag and danced with my friends on the corniche in front of Saad Zaghloul's statue, the historic Egyptian leader. We sang all the songs ever written in praise of Egypt. Even the army soldiers could not hide their smiles behind their military uniforms.

That night after watching the world celebrating with us and raising its hats honoring our revolution, a certain idea haunted me: today is the reason for my existence. I lived to witness this day and taste victory and dignity and tell my children all about it.

For me, it is just . . . the beginning . . .

WELCOME TO UTOPIA!

Amor Eletrebi

Poet, male, 23, Cairo

"Welcome to Utopia!" read the sign. It was the myth, the people's existence, walking around with a harsh grin on their faces—a grin that told you that these people had something to say. You followed the grin and checked the sign a man was holding. You could tell these words were probably the only words this man could write. You could tell he'd asked his friend at the coffee shop, after a game of backgammon and a shared Cleopatra cigarette, to teach him how to write the words. You could tell that he wrote them with the help of his seven-year-old kid. By the colors of the paint, you could tell. And you read the sign. Maybe it was a story about where he came from, a joke, a story about what brought him here, a hint, a wink, or a poem in which he'd chanted names of officials along with names of devils. It was definitely one bite from the tree . . . the tree of knowledge, the tree of revolution—knowledge of your own being and knowledge of the being of revolution.

One sign had the word that brought the rhyme to my heart . . . "Revolution!"

I did not know about any of that. I knew of no revolution. I knew nothing of the rhyme . . . "Revolution!" Yet I knew I could not exist anywhere but Tahrir. No corrupt state television could change the picture. This is big. "Words shall fly, expression shall die, and a poorly pixelated picture shall have, by itself, one sigh . . . and a sigh."

"Now you are telling me that you are ready to go to Tahrir and just die?" said Mother.

"Mother, no one will die," I replied.

"People have died!" Mother said with a worried sigh.

"People I have not met!" I said.

"I do not want you to be one of them," Mother said in reply.

"I already am one of them. I will not die."

For that, it took me a couple of Marlboros to decide to get on a bus heading to Cairo in the early morning hours of a revolution. Everyone held their breath. The bus got moving. The pigeons in the trees along the way had their backs to us. It looked like a cotton parade. But it was the pigeons' white color going bad. It did not take long until we were stopped by thugs. They obviously came from the slums-of-somewhere. You could tell. The police paid them so they would be one more stumble on the way, the Tahrir way. They took away the bus driver's license and said they would keep our bus for the day. A little girl who was with us had a terrified look on her face. She started to cry, and her mother calmed her, "Calm down, love. It's all right. You are the love of my heart, so have no fear in yours." In two seconds, everyone on the bus just felt the need to join in and chant the mom's words. "It is all right. You are the love of our heart, so have no fear in yours." We said it so we would not cry.

I followed a guy who stepped off the bus and went to talk to the big thug. We went up to the big thug, and I started talking in a cold tone with a glimpse of demand, trying to look held together: "Take it easy, bro, let's have a good morning wish for a start. Would you like a cigarette? Here is one." And that was it. A cigarette took the threat away. It was a Marlboro, after all.

The cigarette fell through my fingers while running. Everyone had to run. We'd just arrived at the gates of Cairo five minutes earlier, after a long tense trip on the country road from Mansura city. The bus driver told us he could not drive farther, so we had to walk the rest of the distance to the heart of the city . . . the city's heart that was Tahrir. Thugs attacked us with rocks and live rounds in the air, and we ran. "Maybe we all should just go back to where we came from," everyone thought. Cairo did not seem like a city that could have visitors that morning. I lit another cigarette and tried to look like I did not have a place to go, but I did. I started sneaking onto the farms on the side of the highway and started walking parallel to the road. "I cannot be anywhere but Tahrir." That was the thought.

"Finish your cigarette. We'll be taking you to the military base nearby," said the undercover cop. "They are the ones who will decide what to do to you." There weren't many places for my luck to drive me. I had to run into a group of undercover cops even after walking for twenty minutes through the farms. I got in the car, and we got moving. It was a regular Nissan car with a white cross hanging down from the driver's mirror. One of the cops, a fat, short employee-helpless kind of man, opened the door. "Let me in. Let me sit beside you. There's a place in the back of the car," he said to my grumpy face. The cop who drove the car was a nice tall young Christian with green eyes. I liked the way he held his cigarette and smoked in style. He did not smoke like one of those regular, fat undercover cops/thugs with the thick, mean mustache on his face. After driving for a few minutes, we passed a checkpoint controlled by thugs. "We might as well just give you to these guys, and they'll take you to the army," said one of the cops. "Don't let their looks fool you. They won't hurt you." The car stopped and twenty thugs surrounded it, looking through the windows. They knew these were cops.

They knew I was arrested. "He's an Israeli spy!" one of them yelled. In a few seconds, they were shaking the car, opening the back doors, and I found ten hands and a hand pulling at my chest and my long curls, reaching in from both sides. Each one of the thugs would pull me with one hand, and in the other he'd have a sword, a stick with screws sticking out of it, or a street ivory knife. "We'll cut your head off. We'll peel your scalp off and drag you down the streets," were the repeated yells. For twenty seconds, I had my eyes still and my face frozen. "I'm dead once I get out of this car," I knew. "Maybe I deserve it" I thought and wondered.

"They'll think you are some Jew spy with those curls of yours. Fix your hair or something," Mother had said a few hours ago when I was leaving. She ran after me with a hair brush, and in the kitchen, she brushed my hair a little before I pulled her away with a smile. "It's all going to be all right, Mom," I said. "Leave him alone, guys," said the nice Christian cop. "We'll take him to the military ourselves." He was one nice Egyptian, an Egyptian who, then and there, saved my life. The car started driving away. Breathe . . . ugh.

"For God's sake, say good morning," said the officer. "You got everything you need, Doctor, just stitch it and make it look a bit clean." Blood was everywhere. I could not see a face. I could not see a shirt that was not soaked in blood. The morning light was all shattered in the red shines of blood drops. It had splatters of skin, splatters of a chin, along with splatters of an act of sin. Revolution was the sin, the sin of life. I could see that everyone around me must have passed by and been delivered by the thugs. "You should consider yourselves lucky that we've arrested a doctor along the way," said the smug soldier. I sat on the floor, put my head down, and when I realized that they forgot to tie my hands like they did to everyone else, I held my hands behind my back as if they did and held them still . . . for four hours. The soldiers seemed angry enough to blame me for their forgetfulness.

I kept repeating the same story I made up about flying back to Berlin after a short, ten-day visit to my dad back in Mansura. "Where were you heading?" the huge commando officer asked while walking around in his heavy boots. "I was going to Tahrir!" The old man with his long gray beard and the traditional clothes of a poor Egyptian yelled. And he went on telling the story about his kids he couldn't feed anymore or put in decent schools. He kept looking around and looking into the faces of all the soldiers. I felt ashamed of myself, and I slunk into my own body. "This man is the man I should be," I thought to myself. "Why am I too weak to tell the truth?" I wondered to myself. "I'm going to Tahrir. I'm going to Tahrir. Say it!" I thought to myself.

"Seven of you, get in the trunk," the soldier ordered us. We were the group being released. It was me, a Yemeni embassy employee who looked to be one slow man, three average farmers I knew were going to Tahrir, a lawyer, and a newly engaged skinny young guy who was on his way to his fiancée—I knew he also was going to Tahrir. We got in the back of the big roofless military truck. They tied us all together, joined by one long rope. "Put your heads down so thugs won't attack you. You are supposed to be the lucky ones," the soldiers said to the seven of us.

It had been five minutes since the soldiers dropped us off. I had been walking around with no clue to where I was or how to get to Tahrir from here. I found myself walking by a police station, and I felt scared. I looked away and tried to walk cool. "You there!" yelled the officers who came running out of the station after me. "You got an ID on you?" I gave them my Egyptian ID. "No, we are not going to buy that. You, Egyptian, you? You are Israeli. You are a spy. Come with us," they said and grabbed me. "Gosh, not the spy story all over again!" I thought to myself while rolling my eyes at them. I sat down in the yard of the police station.

As soon as I sat down, a big black police car pulled up. All the cops ran to it and hurried to give their respects to the big general. "Who's he? Who's he?" I asked one of the cops who seemed to have too low a rank to join that paying respect parade. "He's the second man in the Giza state security, General . . ." he told me. "What's this boy's story?" said the general, pointing at me. "Come here, boy," said the big general. I sat with him on the table and told him the made-up story all over again. I told the story with the face of a kid trying to get his toy back. He looked at the stuff they took out of my pockets. "What is this?" he asked me. "It's a pack of tobacco. I brought it with me from Berlin," I told him. "Roll us a cigarette," he said, and I instantly did. Together we smoked the two cigarettes that I rolled and stared off into the view of the street with the sound of the Friday prayers going off. "And what's written on this piece of paper?" he asked while looking at the poem I had written in very bad handwriting while I was on the bus. "Well, it's a poem I wrote on the way," I replied to his astonishment. "Read it out loud for us!" he said. "Everyone come over. This boy is going to read us a poem." I read the poem. He could smell Tahrir in it, but he decided to let it go. And he let me go.

"God, I love this tobacco! What is it called, Jacob?" I said, one morning in Berlin, a few months earlier. "It's Pueblo," said Jacob. Six months, that was how long I spent in Berlin, borrowing bits of Pueblo tobacco from boys and girls around the bar. I enjoyed improving my cigarette-rolling skills. It was one of the few things that I learned living on the streets of Berlin. Berlin was the place that I traded a thousand of my books for—politics books. Politics was one of my teen crushes. And I felt no guilt selling them for money for my escape to Berlin. Egypt and politics were two things among many that I'd given up on.

Those six months came to an end on the morning of January 23. It was a morning that came with a promise I did not know, a promise of a change.

I rolled myself a cigarette while looking at Tahrir far down the long street. I could see the museum and I decided to smoke to that. "Good-looking cigarette," I thought to myself and I took off. If you are wondering, I headed down the long street.

MY EGYPTIAN REVOLUTION

Maha Hindawy

Training and development manager in a car company, female, 37, Cairo

On one night, long before January 25, I saw pictures of Khaled Said on Facebook—I could not sleep at all that night. I joined his support group "We are all Khaled Said" on Facebook. The group started organizing events for which we dressed in black and faced the Nile or the sea for an hour (and in silence) from wherever we were standing. I loved the idea because it allowed me to demonstrate my anger at and condemnation of Khaled's murder in a very civilized way. I could also express my fear of becoming the next victim of the Egyptian police force. I attended several silent protests, one with my mother and younger sister in my hometown, and another alone here in Cairo where I live and work.

On January 25, 2011, the "We are all Khaled Said" Facebook page started promoting the march, which was very well planned in terms of where to meet, what to chant, what to carry and what not to carry, and acceptable types of shoes. The page had all kinds of information, with one exception: the direction and end point of the march. Before the morning of January 25, I had never voted in any elections or taken part in any protests, because I always thought both were dangerous in Egypt. I always associated protests with harassment and very violent police reactions. I recall so many pictures of men and women being dragged through the street, and I wanted to avoid becoming one of them—and yet somehow I trusted the Facebook page. So in the morning, I headed to my favorite coffee place, Greco, in Maadi and met my boyfriend, Tim, whom I was just getting to know better. He asked me if I was joining the protests, and I told him if I did not join that day, then I would regret it for the rest of my life. "I will feel like a coward," I said. I drove from my

house, located in the very quiet neighborhood of Maadi, to Mostafa Mahmoud Mosque in Mohandessin. I arrived after Friday prayer and just in time
for the protests. There were roughly fifty people in front of the mosque, surrounded by police and soldiers, and even more people watching from nearby.

While I was roaming around the circle of protesters, trying to get in, a
police officer looked at me and said, "Do you want to get in?" "Yes," I replied.
He said, "Wassa yabny" (Make room, boy) to one of the other soldiers, who
then let me in. I thanked him, and he said, "No worries . . . we are brothers
and sisters." I learned later that the police were ordered to allow the protesters
to march as they pleased. After I joined the demonstration, I was caught by
surprise as some of the protesters inside wanted to break free. They were holding onto one another in order to form a large mass and push the soldiers out.
In two minutes' time, we broke out onto the street. I suppose that it was sheer
force, generated from the wave of people, that caused all of us to run. As I was
looking around, I noticed a young man. I asked him if he was in the demonstration and he said, "Yes." I asked him, "What do we do now?" and he replied, "Let's just run, like them."

We ran across the Arab League Street in Mohandessin, the area where
people are stereotyped as making lots of money from buying and selling anything imaginable. Adjacent to Mohandessin is the impoverished district of
Meit Oqba. The differences between these two neighboring districts are quite
striking, especially along the bordering street where one can observe elegant
skyscrapers on one side and dilapidated shacks on the other. For every rich
neighborhood in Cairo, there is a slum beside it, thanks to our regime!

As more and more people joined the protests, we chanted, "Ya ahalyina
domo alayina" (Our people, join us). Our march reached the borders of Meit
Oqba where people had a march of their own. A woman waved a flag to us
from her balcony on Arab League Street, and we responded by doing the
same. She threw her flag to us, rushed inside her house, and returned waving
another. I even saw someone on a three-wheeled bicycle operating the wheels
by hand because his feet were damaged. When he joined us, a protester gave
him a flag to use as a scarf. On the street of el-Batal Ahmed Abdel Aziz, I
heard not just chanting but roaring. Cars were driving in the opposite direction honking their horns in support, especially when we shouted "Irhal"
(Leave) in reference to Mubarak and "Enta la aadly wala habib, irhal ya wazir
el-taazeeb" (You are neither fair nor loved, leave, O minister of torture), which
is a reference to the minister of the interior's name, which in Arabic means
"loved and fair." We clapped for the police, who were very kind and allowed
us to march through their barricades and checkpoints. But this sentiment did
not last long.

After marching through Mohandisin and Dokki, soldiers and police stopped us at el-Galaa Bridge, which connects Dokki to Zamalik. In order to overpower them and continue marching, we stuck close together, locked arms, and attempted to push the soldiers out of the way (as we did at Mustapha Mahmoud Mosque), but all our efforts were to no avail. We even chanted "Selmyia, selmyia" (Peaceful, peaceful), which did not work either. I saw two other Maadites standing in the crowd, both of whom I did not know personally but had seen earlier at Greco's. While waiting to cross, an independent journalist asked me why I was protesting, "Because I have been humiliated," I replied. I added, "I do not eat good food or breathe clean air. I do not drive on good roads or feel safe when I'm on the road, because the police have given up their responsibility to the common people and serve only to protect the regime." I even referred to my distress about how our country functioned: "I make a very good salary and pay my taxes, but I never get anything in return; no health care, no education, no roads, no hospitals, absolutely nothing. I do not want to be killed brutally entering a building, as Khaled Said was."

The march leaders then steered us to Agouza Corniche and up to the Sixth of October Bridge to cross the Nile and march toward Tahrir Square. Only two people knew that I was marching: my younger sister Menna and my boyfriend Tim, both of whom were texting me to find out if I was still safe. I was not sure whether I would be going back home safe that day. All the news I had heard or read about protests in the past indicated that they were violent. I was scared, and every minute I expected the police, nice as they had been all day, to attack us. We finally made it to Tahrir and were cheered as we got there, just as we later cheered the Shubra march when it arrived in the square.

I arrived in Tahrir holding Mona, whom I met in the march, by the hand. Neither of us knew what we should do next. There were a lot of people and a lot of Egyptian flags. For the first time, they were raised for something other than soccer games! I was not sure what time it was, but I could see people praying on the square, so probably it was *ishaa* (evening) prayer, which means early in the night. Mona and I sat on the sidewalk because our feet were so sore. Someone came by and offered me a *foul* (baked bean) sandwich. I took it gratefully but then gave it away to other people who were more hungry. We could hear the noise near the al-Qasr al-Ayiny entrance. Suddenly an activist showed up and sat with us on the sidewalk and asked everyone to calm down. People were anxious and asked him what was next. He very confidently said, "Next we should relax. We cannot keep walking and chanting all day long. They have heard our voice today." An older woman who was sitting beside me and Mona suddenly screamed that her son makes barely any money and they live in a rented apartment that eats up all his money and he sits at home, jobless.

All of a sudden, the police became violent, and we eventually walked out of Tahrir Square. No taxis were available, so we continued walking on Falaki Street until we found one. I was surprised that the streets nearby were so lively and people were just going about their usual chores as if nothing was happening. They were probably used to seeing protesters head to the square, and they had started to feel it was normal. Once I was outside the area of the square, I regained my phone connection, and called Menna and Tim and told them I was fine and driving home. At home, I logged on to Facebook and started sharing what had happened to me. The immediate effect of sharing such stories on Facebook was the encouragement they provided to others and the great deal of support I received. For example, my friend Noha, who is from Alexandria and lives in the United States, changed her status and mentioned me in her new status as one of her heroes who is changing Egypt.

After the success of "We are all Khaled Said" Day on January 25, Facebook and Twitter groups posted that January 28 would be "Jum'at al-Ghadab" (Friday of Anger). Because it was blocked, I accessed Facebook through Opera Mini, the software that connected us to proxy servers. We were worried when we heard that the regime was planning to cut off the Internet completely and maybe cell-phone networks, too. An Egyptian friend living in England sent me his number so that if the Internet was shut down, I could text him the news and he would post it on Facebook. On this Friday event, the government did turn off all communication networks, including mobile services, so I could not send any news to anybody. But we eventually made our voice heard by the entire world. Personally, this day gave me the best memories, which I will never forget. It activated a part of me that had been dormant for the thirty-seven years I have been Egyptian.

THE BULLETS ARE STILL IN MY LEG

Al-Mutazbellah Ahmad Ali al-Abd

Arabic instructor, male, 25, Cairo

It was almost 2:00 p.m. on January 25, 2011, in the metropolitan Muhandisin District on the western bank of the Nile River, when shadows of silence were cast over the area. Anxiously, I walked down Arab League Street, hoping to arrive at the given meeting point without being stopped or questioned. When

I got about a hundred meters away, I sat down inside a gazebo, monitored the situation, and waited for some friends to start what we were there for. The time was approaching. I trembled as I picked up my cell phone to call my friends, speaking English as a protective measure. I watched the swarms of black uniforms spreading everywhere as small groups of youth began to appear, scattered throughout the square. One guy approached me and asked, "Are you a member of the April 6 movement?" "No, I am not," I replied. But an inner voice, though unheard, came out and said, "I am here for the same purpose." At that moment, streets flooded with masses of people, and I decided to move ahead and join the small groups of protesters surrounded by huge numbers of black uniforms and a number of armored vehicles that brought to mind scenes in Palestine or Iraq.

At a personal level, it was my first time protesting against the ruling regime in Egypt after many years of oppression and dictatorship. Greatly inspired by the Tunisian revolution's success fifteen days earlier, we decided on that day, Police Day, to say no to the oppression of the Egyptian people at all levels and to the police brutality that was familiar to every Egyptian; we all were in pursuit of our freedom and dignity. We began to shout our demands with mixed feelings of fear and happiness. Because the masses were increasing rapidly and the black uniforms left no space for the new arrivals, it was a time to explode, break down the siege of uniforms, and flee everywhere in the streets, leaving no chance for the black uniforms to surround us anymore.

I was troubled again by a feeling of fright as I was running in no direction, seeing the scattered groups everywhere and fearing the unknown. "What is our destination? Which way should we go?" I shouted, with no reply coming back. Moving ahead toward the unknown, I joined the masses, where we gathered again and began moving in an organized way. Amid the rhythms of the national anthem, we chanted and moved in straight lines, evoking Martin Luther King Jr.'s march on Washington and feeling secure and warm next to one another. Fortunately, another demonstration coming from Cairo University joined us and doubled our numbers so that the security forces could no longer stop or surround us at any point. We marched to Tahrir Square on the eastern bank of the Nile River and near downtown, where we were about to engage in a new round of clashes with the massive groups of black uniforms and the unknown.

The conflict started when a large armored van with a water cannon on top began brutally soaking us, which frightened and angered the masses because of the cultural belief that splashing water expresses enmity. A brave demonstrator jumped on the car, shut off the water cannon, wrestled the police guy there, and got him down on the ground in a heroic scene that is usually seen only in Hollywood movies. The seven entrances of Tahrir Square were blocked by the black uniforms, and I felt that we were in a trap, that it was time to give us a lesson we would never forget. Inside the square, we and the security forces circled each other and engaged in endless negotiations and discussions before the armored vehicles started firing tear-gas canisters and shotguns over our heads. Suddenly, we fled in every direction and separated ourselves from the security circles that ran away from the unbreathable air. Then we found ourselves as a target for the armored vehicles that entered the square and chased us in a useless attempt to get us out of the area.

Attacks and counterattacks continued throughout the day, and the peaceful demonstrations became violent in response to the rough treatment from the police. By nightfall, we could kick the black uniforms out of the square and the masses cheered. With the police rows stationed outside, we started screaming our demands and chanting new songs. It was a moment of self-realization. Victoriously, and with the truth on our side, we held a sit-in till we got responses to our legitimate demands. The masses started to calm down during the night after a long day of skirmishes in pursuit of bread, freedom, and social justice.

At nearly 1:00 a.m., something was about to happen. I was relaxing before the police sirens started roaring, a message that they were going to clear out the crowd violently and viciously. The same scenario was repeated by using the water cannons and firing tear-gas canisters over our heads, and we fled again in every direction to get out from under the white clouds that covered the whole square. A feeling of disappointment hit me when I realized that we might not be able to reenter Tahrir Square after a long day of confrontations with the black uniforms. The masses scattered in every direction, and we could no longer unite. We had to look for a new strategy to survive that night without being detained or injured.

The group I was in started marching downtown in an attempt to get more support and at least spread the word, so we were marching in no particular direction. At the end of each block, we encountered the black uniforms in great numbers compelling us to take a given direction to get out of the downtown area. For me, the dream was vanishing gradually while we were again heading in no direction. Suddenly, we decided to go to an area adjacent to downtown to wake up the youth, since the people of that area were known for their courage and initiative, but again to no avail. The black uniforms appeared before us, but without leadership we could not confront them. Very close to me, I saw policemen in plain clothes kidnap some of us, so I thought it was a wise decision to leave safely so that we could continue what we had started on that day.

I went home late that night, hoping to get back in the next day after getting some rest and watching on local and international media what we had done. I quickly went to Facebook and started sharing news and updates to spread the word more widely and get more popular sympathy for the youth-led movement. The dawn was approaching and I had to take a shower before going to bed, since I was tired. This was not the end of the story, however. Sleep was just a break before starting the second episode of the new series based on values we learned that day. "New scenarios to be figured out and more cooperation to be sought so that we could survive till the end of the story so that generations to come would glorify our names in history." These were nothing but presleep confabulations. To be continued!

A DECISIVE MOMENT

On January 26 and 27, 2011, we kept going down and making small protests everywhere while monitoring the situation developing around us. The idea was to make the police forces stay awake as long as possible, so they could not hold up when the time came. Invitations for revolution on Facebook and other social networks spread like a raging fire and called for the Friday of Anger. As a response, authorities shut down the Internet and even the telecommunications networks in an attempt to stop us. On Friday, January 28, I headed, as did thousands of Egyptians, to one of the many meeting points previously determined on Facebook. Friday is a weekend day in Egypt, and a majority of Muslims living there have to observe the Friday congregational prayer at noon, which presents a good opportunity to gather together as many people as possible. From the same place where I was on January 25, I moved with countless numbers of Egyptians, who represented all social classes and screamed together, "The people want to bring down the regime."

The security forces were not able to stop us at any point, and the first confrontation was on Jalaa Bridge, approximately one mile from Tahrir Square. Again, they started showering us with tear gas and firing shotguns over our heads. The scene was horrible; however, we stood united and kept saying, "Peaceful, peaceful, peaceful." Amid the clashes, I started throwing the gas canisters back at the swarms of soldiers in black uniforms. It was getting worse, but within forty-five minutes the police forces got tired, ran out of gas canisters, and started retreating while we began going forward. The next confrontation was on the Qasr el-Nil Bridge, just two hundred meters from Tahrir Square. For the first time, I could see police forces shooting people with shotguns and rubber bullets. Seemingly, police had no other recourse but to stop us from proceeding to Tahrir Square.

At that time, almost 3:00 p.m., an armored vehicle with a police officer on top moved in our direction. I was in the front lines when that police guy directed his weapon at me and, from a distance of three meters, shot me in my left leg. Suddenly, I crumpled like prey in the jungle with no power to stand up or even stretch my shot leg. My jeans were full of holes through which blood started squirting. Some guys around me picked me up and took me away from the front line to where another guy could drive me to the nearest hospital. When I arrived at the Anglo-American hospital, I saw so many Egyptian youths who had been shot in demonstrations that I received first aid treatment on the ground. My pain got much worse, and the physician decided that I should have surgery in my leg as soon as possible. Since the hospital did not have a major surgery department, they transferred me to another hospital. I was in pain as I waited for an ambulance to come and take me to the other hospital, but to no avail. I could not even call my family or any of my friends, since all communications were shut down, so my fate was in God's hands. I wanted to get rid of the pain even if they had to cut off my leg.

Fortunately, a volunteer Egyptian picked me up and took me to the hospital, where I had an operation on my left leg. The physician opened my leg from both sides, since more than 120 small shotgun pellets had stopped the blood circulating and my skin had started turning blue, a sign of possible gangrene. On my way to the other hospital, the Egyptian guy who had picked me up told me that the police forces had withdrawn; the demonstrators had reached Tahrir Square; armed forces came down; and there was a curfew right now. "Thanks be to God," I replied. I spent seven days at the hospital receiving an intensive course of medication before leaving Cairo and going home to continue the medication program with my family. Ten days later, I had a second surgery to close the open wounds in my leg, which had kept me from sleeping well for twenty days. People say that the most severe pain a human can encounter is a woman giving birth to a child. Not having had the experience of delivering a child, I can assure you that I suffered more than a pregnant woman. Like many other Egyptians, my source of information during that time was the media channels. Although my body was at home, I felt my soul was in Tahrir Square the whole time.

My friends were in Tahrir Square, so I could get even more information about what was going on during the events. Mubarak's speeches were killing me, since each time he came out to give a speech, we expected him to step down, but he used them to tease us while trying to gain more sympathy. On the evening of February 11, Egyptian national TV prepared to broadcast an unusual report. "Mubarak has stepped down," they announced. I could not believe my ears. I was so happy, like all Egyptians who went out to join revolutionists in Tahrir Square and everywhere around the country. I was celebrating with family and friends, who assured me, "Your injury will be all right." My father decided to travel to Cairo that night to celebrate the victory with the demonstrators in downtown Cairo.

Thirty years of oppression and dictatorship had come to an end, and there would be no Mubarak after that day. We fought for our freedom and dignity in a peaceful and peerless revolution that will go down in history. We are the generation that will shape the new future of Egypt and gain the respect of the whole world. Freedom is not free; it has a price and we paid it many times over. We offered 850 martyrs and more than six thousand injuries until we achieved our goal. I got into a physical therapy program, and right now I can walk almost naturally with less pain; however, the shotgun pellets are still in my leg!

IT HAPPENED IN EGYPT!

Aly Hassan Amin Rabea

Purchasing officer in a petroleum company, male, 39, Alexandria

I was not one of those political activists or those who join demonstrations with angry faces and fiery chants. I barely made it to some of the demonstrations scheduled in advance and announced through social networking sites. Yet when I started going to the demonstrations in Egypt, my main purpose was to document what was happening by taking some pictures and uploading them on Facebook. But what happened on January 25, 2011, was quite different and changed my attitude. The day before, I had arranged to meet with my friend Abdullah Sharkas, a director and photographer from Alexandria. We wanted to take some pictures of the demonstrations that we heard would be all over Egypt. We met in Manshyia Square, the largest square in Alexandria. Dating back to the late nineteenth century, it has a wonderful statue of Mohammed Ali Pasha in its center, and it is a testimony to the great historical era of Alexandria when it was a cosmopolitan city—before everything changed after the revolution of July 1952. We did not feel optimistic that the demonstrations would be very effective or even that they would be launched throughout

Egypt. The source of our pessimism was our previous experience with demonstrations over the past few years. They used to be as small, with only a few dozen or a few hundred people, who would end up receiving beatings with the sticks of the Central Security Forces and whose leaders would face arrest. Nevertheless, we decided to go and film the event, which was supposed to be during the Police Day holiday in Egypt.

It was two o'clock in the afternoon when we arrived at Manshyia Square. We were not surprised that almost nobody was there to demonstrate, particularly because the place was filled with the Central Security Forces ready to surround and beat the demonstrators at any sign of movement. Because of their small numbers, those who came to protest were looking at one another in fear and did not know if it was wise to start chants or if they should return to their homes. Even though the situation was not a surprise, we felt disappointed. Then, we decided to go to a café to drink tea and sit a bit, hoping that something new would happen. We headed to Ali al-Hindi Café, which is located in a special place: a corridor between four historic, European-style buildings. This place is covered in black because of pollution or sadness caused by neglect and ignorance. Having finished sitting in the café, we went to the square again and saw that the number of demonstrators had begun to grow, but it was still just a few dozen standing around timidly. We decided to stand for a little bit, hoping that something would happen, and soon a veiled woman and her daughter approached us. She asked us to take heart and start gathering together and chanting. Suddenly three huge, angry-looking men surrounded us, and the lady was quick to pull her daughter and flee without finishing her speech. We realized that these men belonged to state security and that we had to act wisely and quietly because we were in real trouble.

We had a dialogue with the security officer, which went as follows:

STATE SECURITY OFFICER: Who are you, and what are your names?
WE: Ali Hassan and Abdullah Sharkas.
OFFICER: What is your occupation?
ABDULLAH: I am a film director, and my friend works for an oil company.
OFFICER: And how did a Moroccan get together with a Shami? (that is, how did you get together when you do not seem to have anything in common?)
ME: Is it necessary to work in one place to be friends?
OFFICER: So what are you doing here in Menshyia?
ABDULLAH: Today is a holiday, and we decided to come here and walk downtown and have dinner at a restaurant.

Noting the professional camera that Abdullah was carrying, the state security officer asked him: 'What are you filming now during a holiday?'

> ABDULLAH: I told you that I am a director, so I need my camera with me to shoot any scene that I like while walking around.

At this moment it seemed as if the officer had lost interest or noted some of the other protesters and wanted to interrogate them. He said to us: "Photography is prohibited here. To avoid any problems, please do not do that." He turned away arrogantly and started walking away, followed by his subordinates. Abdullah answered him: "OK, but you did not tell us who you are?" The officer just looked angrily at Abdullah, not wanting to escalate things. I think it was divine providence that he only turned away egotistically while telling us his name. We did not get his answer about his occupation but did not dare to ask him again. When Abdullah realized that his defiance had upset the officer, he smiled maliciously and said to him: "You are welcome, officer!" When the officer was gone, I was relieved and asked Abdullah: "What do you think?" and he replied, "Things are getting more interesting!"

We proceeded to the center of the square and saw a few protesters, who began to sing the national anthem and wave the Egyptian flag. I was surprised by the quick reaction of the Central Security Forces, which immediately circled the square and completely contained the demonstrators. Nevertheless, the chants began to escalate, expressing love for Egypt. Finding themselves surrounded, the protesters were quick to move to the streets outside the square, causing the security forces to panic. Interestingly enough, pedestrians began to join the demonstration, which became like a snowball headed down a high hill and rapidly growing large and uncontrollable. This was beyond my expectations—in previous cases, pedestrians usually pass by demonstrations, stand far away from them, watch the protesters being arrested, and sometimes even run away from the scene quickly for fear of being beaten or arrested by mistake. As hundreds of demonstrators filled one side of the square, the security forces finally overcame their confusion and succeeded in organizing themselves in one of the downtown streets. Appearing to receive orders to attack the demonstrators, they pulled out their batons and advanced toward them, only to be met with their heroism. The demonstrators then shouted, "Peaceful, peaceful, go back, go back," forcing the security forces to stop the attack and retreat to their previous position.

As we moved from one street to another, we found that the number of people was increasing, and so were the perplexed security forces. Arriving at

Saad Zaghloul Square, the demonstrators could see the provocative campaign posters for Gamal Mubarak's nomination for the presidency. Suddenly, some young people climbed the columns and walls and, in an exhausting and challenging process without using any tools, succeeded in bringing down all the posters. Demonstrators gathered around the banners to shred and burn them amid loud shouts of joy, all in front of the security forces, which seemed to have lost control completely.

Now covering most of the streets in the city center, the protesters clearly were determined to do something new and to bring about real change on this day, not satisfied with what had already been achieved. We started to leave downtown and headed to Port Said Street, a main street that passes through several of this middle-class city's residential neighborhoods. By using such slogans as "Come out, fellow Egyptian citizens!" we tried to urge more people to take to the street and join the demonstrations. The people's response was positive, and many participated in the demonstrations. Some of the women who could not leave their homes and join us helped the demonstrators by tossing them fruit and plastic bottles of water.

The number of demonstrators increased into the thousands, and they marched down Port Said Street for a long time until they reached the end. As night began to fall, the protesters stopped to perform the *maghrib* (sunset) prayer on the street, which had helped the security forces surround the front line of the demonstration, where I was protesting, and isolate it from the rest of the demonstrators. We realized that they would beat us if we moved forward, so the protesters sat down on the ground, chanting their famous slogan, "Peaceful, peaceful." Still, it was clear that despite the demonstrators' peaceful state, the security forces had decided to handle the situation with violence, hitting the demonstrators with their batons, and the officers ordered them to shoot into the air. Because of the panicked moving and pushing of bodies, I was isolated with a small number of demonstrators, and the soldiers began beating and insulting us, and I was hit twice on my head. I was about to lose consciousness, and all that was happening to me physically seemed like a bad dream.

I could not think of anything at that time except being beaten on my head. I thought they would arrest us as soon as they were finished with the beating. But one of the officers ordered them to stop beating us, and the soldiers blindly obeyed, stopping immediately, just like a scene in a sci-fi movie when a crazy scientist presses a button and his robot soldiers suddenly stop. The officers then allowed us to get out, one after another by opening a passage past the security soldiers. As I was looking around, I saw some demonstrators with heads wounded by the severe beatings, and some were trampled. I could not believe that I was released so easily. All I thought about when I walked away was, Why didn't they detain us? The answer was clear: it was the huge number of people joining the demonstrations. In the past, they could arrest the few who came out to protest, but now what could they do with those thousands? The solution, for the regime, was to attack some of the protesters in hopes of terrorizing all of them and forcing them to return home. I branched off into the side streets in search of transportation to get home but found another demonstration at the corniche coming from the opposite direction. The entire city was demonstrating, and people were coming from all areas and from all streets.

What happened in the following days in Cairo, Alexandria, and most of the governorates of Egypt is known and has been documented, as should the determination of the Egyptian people in bringing about change and insisting on a nonviolent revolution, despite having been killed, dragged in the streets, beaten, and arrested. But in my humble opinion, such determination, persistence, and peacefulness are not less admirable than the demonstrators' civility and sense of community.

Over the last thirty years, the former regime worked to impoverish and humiliate the Egyptian people. These people believed that their taxes had been stolen in broad daylight by members of the government and parliament, who in return gave them public hospitals and other services in deplorable condition. I am not exaggerating when I say that "public hospitals" are just big words hung on some buildings; in reality, these places are not suitable even to treat animals. The state officials devoted their time and efforts only for personal gain and their own affairs, and they used their positions to achieve these selfish goals. They despised the rights and hopes of individuals, often treating them as second-class citizens. As a result, the average person internalized the same spiteful attitude: Egyptian citizens, too, selfishly cared about only their own affairs and thus hurt the interests and freedoms of other individuals and the interests of society as a whole. Yes, the Egyptian people forgot or were made to forget what society means. Although we lived in one place, every individual was speaking his or her own language and pursuing his or her own interests.

During the Egyptian revolution, particularly on January 25, 2011, we discovered an astonishing new reality. The protesters treated their revolution and one another with the highest degree of civility—I saw girls walking through huge crowds without fear of being harassed, and I saw young Christians protecting Muslims during their prayers. I saw people buy bottled water to distribute it to their fellow revolutionaries without keeping any for themselves. And I saw the rebels clean the public spaces and paint the squares immediately after Mubarak stepped down. These scenes are a few of the many other fascinating realities the Egyptian people created during the revolution. They instinctively realized that their real power lay in working together on one goal and that this unity would not be possible unless each and every one of them preserved the rights of other individuals and took care of his or her responsibilities before pursuing personal rights. Indeed, the whole world was shocked and so was the regime, and I am not exaggerating to say that even the Egyptians themselves were taken aback by their ability to adopt this civilized behavior.

The former regime, which had applied the principle of divide and conquer during the past thirty years, was toppled by the same people whom it had earlier made enemies of one another. By turning people against one another, the regime tried to remain in power, but it was surprised by a different, united, society, whose members were aware of their duties and their national goal. The regime during and after the revolution acted according to the same mob mentality that defined its rule. That is why some of its members tried to flee with stolen money or set fire to buildings containing documents that would convict them. Some officials even freed thugs and prisoners to cause confrontations and havoc in our country. There obviously is a startling contrast between the behavior of Egyptian society and that of its regime, with the latter revealed as it really was: demagogic, weak, and pathetic. And that is why it fell.

I know very well that what happened during the revolution was an extraordinary response to exceptional, difficult circumstances and that the most beautiful days of the revolution are over. The wonderful community spirit was over when the struggle for power between rival parties and movements began. After the revolution, uncertainty and confusion emerged because for the first time, people can choose their elected representatives. Regardless of these developments, human memory and history books will retain those wonderful scenes of revolutionary Egyptian society, which in moments of distress was able to make use of a great nation's civilization.

DIARY TO DEMOCRACY
(*INSHALLAH* [GOD WILLING])

Claudia Wiens

German photojournalist, female, 39, Cairo and Istanbul

You might ask why a foreigner is writing here about her experiences during the revolution in Egypt. And no, I'm not part of the foreign conspiracy that the regime claimed was supposedly instigating the revolution. To illustrate the farcical nature of these claims, the Egyptian satirical online newspaper, *el-Koshary Today* (http://elkoshary.com/), identified these foreign forces as Australian koala bears.

Since 1994 I have simply loved Egypt unconditionally—it has always felt like home. Being in Egypt during the revolution was not just a professional experience as a photographer, but something that turned my life fundamentally upside down. The intensity of events and emotions that would change by the hour during those eighteen days left me emotionally confused and exhausted for a long time. I started writing a blog called "Diary to Democracy" partly to detangle my own feelings and calm the cinema in my head.

The blog is ongoing, just as the revolution is, although whether the title Diary to Democracy still is appropriate, having being born out of overzealous optimism, remains to be seen. So far, although the first parliament elections are just about to take place, nothing really has changed in Egypt. The Supreme Council of Armed Forces (SCAF) is ruling the country in a way similar to how Mubarak did, with the same corrupt businessmen holding on to power, and even the infamous emergency law has not been dismantled. There even is talk of extending it until June 2012. With limited space to write here, three days stand out for me personally as being important to describe: January 25, the day it all began; February 1, when maybe up to five million Egyptians across the country peacefully demonstrated against Mubarak and his regime; and February 18, when a million people in downtown Cairo perhaps naively celebrated their unbelievable victory.

JANUARY 25, 2011: THE DAY IT ALL BEGAN

When the first demonstration on January 25 was announced, nobody was quite sure what would happen and how many people would turn up. Historically, demonstrations had always been quite small, with demonstrators normally being far outnumbered by police. Nobody knew what to expect, and I had the feeling we were in for a surprise. Nobody really knew where the demonstration was taking place; it started very randomly with small groups appearing from many directions. Around noon, a few thousand people arrived and started marching along the corniche (riverside) from downtown, calling for all Egyptians to join in and fight for democracy together. Prominent figures like Ayman Nour, who ran for president in 2005 and is the head of al-Ghad Party, were among the demonstrators. Protesters gathered in front of the much hated, pro-Mubarak State Television Building, from which the interminable broadcasts of propaganda stopped only the day before Mubarak stepped down.

It was then understood that their ship was sinking. Egyptian broadcasters finally admitted that there were more than a handful of protesters on the streets.

There were a lot of security forces present, but things were different this time—the authorities let the demonstrators walk freely through Cairo. One supposed that this was just a hopeful strategy that they would soon tire and go home, but little did they know. I followed the protesters all the way to Shubra, quite a few kilometers from downtown, taking photos of them and the onlookers. They paused beside the TV building and other media offices, calling for Egyptian journalists to respond. The atmosphere was really strange, a mixture of courage, apprehension, and determination—adrenalin was in the air. Astonished people in the poor neighborhood of Bulaq Abou Eila were watching with curiosity as hundreds of protesters walked through this *baladi* (local) area calling for every Egyptian to join in.

For decades Egyptians have felt that they did not have a voice, with many too scared to speak out. On this very first revolutionary day, most ordinary Egyptians still did not believe that this time things would be different, and they could even less imagine that it would take only a few days for many of them to join the uprising. I will never forget the expressions of utter disbelief and how many citizens were transformed from total passiveness, resignation, and apathy to courageous activism. It was as if the genie had finally granted them a wish. This revolution took everybody by surprise, although deep down many knew that it was more than overdue.

Having experienced many demonstrations in Cairo before, I was highly alert and uncomfortable, this time expecting something untoward to happen at any moment. Previously, you might have expected to have seen a crowd of a few hundred people (if that) stationed in front of a public building surrounded by far greater numbers of police. Protesters would chant their slogans, police would flex their muscles, and a few hours later the whole thing would be over. We just kept walking, winding through many neighborhoods that had never seen a protest march before. On the main road through Shubra, we passed a number of unarmed police, which looked somehow suspicious. I found a concrete plinth between two cars to take a photo, and as people from the crowd came toward me, I suddenly heard screaming from the other side. I realized we were trapped by armed police charging at the protesters from both sides. Panic broke out, and with no means of escape, people were running in all directions, protecting themselves from being beaten. The police were running directly toward me, and since I was stuck between two parked cars, I had nowhere to go except climbing on top of one of them, hoping nobody would harm me. I was very scared by this sudden outbreak of violence, which was only a glimpse of what was to come later in Tahrir Square.

I was scared for my life—the longest seconds of my life, I think—but I was really lucky not to be harmed by the fleeing masses. Then one of the police officers left the line and came toward me. A blond, foreign woman taking photos of a demonstration in a part of Cairo where tourists were not normally to be found was perhaps asking for trouble. But to my surprise, he said to me, "Give me your hand and I'll take you out of here." I first refused to climb down from the car, but he insisted. Hesitantly I gave him my hand and let him help me, and sure enough he led me behind the fighting and delivered me unharmed. He also apologized with the words "I'm sorry for that."

Obviously on this first day of unrest, the police did not yet have clear orders to attack journalists or foreigners. Anyway, I was shaken by the whole scene and got into a taxi to escape. The taxi driver looked at me and said in a fatherly voice, "What happened to you? You look terrified; I think you need some juice." And without further ado he drove to a small shop and bought me a juice. From being scared to death just minutes before, I felt now really touched by this kind gesture. I got a taste of the emotional roller coaster that was to come in the next weeks.

FEBRUARY 1, 2011: THE ONE-MILLION-PEOPLE MARCH

It is thought that more than five million people took to the streets all over Egypt, including the One-Million-People March in Cairo (perhaps even *two* million). I still have goose bumps and tears in my eyes when I recall that day. It was amazing to see all these Egyptians united in their wish to end Mubarak's dictatorship. For many years I told Egyptian friends that if they took to the streets in massive numbers, nobody could stop them, but to no avail. Repeatedly I had to listen to "You cannot mobilize Egyptians" and "People are too scared of the security apparatus." My usual reply was, "But you constantly complain about the government and the corruption; I do not understand why you do not fight for your rights!" "So what can we do?" "There is no hope" was normally the end of the conversation. I knew that my nagging was somewhat naive and that I could never fully appreciate their fear, having grown up in a free country and not having been conditioned to live in fear and be silent. But I kept hoping and strongly believed the day would come when Egyptians would break their "chains," take to the streets, and fight back.

I believe that February 1, 2011, actually was one of the best days of my life, as I was so full of hope and everything seemed possible. At 9.30 a.m. I was standing on a balcony overlooking Tahrir Square and its adjoining bridges. I could see endless streams of people heading slowly but surely toward Tahrir, to join the first ever one-million-person march. That was the moment I knew the Egyptian people would be successful, that it was only a question of time. The energy was so overwhelming I cried—so peaceful, hopeful, and powerful. It reminded me of Gandhi's so-called Salt March. People were determined to reach their aim peacefully, no matter how long it took. For an hour or so I watched people crossing the Nile bridges, walking down the corniche and advancing from Qasr al-Aini Street. Then I joined them in Tahrir. Everybody was there—whole families, students, professors, rich and poor, al-Azhar clerics, Coptic priests, young and old. It was a vast and comprehensive mixture from all walks of life that I had never ever seen gathered together. Unfortunately, Egypt has a very segregated society, with rich and poor never integrating on such a level. The atmosphere was so powerful that without seeing it for oneself, words cannot really pay it justice. The masses on the streets from all levels of society, who were united in their wish to end Mubarak's reign, created an unbelievably powerful energy that touched me to the core.

February 18, 2011: The Friday of Victory

Hundreds of thousands Egyptians went to Tahrir Square once again on Friday, February 18, to celebrate their victory, exactly one week after Hosni Mubarak stepped down on February 11. They called it the "Friday of Victory," and in fact it was also the Friday of utmost freedom and joy. Where else in the world can citizens decide to turn the center of their city into a one-million-people party without needing an official permit? Social media and text messaging spread the word, with rich and poor of all ages turning up to celebrate peacefully! This was a drastic change from only four weeks earlier when the very notion of such great numbers gathering in a public space was not only inconceivable but life threatening.

People were commemorating the "martyrs," as they called the victims of the revolution, displaying their pictures and praying for them. Everybody was waving flags and chanting "Irfaa rassak foq, inta masri" (Hold your head up, you are Egyptian), expressing their newly found national pride. During the twelve years I have been living in Egypt, I have listened to people expressing their hopelessness and lack of courage to change even the smallest thing—everybody was caught up in a big corrupt machine. I was delighted to see that people were now able to speak out against injustice. Downtown was like an enormous version of Speaker's Corner in Hyde Park, London, with many giving speeches about their ideas for the future and how to improve the society or sharing political ideas with anybody who would listen. Others were giving out fliers with pleas like "Do not take bribes" and "Do not drive the wrong way up a one-way street"!

A military band played for the masses, who had come together for the Friday prayer that was held by the famous sheikh Yousef el-Qaradawi, head of the Islamic Conference. He announced, "Today I will not only address Muslims; I'm addressing Muslims and Copts, I'm addressing all Egyptians." The song "Ya habibti, ya Masr" (My Darling, Egypt) by the famous singer Shadia, about her patriotic love of Egypt, blasted out, and people were dancing wildly in the streets, singing along at the top of their voices. It might sound kitsch, but there is no other way to describe it: it was an atmosphere of love and peace, an Egyptian Woodstock!

Unfortunately these days, hope is not really in the air. The initial optimism has diminished, partly because people realize that in order to have real change, society also has to change, and this means that every person's behavior has to change. It began to dawn on people that the responsibility lies with them and that a true revolution does not happen overnight. One Egyptian said the other day, "If I had fallen into coma at the beginning of January and had woken up now, I would not see any difference."

This represents the feeling of many Egyptians, but if one takes a closer look, one will discover many small projects that are working toward a freer and more responsible society. Projects like Open Space, the Flash Hub, Mashrou al-Mareekh (open mic). Even though I came to the realization that it all will take much more time, I still feel optimistic and strongly hope for more days of freedom and joy like February 18.

TELLING MY SECRET

Kholoud Said Amer

Editor and translator at Bibliotheca Alexandrina, female, Alexandria

How do I start my revolution story? It is in fact not only my story—it is the "story of the people," like the title of the famous song by Abdul Halim celebrating the construction of the Aswan Dam in the 1960s. During the eighteen days from Tuesday, January 25, until Friday, February 11, 2011, the best days of my life by far, we related to this classical song because it talks about Egyptian resilience. For many years, I have been occupied with public action in a nonpolitical and nonideological manner, particularly in social movements and civic work. I also was involved in youth activities in the areas of dialogue, informal education, and different community service opportunities. Since around 2009, Egypt's social media network has allowed a public space not only for expression but also for mobilization. The information that was blocked before has become virtually impossible to control now. The truth has become completely exposed.

For some reason, the Khaled Said incident persuaded me and other people to become politically involved, and his death sent a message that nobody could be safe from the regime's aggressive rule. My brother, for example, goes to Internet cafés in the middle of the night without an ID card, and the last thing I want to see is a Facebook page dedicated to his memory, which was the fate that Khaled Said faced at the hands of the authorities who picked him up from an Internet café and killed him. We realized that being passive was no longer acceptable because even those who did not get involved in any political activities were not spared from oppression. The first time I participated in a demonstration was the one that followed the funeral prayer for Khaled. (I always refer to him by his first name only and still feel unpleasantly cold and sorrowful when I see his famous picture with his smiling eyes, or when I see his mother, Layla, dressed in black at a demonstration or in a picture.) I then participated in several demonstrations close to his house and mobilized a lot of my colleagues to join. I also met a number of activists with whom I have developed strong relationships.

With the call to take to the street on January 25, 2011, which coincided with Police Day, I had mixed feelings of enthusiasm and frustration because of some activists' dismissive attitude: many of them ridiculed the call because it was scheduled ahead of time, something they were not used to. Later, I understood their position, but I still cannot forget the feeling of regret I had because I felt that some of them let down the people. On Tuesday morning, I checked out the streets and the reaction of the people, and everything was quiet and there was no evidence of anything abnormal. But my frustration disappeared as new demonstrations spread, and I was walking fast in the street trying to find one. Finally, we saw the Central Security soldiers preparing to move somewhere. We walked cautiously next to them because I knew where they were going. The voice of the people was our guide, and I melted in its melody. I have never seen such a scene before: men, women, young men, girls, adolescents, children, and even the elderly were present, some wearing shabby clothes and some the latest designs. We saw people closing their shops to join us while others waved to us from the balconies of their houses. I saw a staggering number of Egyptian flags, along with enough love to fill the entire world.

I tried to escape from the Central Security soldiers because one of them hit me while, ironically, another helped me out. I chanted with the masses and met my brother at the demonstration, where I caught him by his shirt and trembled when he disappeared for a moment. That's when I knew why my father would scream every time I left the house to join a demonstration. In the evening I was really tired, and my brother helped find a taxi to take me home around 6:30 p.m. But I soon realized that the protesters were suffering an unprecedented attack with live and rubber bullets and tear gas. During the night, I made sure that everyone was all right and, with one of my friends, wrote a report about the day's events and published it on Facebook and several blogs. With a feeling of euphoria I followed up the news about Tahrir Square sit-ins and shouted in front of my computer with them, "The people want to overthrow the regime." It was a great and overwhelming feeling, and I cannot easily describe it. As I was about to go to bed, I was surprised by the news that security forces had broken into the square, and I started to scream "electronically" with the rest of my friends: "Help them; save them; join them!"

When I went to work on Wednesday morning, the day was not like any other workday. I was surprised to be labeled by my coworkers as the "revolutionary veteran." (I was one of the few employees who participated.) Everyone gave me a great deal of encouragement, with the senior colleagues expressing some serious concerns and the junior ones showing jealousy in the sense of "I wish I had been there too." Everyone followed the news of the Suez governorate, and it was clear that its people were more likely to win. We also were concerned about those who were arrested on Tuesday and Wednesday in Alexandria, and we tried to do something to release them or provide legal support for them. I received many telephone calls asking me about someone who was missing and whose family did not know where he or she was.

I also was very disappointed not to see organized demonstrations on Wednesday and Thursday as planned, but it was very clear that Friday, January 28, 2011, was the decisive day. Mobilization for that Friday continued, and tips on how to deal with security forces spread as well, mostly coming from our Tunisian brothers. A large number of nonpoliticized individuals were ready to participate, along with those who had clear oppositional positions but did not participate in the earlier days because of family circumstances. I remember very well one of my friends who suffered from the grip of her protective family. She was crying, "People are dying outside and I am sitting here, all I can do is 'share' and 'tweet!'"

On Thursday, we started to use landline telephones because we were increasingly aware of the regime's surveillance. One of my best friends told me about the "war" between us and the security forces before I bid him farewell that day as if he were going to a holy war. I wanted to cry and tell him not to put himself in danger, but he responded by teaching me the tactics of dealing with different situations in case the security forces attacked us. That day I knew I had an important role to play, but when I returned home, I realized that the regime had shut down the Internet, messaging services, and mobile phones. The first thing I saw on TV was a video on Al Jazeera showing a protester from Sinai who had been deliberately shot. I collapsed in tears and cried with a pain I had never felt before. My family was talking about those "who organize demonstrations," without knowing that my brother and I were among those people! We did not reveal that we were participating. My father tried to stop me from going out that day, but I convinced him that I was going to watch the news with my friend, who also used the same (trick) to be able to get out. Two of my friends and I joined the protesters after Friday prayer, which was a majestic scene without soldiers among the people. We passed many police stations and did not see anything unusual. By the afternoon, my friends were tired of walking, so we decided to go to the house of one of them to rest before setting off again. In her house we watched the news, and we found out what happened at al-Qayed Ibrahim Mosque in Alexandria where the security forces threw tear-gas canisters at the worshippers before they had even finished their prayers. The news said that the prime minister had called for an urgent meeting of the government on Sunday.

When we got back to the streets around four o'clock in the afternoon, we saw uproar and chaos and realized that the Bab Sharq police station had been set on fire. We had never seen such destruction and thick smoke before. A black cloud was covering the sky of Alexandria. As darkness fell, my friend's husband suggested that we go home. The al-Muntazah Building, which is close to my home, was on fire, and the road to my house was closed. I felt very scared—there was fear inside me for my country and its future. It took me a long time to find another road to my house, but as soon as I arrived, I heard my sister screaming, "Someone's coming." My mother was talking on the phone, almost collapsing and saying "I want my boys!" I read on the newsflash of the Egyptian television channel 1 that a curfew had been issued and that the military forces would move into the streets. At that time I realized that we had done something: we had started a revolution. This thought lasted for several seconds before I recalled my mother saying "boys" and not "my daughter."

My brother was taking a college exam, and we were worried about him, but he arrived home a few hours later. He brought videos and pictures of the deployment of the army and its tanks. He took the footage while walking from the college to our house, almost from beginning to the end of Alexandria

Corniche. His exam had been held on the fourth floor of the college build-ing, but all students were sick as a result of the tear gas, which was sprayed at demonstrators on the street. "My God!," I thought, "What happened to the people who had canisters thrown at them?" We waited from eight o'clock to midnight to watch Mubarak speak. Political analysts on satellite channels were competing to guess how his letter of resignation would be worded. It was ecstatic to think that we could beat him in three days, but he soon ap-peared to have slapped us on the face with an arrogant speech in which he described us as people destroying public and private property, adding that he had asked the government to resign.

Personally I did not hate Mubarak before then—despite my interest in pub-lic affairs and my knowledge of the Egyptian political scene. I considered him a very old man fooled by those around him to exploit power. I did not feel that the problem was only Mubarak, and that is why I did not shout "Down, down, Hosni Mubarak" during the demonstrations for Khaled Said. But one sen-tence or incident was enough to change my mind. It happened when the for-mer president was visiting Upper Egypt, supposedly to open a bridge or a farm or something that does not matter in the context of what he said. Television showed that he had accepted an invitation to drink tea with a farmer! In fact, his aides brought someone, with his wife, to pretend to be a farmer living in a beautiful house overlooking the Nile. They kicked out the real owner of the house to stage this show. The broadcast dialogue was superficial—the presi-dent was asking, "How are you and your children?" and the man was replying, "Thank God, we are living in prosperity, thanks to you." But when the presi-dent asked him how he got to his work, the man replied that he took the ferry. "Is it one of those that sank?" the president asked as he burst out laughing. He was referring to the Egyptian ship that sank in the Red Sea in 2006, drowning about a thousand workers returning from Saudi Arabia, a tragedy that aroused intense anger toward the regime.

His laughter and insensitive reply shocked me as nothing had before, and I realized that he was aware of what was happening in Egypt. He knew about all our calamities and never spoke about them or, even worse, he made fun of them. The lives of one thousand people were lost while traveling on a ship that belonged to one of his friends, and his authorities did not even try to save them. When he gave his first speech during the revolution, I suppressed my rage and desire to spit on the TV screen. If he had stepped down then, he would have saved some of his remaining dignity, but he refused to do so.

On the morning of Saturday, January 29, I went to the demonstration with-out telling my parents. Two of my friends who lived in my neighborhood joined me to take a taxi to Manshyia Square. We did not know about the situation there after the regime shut down all means of communication. We saw thousands of people, but police cars and security vehicles were burned and the army tanks were surrounded by people. Everywhere I looked I saw smiles on the faces of protesters, and I was smiling back. It was a solemn scene, yet we were talking and encouraging one another. At that time, I knew that we were determined to end Mubarak's reign.

But we made a mistake by leaving the streets and squares after he stepped down. We will continue. God is with us, and people who have a right always win.

THE FALL AND RISE
OF AN EGYPTIAN UPRISING

Samaa Gamie

Professor of English at Lincoln University, Philadelphia, female, 38, Alexandria

For years I have wondered what it meant to be an Egyptian: Was it something that came with birth? Was it that once someone was born on a land, it became his or hers by default? That was not the case with me. I was not born in Egypt. Being born in another country took away my sense of belonging to what I should perceive as my homeland. Even after moving back to Egypt and spending most of my youth and adult years there, the question of what made me an Egyptian lingered. I always wondered who I saw myself as. Was my homeland determined by the fact that I was born to Egyptian parents? Was I determined to be an Egyptian by blood, inheritance, passport, or default? I could never pinpoint who I was. I was an Egyptian based on a birth certificate and a passport that claimed my nationality was Egyptian, but there were questions in me that lingered about what made me an Egyptian and how it was that I felt so little attachment to the land that claimed to be mine and that I belonged to it.

I guess my sense of unbelonging and the question of who I was started with my younger years. I went to an English school and learned to take pride in all that was not mine. In the language of a British teacher and every attempt on my part not to sound Egyptian, I found my calling. It was the shame that followed the idea of an Egypt that I never felt belonged to me or that I belonged to it. A country that, despite its long history, goes back thousands of years has succeeded in alienating millions of its youths and making them ashamed to feel like they belonged to it. The shame in learning that you, as an Egyptian, do not matter, that the blood of your family, your children, and your brothers and sisters has no value; when you see your friends killed and the knowledge that those who killed them roam freely; this was when I learned that Egypt did not belong to me and that I, in turn, did not belong to it.

Growing up, I wanted to scream out my political views, and in college, my friends and I would start political debates, and to their dismay, I would not tone down my attacks on Mubarak, his government, and their corruption. It became a routine to end my vehement conversation at school and, on my way home, regret that I ever opened my mouth. My mother's words that one day I would be arrested and taken to a detention camp where I would never be seen again constantly plagued me. I regretted that I had said anything, and every time I spoke again and every time I visualized late at night our door bell ringing, I saw myself being driven out of my room into the shackles of darkness by strange men in civilian clothes, probably undercover cops. The same story repeated itself in phone conversations with my best friend and the fear of what would follow my arrest. The horrors of what would happen to me never stopped crossing my mind, but nothing ever happened. I was lucky or maybe irrelevant. But I learned that silence was what was expected of me and everyone who wanted to live in peace in Egypt. I learned then that being careful was not a bad thing. It was a survival tactic that I learned well and exercised masterfully.

Growing up, I had rarely seen people hungry or homeless. It could be because I was living in my little middle-class bubble, and through that narrow prism I could not see the misery of those surrounding us, those whom I and others, deemed privileged, never bothered to think of or wonder how they could feed themselves or their families if they lived on less than $50 a month. These were questions I never asked and never tried to answer. I felt a sense of privilege and entitlement when I lived in Egypt. I had an English education and graduated with a degree in English, was fluent in English, and had an impeccable American accent that was the cause of others' envy. I felt I had it all.

Years passed. I graduated from college and went to the United States for graduate school, which I eventually completed. It took going to the United States to learn how to see myself and what I had accomplished. I was an Egyptian studying English, thinking I would be better at it than American and British native speakers themselves. But did it matter to me? Was it that when I learned that this language about which I prided myself would never be mine? I learned to resist the hold that the English language had on me. I would often slip in an Arabic word in class as I was speaking, sometimes consciously and sometimes not. It gave me a sense of pride that I could speak my language and not feel that I had to prove I was someone I was not. I took pride in telling

my students where I came from and learned to live with my students' preju-
dice, 9/11, and comments about my pronunciation and funny accent that often
was an odd mixture of British and American. I played the role expected of me
as an international student and teaching assistant. I learned to question what
I valued (and why) about an education that had stripped me of pride in my
language, my history, and my literature but that had inadvertently empowered
and taught me the value of freedom from all the shackles of language, preju-
dice, race, religion, history, and absolution.

In the United States, I learned what social and economic justice meant;
I learned the meaning and value of democracy and freedom. I envied my peers'
and students' right to vote and preached to them the need to do so. Around
election time in the United States, I watched everything with amazement and
relished finding a country in which the concept of democracy was vastly different from Egypt's. It was not that I had never read or heard about the U.S.
presidential election before, but being part of it, even if only as an observer,
made me feel a great sense of joy and pride to be part of the making of the
history of a nation. That concept of democracy was not a referendum on a president, as in Egypt's case, who had ruled a country for decades and in which
the only options were a yes or a no to elect that same person and the president
always ended up getting 99 percent of the votes at the time when everyone
knew that no one voted. The joy of feeling that a citizen's voice mattered
somewhere in the world contrasted sharply with that intangible sense of oppression and the insignificance of my own voice that I felt in my country.

I still could not pin down what tied me to this land of the pharaohs and
what kept me going to spend every summer with my family, despite my discontent with everything I saw and despite my clashes with my family over politics,
civil rights, personal freedoms, and U.S. democracy. It was not in the history
of ancient Egypt that I found consolation: For me and probably others, Egypt's
ancient history was a distant past disconnected from our reality. It was something to view with wonder and not something to give meaning to our present
life or future, which appeared to be void of the hopes and dreams of our youth,
in a country in which we were meant to lead but instead ended up occupying
its morgues, prisons, or long unemployment lines. Meanwhile, the country
was ruled by a government of sixty-year-olds who had no understanding of the
dreams of our youth and no vision for the country's future.

With time, my visits "home" became marred by more bitterness. I no longer
saw Egypt as home. It was the place where people's dreams suffocated, where
the stories of friends who had been killed at the hands of the police or on
Egypt's unruly highways tainted the idea of a home and a haven, where the
horrors of administrative detention and political prisoners, torture, discrimi-

nation against Copts and non-Muslims, nepotism, and the exploitation of the poor became the new realities to which I had long been oblivious. My visit to Egypt underscored the misery of a land shackled by fear and people broken and humiliated by oppression, poverty, and need. For the first time I learned that the subjugated place I was expected to occupy as a citizen of Egypt and as a woman occupying a lowly place in a patriarchal society that gave all its privileges to men over women.

My realization of my smallness as a citizen unraveled on one summer visit to Egypt, when my father went with me to a police station in Alexandria to finish some paperwork for my international driver's license. The crowded hallway was filled with the stench of the sweat of people waiting for the young police officer to allow them to proceed to the next room to get their paperwork signed. The young officer took every opportunity to shout at everyone as he checked the loud crowd. Despite that, no one complained; everyone smiled at the officer and showered him with praise. Everyone seemed to know the drill, which was based on the officer's preference of who went in and in which order. My father, whom I had always viewed as formidable and proud, knew the drill too; he meekly called him *ya pasha* and showed him our paperwork. There was a deference in my father's voice that I had not heard before. It did not make sense to me that my father would call this man, who was younger than his youngest daughter, *pasha*, a Turkish word that had become a staple in Arabic conversations whenever one wanted to indicate someone's superior title. I could not understand then what made my father, the man I had always looked up to, speak like a meek woman to anyone. At that time, my father was at retirement age. Most of his friends who were police officers and who usually gave us special treatment, had retired as well, so this was my first time seeing my father play the role of an average citizen who had to get his paperwork completed like everyone else. It was no longer possible to cut in the line, be offered a seat and a hot drink by the high-ranking officer while someone else got all the paperwork done for us and while we took someone else's turn who had been standing in a long line since the morning.

I wondered how many times we had victimized others that way and what made us think it was our right to be treated differently. I wanted to shout in the officer's face: "What makes you think you are better than everyone else? We are equal citizens of this country and your job here is to serve us." I bit my tongue and looked at my father, who averted my gaze. As we walked to the other room, I wondered when we became slaves and others masters. Was it another era of intangible and invisible colonialism in which we lived? It was not the Ottomans, the French, or the British who had colonized us; it was the remnants of the power left by those colonizers. It was the sense of privilege over the inferior masses that had been taken over by the bourgeois that had claimed the privilege over all of us, using the state structure to disempower the rest of us, to keep us down, and to enslave us in mind and spirit. I felt my father's smallness, and I know he felt it too.

It was at this point in my life that I became more aware of the exploitation of the poor, the corruption in government institutions, and the power of capitalism to make billionaires and turn 98 percent of the population into paupers and beggars. These underprivileged lived paycheck to paycheck, and without laws protecting against work-related injuries. If they are injured or become ill, poverty and homelessness are the only outcome. I asked my father why he called the police officer *pasha*, but he did not answer. I knew that his silence held the answer. He and millions of others had been bred on silence, and the few who dared to speak up were humiliated, beaten up, or arrested. My father, then sixty-six years old, had long ago learned the lesson.

With every visit to Egypt, I saw more of the people's suffering. I heard stories of those who had been killed or tortured at the hands of the police. These stories always took me back to the murder of a former classmate of mine by the police back in 1996. I had heard about his murder from another old friend of mine who died, a few years later, with her husband in a car crash on Egypt's infamous highway, only a few months after her wedding. I heard stories of other friends and colleagues who had died on the Egyptian highway, which had become one of the largest graveyards for our young. On the passenger seat in every taxi, I heard heartbreaking stories of those suffering in a country where the growth rate was poised to be more than 5 percent and where the number of millionaires and billionaires had increased exponentially. Even so, we had people living on less than fifty dollars a month who could not even afford to eat plain bread every day. I heard the stories of workers at blood banks who sold the donated blood collected from blood drives on the black market for a hundred pounds a pint. I listened keenly to the anguish of a taxi driver who had to buy his young daughter blood for her transfusion, which he moaned cost him more than a hundred pounds, money he did not have. He moaned that she would die, but he had no choice. I reached into my pocket and gave him all I could. Whether he was being truthful did not matter. Nothing I did made me feel any better. With my silence and my choice to leave the country and turn my back on everything in it, I was as much an accomplice in these people's suffering as any corrupt politician or official.

The list of problems that plagued Egyptians was endless. In the newspapers, doctors and researchers warned about drinking Egypt's contaminated drinking water, which, they claimed, led to kidney failure and advised people to drink bottled water instead. Can this be possible in a country in which almost half the population lives at or below poverty levels? I empathized with the story of our porter, a single mom suffering from kidney failure who has to undergo kidney dialysis twice a week. To my naive question as to why she did not get a transplant, she responded that she could not afford one because it would cost fifty thousand pounds, which was more than she could ever afford.

Article after article talks about the problems of the millions of unemployed Egyptian youth, many of whom are college graduates, who have lost hope of finding employment or having a future. Yet the government has never felt these countless problems to be urgent. The hundreds of pictures and stories of dead Egyptian young men who resorted to traveling illegally to Europe and paying thousands to illegal smugglers in search of a job, a future, and a life broke my heart. It was in these young people's shattered dreams, those who killed themselves or drowned in the Mediterranean that I saw the ugliness of a country that killed its youth's spirit even before it came after their bodies. Egypt became to me a monstrosity, a mother that ate its children and fed on their souls and flesh. The shocking newspaper articles about the high cancer rates in Egypt caused by the hormone- and pesticide-infested foods due to the lack of regulation and the contaminated fertilizers imported by government officials were nothing short of an outrage. The constant ache and suffering of the people were undeniable. Poverty, illness, and injustice all were marks of the new Egypt that I had long failed to see and chosen to abandon. I felt anger at my helplessness. I wondered how come there could be such injustice and suffering, but nothing is done.

I always told my mother there would be an uprising. On my last visit to Egypt in December 2010, I told her that one day the people would stand up for themselves and say enough is enough. I wondered how long it would take before injustice could no longer be tolerated. I told my mother to mark my words: "It is a matter of time and we will have a revolution." I always believed that even though freedom was a dream as elusive as reaching the surface of the sun and even though it burned those who sought it or called for it, I knew there were people who yearned for it and craved this new dawn. A country like Egypt needed a full-fledged revolution that would change the course of its modern history, which had been marred by colonialism and corrupt military rulers, and would make the people feel that they belonged in their homeland. I knew that day was coming.

I do not know how I came to learn about the outbreak of the January 25 revolution and the first Friday of Anger on January 28. All I know was that I found myself in the midst of a story that I had long hoped would come true, a dream that had been elusive for many of us. It was the start of the rise of the people of Egypt against corruption and oppression, in a country in which

30 percent of the population is illiterate and 40 percent live at or below the poverty line. On television, I saw the Egypt that I had long searched for in my heart but had never found before. For the first time, I felt a deep sense of pride and belonging to those who had the courage that I myself lacked, to call for freedom and democracy and stand up against corruption and injustice. I saw in the faces of the young people who started the revolution my lost youth and dreams. I heard in their voices the voice I had long suppressed in my endless debates between fear and indecision.

During the revolution, I found myself glued to the computer and television, watching the live reporting on Al Jazeera, CNN, and even Fox News and reading as many national and international newspapers I could get my hands on or find online. I did not want to miss any part of the revolution; even if it was only in my role as a distant observer, I wanted to do it well. In my classes and in the height of the revolution, I talked to my students about the revolution in Egypt and the long-standing corruption of the Egyptian government and the president, with which many were unfamiliar. I could not help tearing up when talking about the brutality with which the government security forces faced the young protesters. At work, between my classes, I constantly checked the Egyptian newspapers, CNN, and some of the revolution blogs. During those days, Facebook became my news hub. My Facebook friends and I, most of whom are Egyptian, some of whom live in Egypt and some in the United States, became avid Facebookers. Every time one of us found an important article, we posted it; we exchanged views and news and sometimes argued. We were more like amateur reporters and political activists; we compiled all the news we could collect and made sure everyone got updated. Posting and following the news took hours out of my day and made me lose hours of sleep. There was an unspoken spirit of competitiveness among us. Each one wanted to get the news out first, but despite my efforts, the six-hour time difference always took away my lead and forced me into playing catch-up.

February 11 was the day we all had been waiting for. Friday was the day that always coincided with every *millioneyah*, or million-person march in Egypt's revolution. I finished my teaching at 3:00 p.m. as usual; as I walked to my office hurriedly, I ran into one of the English professors who asked if I had heard the news. "What news?" I answered puzzled. I wondered what could have happened in the two hours since I left for class. "Mubarak has stepped down. They have just announced it," he replied with the biggest smile I had ever seen in my life. I was at loss for words. "Are you sure? Is this real?" was all I could say. I thanked him hurriedly and ran to my office, with my heart feeling as though it were pounding its way out of my body. My hands shook as I opened the online page for *al-Dostor*, an Egyptian opposition newspaper, and there it was. Mubarak had stepped down; after eighteen days of protests, he had finally been forced out after more than thirty years as Egypt's president, an office he had taken, as acting vice president, following Sadat's murder in 1981. The euphoria seen on the faces of the millions who went to Tahrir Square and the major streets of every city in Egypt to celebrate the end of Mubarak and the fall of his regime and to embrace the hope for freedom was unlike any I had ever witnessed before. The young men and women who had bled and stood side by side during the protests could now celebrate freedom. For the first time, they had achieved the dream not only for themselves but also for more than eighty million Egyptians. At this moment, one could not help but remember and pray for all those who died or were injured or imprisoned to make that day a reality. This moment marked the culmination of more than two weeks of protests that had overtaken Egypt and the realization of everything we had dreamed of, the end of oppression, corruption, brutality, and injustice—or so we thought.

Eleven months have passed since the start of the Egyptian revolution, which succeeded in two things only: bringing down Mubarak and his sons, who are now facing trial for nothing less than the killing of unarmed protesters, and bringing a few corruption charges against some of his ministers and top officials. These trials started after millions of people took to the streets in Tahrir and all over Egypt demanding justice for those who were killed during the revolution and for the millions of Egyptians who had to live in abject poverty so that Mubarak and his sons could live in absolute wealth. But with the destruction of almost all evidence and the recanting of almost all the witnesses' testimony, Mubarak's innocence is more than likely assured.

The illusion that the regime had been taken down or that the era of corruption, injustice, oppression, and police brutality had ended was just that—an illusion. The military took over after relentless protests against Omar Suleiman, the former head of intelligence and the vice president appointed by Mubarak after the revolution broke out, and later against the two prime ministers appointed by the military. After taking power, one of the first orders of business of the Supreme Council of Armed Forces, SCAF, was criminalizing protests and renewing the emergency laws indefinitely, as was expected. Under military rule, while thugs and criminals roam the streets freely terrorizing and attacking civilians, more than twelve thousand people who had actively participated in the revolution have been arrested and forced to undergo harsh military trials, which thugs, criminals, and murderers did not have to face. These young activists face torture and heinous conditions in military prisons, not to mention the virginity tests that the military forced young Egyptian women to undergo after their arrest.

Under the rule of the Egyptian military, which is governed by the SCAF, which in turn was appointed by Mubarak, two massacres took place. The first was on October 9 in Maspero, in which more than twenty-seven unarmed protesters were killed and hundreds were injured after being shot at and run over by armored vehicles. Most of the protesters were Copts, who took to the streets joined by Egyptian Muslims to protest the destruction and burning of a church in Aswan. The second massacre was on November 23, in which the police used an internationally banned nerve-gas agent in their tear gas and live bullets against the protesters in clashes around the country, resulting in the deaths of more than thirty protesters and injuring more than a thousand. The military and police claimed no role in any of these massacres, and the government-sponsored media were quick to point out that a third party must have had a hand in that, despite the uploaded YouTube videos that circulated showing police shooting at civilians. These actions by the SCAF contrast sharply with the chant popularized during the revolution: "El-geesh wa el-shaeb eid wahdah" (The military and the people are one hand). This statement no longer holds true for me and many others who had long hoped and fought for change in Egypt.

The recent protests that broke out throughout Egypt marked what some people call the "second revolution of rage" and came out of the realization that the first revolution in January was never completed. Most of the protesters went home after Mubarak's ousting and later trial, though nothing had changed in Egypt in any meaningful way. The recent protests underscored the disappointment with the SCAF's failure to manage effectively the transitional phase after the revolution. Its failure to ensure that security is restored in Egypt has been the cause of discontent among the people, many of whom have chosen to blame the protesters rather than the military rulers who are now governing the country. The almost nonexistent social or economic reform and the continuation of almost all the corrupt officials in their posts and their business-as-usual mentality have caused more disappointment within the ranks of the protesters and activists. The continuation of the military trials of protesters and police brutality and torture, whose victims have always been young Egyptian men, have marred the period of military rule in Egypt after the revolution. The bulk of the protests now call for power to be handed over to a civilian national government that will take over that transitional phase in Egypt. Whether these protests and sit-ins in Tahrir will result in any tangible change is unclear.

In response to these protests, the SCAF had gone forward with the parliamentary elections, the results of which came out last week in which the Islamist parties, the Muslim Brotherhood and the Salafists, made huge gains and are poised to control more than half the parliament. The theories that the SCAF and the Islamist parties agreed to hand power over to the Islamists in exchange for not pursuing any further investigations into government corruption and not interfering with the military's budget or finances are quite compelling and have been circulating widely. The absence of the Islamist parties from all the recent protests and their decision to disappear and constantly tout their support for the military rulers, despite the recent massacres, were at the root of such theories. Nevertheless, with the recent talk of the winning party's forming the government, it is more than likely that the Muslim Brotherhood will form a government as well.

Despite the Muslim Brotherhood's reformist agenda, there is no guarantee that once they take power they will not resort to their former conservatism. The recent rhetoric of ultraconservatism by the Salafists, with their Taliban-like religious ideology, took the moderates by storm. The ultraconservative agenda is one that aims to take from women their rights to vote, work, be educated, and hold public office. That agenda most likely will turn Egypt into a new Afghanistan as these Salafists who run for public office assert that democracy is apostasy and claim people should not govern because God is the one who governs. They advocate a supreme ruler who will have absolute authority and claim that anyone who defies the ruler is an apostate. These religious clerics were the same people who, during the revolution, said that going against Mubarak was a violation of religious laws, even though they saw fit to run for public office after Mubarak's regime collapsed.

These recent gains by the Islamists mark a change in the direction of the Egyptian political landscape and the shift of the country toward a conservative Islamist agenda. The obvious failure of Mubarak's liberal policies to realize any kind of reform or equality has led to a popular mistrust of liberalism and secularism, which, to the public, have become synonymous with atheism. As the West feels its way around the growing power of political Islam, the moderates, liberals, and Christians in Egypt find themselves squeezed between the Islamist parties. The popular support of the Islamist agenda came after decades during which people were besieged by impotent Western policies of supporting friendly authoritarian regimes. No one can doubt that in Western foreign policy, the consensus has been to support friendly but corrupt leaders to become president for life and to legitimize, arm, and fund them to serve the geopolitical interests of the democracy-toting West. That glaring hypocrisy and double standard, about which the West has long acted as if everyone were oblivious to its blatancy, increased the credibility of the Islamists, who had long been the only vocal opposition against the Western-backed Mubarak. This has made many view the Islamists as the only ones capable of carrying out the reforms needed to rebuild the country after the revolution and to establish economic and social justice.

Whether the Egyptian revolution has reached a conclusion is unclear. Whether Egypt will follow Turkey's, Saudi Arabia's, or even Afghanistan's model also is unclear. One thing I know is that thousands have and still shed their blood for Egypt; hundreds of young men have lost their sight and become crippled; and hundreds sacrificed their lives for the people of Egypt to be free and live with dignity and pride. My question is, How will history regard the people of Egypt? Will it say that the revolution failed because the people traded the blood of their young men and women for grocery bags, meat, and cell-phone charge cards, which were distributed by the Muslim Brotherhood and the Salafists before and around election time? If the parties representing the January 25 revolution youth were able to win only 3.2 percent of the votes in the first round of the parliamentary elections—a scant number compared with the 58 percent of the votes for the Islamist parties—then what does it say about us? When people vote for those Salafists who called our brave protesters heretics and apostates because they defied a Muslim ruler, then what does it say about the millions who have voted for them? When we vote for people who call democracy apostasy, don't we defile the memory of our dead whose blood has not dried yet?

My frustration with the outcome of the revolution is indescribable. The great euphoria, following what seemed like the success of the revolution, was replaced by a great sense of misery and uncertainty over what the future will bring in an Egypt poised to be ruled by political Islam for the first time in its modern history. The great sense of belonging to "my" Egypt was replaced by the question of whether the young girls and other young women will be allowed to reach their full potential and to exercise their freedom of expression and speech as I had always envisioned in what I call my homeland. I am left to wonder whether I will ever fully belong to a land that is now questioning and casting doubt on my rights as a woman to be free.

The words of the last poem I wrote about the revolution echo in my ear:

In a fog-blinding leap of fate,
I heard a scream shake the gallows of dreams
I felt the earth shudder at the force of a millions' march
I galloped through the meadows of noise and echo
Of pictures, motionless and animated
Of a rage of colors: red, black, blue, green, white
I was amazed at the horrors it unleashed
When the world was going up in flames of pain

I have long wanted to be a hero in a world without heroes
But the day the voice erupted through the waves
A "hero" was reborn
In your thighs when it melted with the stuff of this earth
In your blood when it froze the sea waves.

It was in the sacrifice of the heroes of the revolution that I found my homeland. I wonder if in death, I and others will find our dream.

THE SPIRIT OF TAHRIR SQUARE:
"LIKE GOING TO MECCA ON A PILGRIMAGE"

Al-Sayed Abdulmughni

Owner of a bread bakery, male, 46, Mait Ghamr

My name is al-Sayed Abdulmughni, and I am also known as al-Sayed Falafel
(or Mr. Falafel) because I used to sell falafel at one point in my career. When
I reflect on my life, I claim to be a self-made Egyptian citizen because I have
taken financial responsibility for myself since I was in fourth grade. While working hard in different jobs, I earned my diploma of commerce in 1984, the most
education I could ever receive. Working hard was the staple of my life in my
multiple careers, sometimes working for eighteen hours a day. Thank God I
now have my own bakery for making bread, which I have had for the last ten
years, a small business that I consider my sole source for living. Thus, my financial situation is reasonably stable, but I have many commitments, particularly my five children, who are in various stages of education. They need my
support for their education, work, and marriage.

The reason I joined the revolution was not materialistic and was not directly related to my financial situation. I participated in and will always be
part of the revolution because I hate nepotism and bribery, which the regime
encouraged, and I believe that the rights of people must always be granted to
them. I joined the Egyptian revolution because I believe that all Egyptians
have the right to live with dignity. We have to live in a country where we are
not subjected to humiliation if we seek our rights as free citizens. But I should
mention that my participation in the Egyptian revolution was not the first
time I joined demonstrations against the regime. I had participated in the

demonstrations that were organized by the Egyptian civil movement Kifaya, one of the first opposition groups that openly and totally rejected the succession of Mubarak's son to rule after his father. I also joined the demonstration in support of the Egyptian journalist Ibrahim Eissa, who was one of the well-known dissidents against the Mubarak's rule and who was arrested and imprisoned in 2007 for publishing alleged "rumors and false news" about the deteriorating health of President Hosni Mubarak.

I live in the city of Mait Ghamr, which belongs to Addaqahliyah Province and is about eighty kilometers from Cairo. When I learned from the *el-Massry* newspaper that there would be demonstrations in Cairo on January 25, 2011, I traveled with my friends to be part of them. I was motivated because I read that some of the slogans would be calling for life in freedom and social justice and denouncing Minister of Interior Habib el-Adly. So I firmly decided to take part in these demonstrations, and along with a group of friends, I decided to travel to Cairo. We arrived on January 25 and immediately headed to Tahrir Square, reaching it around the time of the *assr* (afternoon) prayer. After the prayer was over, I joined the demonstrators, whose numbers gradually began to grow. But in different areas of Qasr al-Ayiny Street in Cairo, clashes and skirmishes started to take place between the security forces and the demonstrators—with the latter bravely succeeding in stripping central security soldiers of their sticks and helmets.

Between the *maghrib* (sunset) and *isha* (evening) prayers, some people set up a station to circulate news and information in the square, and the idea of staying overnight spread among us. Some activists told us that if we succeeded in staying in the square until the next morning, more people would join us, and so we decided to spend the entire night there. I left only to bring back some blankets to protect us from the cold weather. At about 11:00 p.m. I was very tired and tried to sleep with the background noise of dialogues and clashes coming from afar. In this anxious attempt at sleep, news got to us that there was an attack being prepared against us. About 12:30 a.m. we started to hear noises of armored vehicles and tear gas guns. Panicked, we did not know what to do, so we began running in the direction of Abdel Moneim Riad Square. I remember that I was running until I reached the Journalists Union, and on our way there were warnings that an ambush by the police might be waiting for the escaping people. I saw some thugs breaking stores' security gates, trying to exploit the chaos.

But eventually the demonstrators reacted bravely, and their reaction was strong. People spent the rest of the night shouting against the regime, declaring that it was no longer legitimate and that Mubarak had to step down. Some of the slogans that I remember from that night were "Step down and leave,

Mubarak!" People also condemned the minister of the interior by demanding, "Go Away, Minister of Torture, there is no vandalism or sabotage!" Some shouts were encouraging more Egyptians, Muslims or Christians to join the revolution: "O Muhammad, O Paul, stand up, and let Egypt follow Tunisia!" When I returned to my family and friends, I happily told them about what happened before I succumbed to a deep sleep. When I woke up, I saw on Al Jazeera that people were still in the square, so I decided to go back and join them.

Demonstrations also started in my city, Mait Ghamr, on the Friday of Anger (January 28), by a diverse group of Egyptian citizens. Nevertheless, this time it was a lot harder to get to Tahrir Square. On my way, I saw break-ins and beatings and realized that there were thugs and thieves in the area. I saw members from the Muslim Brotherhood, al-Karama Party, and al-Tajamu' Party. We all left Alzenfali Mosque, went through the vegetable market, and finally stood in front of the police station. We were collectively chanting, "Be strong, O my country, freedom is being born"; "Unite with me, shoulder to shoulder"; and "Raise your voice, raise your voice, Egypt will be greater and will not die." Addressing the government, we chanted: "Raise the prices of sugar and cooking oil, tomorrow we'll sell the furniture in our homes" and "Change is legitimate against injustice and hunger." We also directed our chants against President Mubarak: "O Mubarak, ghore ghore (pejorative and slang for "leave") so that our country can see the light," "Leave, leave like King Farouk, our people became strangled by you," and "O Mubarak, O the one who made us poor, tell us what you did with our money." After that afternoon, we received news from Cairo that more demonstrations were taking place all over Egypt, which increased my certainty that the beginning of an independent Egypt had arrived.

I still feel that the spirit of Tahrir Square, the sit-ins and the demonstrations we had in it, was like performing a *hajj* (Islamic pilgrimage) to Mecca! People were great there—everyone had the attitude of cooperation and love. The people around me were simple people who had long felt that the regime created injustice in the country. They felt this injustice because they were suffering from either poverty or disease or both, and they insisted that there should be real change in Egypt. This spirit and the sense of determination were not only in Tahrir Square but in all the places that witnessed the revolution against the regime. When I participated in the demonstration in Mait Ghamr, some of the National Party officers and members tried to organize themselves, inciting and paying for thugs to harass us, but we did not let them spoil our demonstration and forced the thugs to run away.

As I am writing now, almost one year has passed since the beginning of our revolution. I am sure that positive change is coming. Despite the counterrevolution and those involved in destroying our revolution, I believe that we will succeed in achieving our goals and ambitions. We should not forget that the Egyptian revolution was possible because there were people who spread awareness among us, such as Attiya al-Sayrafi (1926–May 31, 2011), the author and political activist from the National Progressive Unionist Party who was well known as the "Egyptian Worker." He inspired me to love reading about our country's issues, and he had the greatest impact on educating me. He— may God have mercy on his soul—used to say, before the revolution started, that if 200,000 demonstrators went to Tahrir Square, our revolution would succeed in toppling Mubarak. I also love Dr. Mohamed ElBaradei, a decent human being and a sincere and noble politician. I always see him as someone who is like Gandhi from India! We, in fact, chanted for him during the revolution: "O ElBaradei, we will not fail you, you are our fate and we are yours!" But I blame him for being away from the public sphere despite our need for him. I believe that when it comes to who might be a president for Egypt, there are many good people, such as Hamdeen Sabahi, Dr. Abdul Munim Abu al-Fotouh, Judge Hisham el-Bastawisi, and Dr. Abdallah al-Ash'al. Any one of them could be an authentic president for Egypt, whose freedom we attained and who will not leave us.

Yes, I am optimistic, and without optimism, I would die!

NOTES

1. Wajih al-Saqqar, "The Demands of Revolutionaries Unanswered," *al-Ahram*, January 25, 2012, 18.

2. Wael Ghonim, *Revolution 2.0: A Memoir* (Boston: Houghton Mifflin Harcourt, 2012), 76–77.

3. Friday, the Islamic holy day, is often chosen for major protests and was frequently dubbed "Friday of Anger" by protesters to refer to topics related to the unfolding events in the revolution.

4. See Ian Black, introduction to *The Arab Spring: Rebellion, Revolution, and a New World Order*, by Toby Manhire (London: Guardian Books, 2012), vii.

5. Ibid., viii.

6. Ryszard Kapuściński, *Shah of Shahs* (San Diego: Harcourt Brace Jovanovich, 1985).

3. *Libya*

On February 15, 2011, the Libyan authorities in Benghazi arrested the lawyer Fathi Terbil, who was representing the families of those killed in Abu Salim prison in Tripoli in 1996. The prison was the scene for a massacre of about twelve hundred inmates, who were imprisoned because they were opponents of the regime. The event took place after the prisoners had taken some hostages inside the prison and demanded better conditions, and it left many families of the victims seeking justice. When Terbil was arrested, the families joined the lawyers and judges who protested in front of Benghazi's main courthouse. Thousands of Libyans took to the streets in Benghazi, demanding the departure of Colonel Muammar al-Qaddafi, who had ruled Libya since 1969 after leading a coup against King Idris al-Sanousi.

Qaddafi's militias in Benghazi and four of his sons were in charge of crushing the uprisings by instigating systemic hostilities. On February 19 and 20, 2011, the protesters of Benghazi were hit hard by the Qaddafi forces, but their resilience and a few military defections allowed them to take control of some military bases. After the city was taken by the rebels, who pronounced it "liberated," they used it as a base from which to free the entire country. More cities were liberated, and on March 19, NATO began its military intervention, allowing the rebels to enter Tripoli and start the hunt for Qaddafi, who was killed in Sirte on October 20, 2011.

The use of armed force, rebellion, and the support of the NATO forces left Libya struggling with many problems, not the least being that rebel groups were unwilling to put down their weapons. On February 27, 2012, the military defectors, rebels, and activists managed to form the National Transitional Council of Libya as the legitimate replacement of Qaddafi's regime. The former justice minister, Mustafa Abd al-Jalil, chaired the council, which immediately received international recognition both during and after the Libyan uprisings. Then in November 2012, a new government was formed, with Abd al-Jalil as the temporary head of a state. The government's tasks included working on a new constitution, parliament, and eventually presidential elections. Libya's main challenge remains the continuing unrest and existence of militias that did not give up their arms. Partly as a result, on September 11, 2012, the U.S. ambassador to Libya, Christopher Stevens, was among four Americans killed in an attack on the U.S. consulate in Benghazi. On July 7, after taking steps to distance Qaddafi-era officials from politics, the first free elections in Libya were held for the General National Congress (GNC) as its ruling body. Nouri Abusahmain, chair of the GNC, resumed his duties as the interim president on June 25, 2013.

MY MISSION IN THE LIBYAN REVOLUTION

Mohammed Zarrug

Coordinator of an information department, male, 44, Benghazi

I want to start with a disclaimer: It is really embarrassing for me to write about my role in the Libyan revolution when I remember the blood of the martyrs. It is equally embarrassing to try to describe only my own role when the revolution was indeed the outcome of millions of Libyan people. But I will write about my experience because I was asked to do so. I will write because I witnessed and participated in major events—even though everything I did does not equal one drop of the blood from the glorious martyrs who suffered death as the penalty for joining the revolution.

During the revolution, a French journalist crossed the Libyan border and arrived in Benghazi. After he entered our house and talked with my father, he told us he had noticed that our car and house showed we were better off financially than the average Egyptian and Tunisian. So he wondered why we would revolt against the government when we were not suffering financially.

I needed a really long time to explain to him that our revolution was not a revolution for bread; at the same time, this did not mean we were living a life of luxury. Many average Libyan families lived below the poverty line, and salaries in the public sector often did not meet their needs. In addition, getting a job in the public sector was a complex process that did not reward all college graduates, whose qualifications were often not considered. Moreover, the attempts at reform attempted by Saif al-Islam, son of former Libyan leader Colonel Muammar al-Qaddafi, began too late, were too slow, and deliberately followed his father's policy of making people poor so they had to rely exclusively on him.

This unethical policy fits the old Arabic saying, "Keep your dog hungry, and it will follow you." Such alleged reforms were adopted after the Lockerbie crisis was resolved and the regime tried to address human rights concerns in Libya. Before that, Libyan citizens had the lowest standard of living ever; it was common for the per capita income to be less than ten dollars a month, even though our country is situated on a huge lake of oil and has a number of gas reservoirs. Thanks to our government, poverty existed in a country that covers nearly two thousand kilometers of Mediterranean coastline in addition to having viable economic resources, such as historical and tourist attractions that can bring in global investments.

Later, in Lebanon, someone else asked me whether we, the Libyan people, started our revolution as a kind of imitation of the Egyptians and Tunisians. I replied that such an assumption was one of the fallacies about our revolution and is refuted by the fact that an invitation to demonstrate on February 17, 2011, was posted on Facebook seven months earlier.

But in addition to other factors, the revolutions in Egypt and Tunisia certainly helped motivate our revolution and make it successful. We cannot deny the help and encouragement we got from these revolutions, just as we cannot deny the grace we received from God to achieve our revolutionary goals.

One of the immediate factors that sparked the Libyan revolution was the arrest of a lawyer from Benghazi who worked to defend the rights of about twelve hundred prisoners unjustly killed in Tripoli's notorious Abu Salim prison in 1996. The families of the persecuted prisoners went at night to the headquarters where the lawyer was detained and demanded his release. This happened two days before the official start of the revolution on February 17. People were already angry at the regime, and once there was a call to demonstrate, they immediately rushed to join.

But one can also ask, "Why did it take you all this time to revolt?" In fact, there had been attempts to overthrow the tyrant Muammar Qaddafi during the first few months of his rule, which began on September 1, 1969. He dealt with them severely, however, and since then has established himself as someone who would kill anybody based on mere suspicion. That's why anyone who would even think of uprising against the regime would also consider the possible reprisals against his or her property and family members.

Twice I witnessed the Libyan people taking to the streets in Benghazi: once after the events at the al-Ahly Club in 1996 and again at the Italian consulate on February 17, 2006. These two protests against the regime showed the residents of Benghazi that the regime was fragile and that the legendary grip holding the reins of things had slackened considerably.

There is no doubt that the revolutions in information and communication technology have contributed to the delivery of opposing voices to every Libyan citizen. Although Libyan citizens generally opposed Qaddafi, he was involved in every aspect of their lives, including naming their country and preventing some Libyans from using certain names for their sons and daughters.

Ironically, it was Qaddafi who introduced the Internet to Libya in the late 1990s, but he limited it to his sons' offices and selfishly prevented the public from using it, at least for a while. When the Internet eventually did become accessible to the public, the connection was very weak. This forced many people in Brega, in the eastern region of Libya, to rely on their own Internet service by using two-way technology that allowed customers to connect via satellite.

Despite the expensive price for such a service, it had the great advantage of not being under the surveillance of the government, which used to block any sites that disseminated ideas critical of the tyrant. Thanks to this uncensored access to the Internet, I had the opportunity to communicate with some opponents and read their writings, especially during the protests at the Italian consulate in 2006. I went into the street and saw what happened, then wrote about it, and reported it to the Al Jazeera and Al Arabiya websites. I also sent information and postings to the banned Libyan sites using aliases.

The government eventually improved the Internet quality, and the price for service went down while the speed increased. This gave many Libyans the opportunity to use government servers, even though the regime still blocked certain websites. Although YouTube and Facebook initially were allowed, YouTube was blocked shortly before the revolution started. Facebook remained accessible, though only until Benghazi was freed. But when the regime retook power, access to major websites, including Facebook, was restricted.

So my mission was to teach people how to unblock restricted websites by using different proxies or ultraservers. Eventually, when the regime found that blocking the Internet had not worked, it completely disabled any connection to it. This was, if memory serves me correctly, in March 2011. Interestingly, mobile phones continued to work, thereby allowing the rebels to keep communicating with one another.

During the evening of February 15, 2011, I was watching television when my brother-in-law called and told me that a demonstration had started and that it had passed by Benghazi's Security Directorate. This surprising news made me wonder. First, it was rather strange because the previously arranged date (February 17) had not yet arrived. I also recalled that based on what happened five years earlier, demonstrations usually began during the day, not the night.

I asked him about the demonstrators' chants, and his reply was that they were saying, "O Muammar, where are the promises, for we saw only restrictions." Appalled, I did not understand what they meant by the word "restrictions" and quickly interpreted it as written documents (or government bureaucratic paperwork) and the slow progress of the promised reforms. But then I thought that maybe what he was describing had been staged by Qaddafi loyalists as a proactive demonstration in favor of his regime. But my brother-in-law assured me that the pictures in the demonstration belonged to the fallen heroes of Abu Salim prison.

To make sure, I called my friend Khaled and asked him about the demonstration. He told me that he also had heard about it and was about to join it. When I expressed my doubts to him, he promised to call me back. I knew then that the demonstrators had marched for several kilometers, crossed al-Ishreen Street, and ended at Shajara Square in the city center.

I waited for what seemed like a long time before Khaled called me. He said he had already been in the middle of the demonstration. When I asked again about the slogans, he let me hear them directly through his cell phone. And yes, I could hear my Libyan people clearly saying, "The people want to overthrow the colonel."

At that point, I understood that "restrictions" was intended to mean the shackles created by the regime. I then left the house intending to go to Shajara Square, but I was surprised by the traffic congestion extending for more than three kilometers away from the square. At first I thought about walking there, but it was almost midnight, and I was exhausted and sleepy. When I called again to see if the demonstration were still going on, Khaled said that the resonant slogans were filling the sky over the square, demanding the end of Qaddafi's rule.

The next day, not only was Benghazi rebelling, but we also heard the news that the city of Bayda, which is two hundred miles east of Benghazi, also was joining the revolution. This city sacrificed the first two martyrs in the Libyan revolution. Located in the western mountains of Libya, Zaltan city also revolted and achieved its freedom. The uprisings in Benghazi continued, but the police and thugs tried to suppress them using clubs and machetes, as well as cars spraying boiling water. These measures failed to stop the demonstrators. They threw stones, targeting the pro-Qaddafi forces, who were set up in tents scattered throughout the city.

February 17 arrived, the day when Libyans decided to take to the streets against Muammar Qaddafi. That morning, I was in my office and I called to find out what time Khaled would join the demonstration. He told me that he already was on his way to the courthouse where a sit-in was in progress. There, Libyan lawyers and judges were demonstrating as a gesture of solidarity with the general public. We decided to go to the courthouse together and picked a meeting place in the neighborhood of Sidi Hussein.

After I met with Khaled and his friends, we headed over to the courthouse. On the way there, we were confronted by yellow-hat mercenaries, who appeared on the scene for the first time. I looked at my friends and asked, "How on earth do they know we are demonstrating? Is it written on our faces?"

I found out later what was going on. Apparently, Muammar Qaddafi's son Saadi and the Libyan intelligence chief, Abdullah Senousi, already were in Benghazi. So everyone walking was assumed to be going in one of two ways: toward either the savings bank that, Saadi Qaddafi promised, would give people money (to ease the tension) or the street that led to the courthouse where the proregime forces were stationed.

We threw stones at the mercenaries, and they began to retreat. Then we heard the sound of gunfire but could not determine its source. At this point, people started running away, and I could not see where I was. I was then startled by some young people with a man they had detained. They firmly believed that he was a yellow-hat mercenary whom they assumed had dropped his hat before they stopped him. The man swore to God that he was one of the demonstrators, but he was not convincing them.

One of the young men raised a dagger and was about to stab him, but I grabbed his hand and demanded, "How can you kill him based only on suspicions?" Although I did not know either the suspect or the young man, the latter listened to me and released him. I was satisfied that I had rescued someone, even though I did not know his real identity or whether he belonged to the yellow-hat gangs. The shooting increased, and during the gunfire, a boy fell in front of me. He was about sixteen years old and had been hit in the stomach by a stray round.

After some people drove him away, I started to feel a wave of anger engulfing me and began to shout in the street, "Shame on you! Why? This is just a young child!" I was then startled by someone pulling me away and telling me that I was in the line of fire and should take cover so I would not get hit. I hid behind a nearby wall where I found one of my friends, Idris Abdeljawad. I told him to get out of here because of all the random shooting.

I stayed and tried to contact Khaled, whom I had lost in the crowd. Only after several attempts did he finally answer his phone. He told me that he had been shot in the shoulder. Because I was afraid he would be arrested, I said to him, "Don't go to the hospital; I'll try to get a doctor to come to your house." I thought of contacting one of my relatives, who is a doctor, and go to his house. But as soon as I arrived at the house, Khaled called me and said that he already was at the hospital. I quickly went to the hospital and discovered that one of the reception staff was someone I knew. When I asked him to look up Khaled, we realized that the last page of the register had more than a dozen names of patients with gunshot wounds. I could not get inside the hospital to see Khaled because of the security.

But while I was there, it occurred to me that the injured people being treated were probably either demonstrators who were hit by bullets or the yellow-hat mercenaries who had suffered only scratches and whose wounds were caused by stones.

I saw one African mercenary being carried in on a stretcher, suffering from a wound to his head, and I wanted to kick him in the face—an impulse caused by the image of the child who had been shot right in front of me. I could still see the child's lifeless body, yet I had pity for the wounded mercenary.

I left the hospital that evening and headed down to the sit-in in Shajara Square. Huge crowds of people were walking over Gelyana Bridge, which is in the middle of Benghazi. They walked in a line a few kilometers long, and because I was in my car I could not join them. But as I was driving away, I heard the tyrant's security agents shooting at the demonstrators again, killing several. Amid the panic, I also heard rumors that the wounded in the hospitals were being killed by the regime's secret agents. But when I called to check on Khaled, he told me that he already was home after being forced to leave the hospital. Despite his wounds, a doctor kicked him out because he had quarreled with some of the injured mercenaries. Strangely, the doctor also wrote in the hospital report that it was Khaled who refused to stay in the hospital! As for the rumor about killing the wounded, he told me that it was groundless.

The next morning we went to the courthouse, where the sit-in was being held, intending to perform Friday prayers and attend the funerals of those who had been killed in the demonstrations on Thursday. The martyrs' funeral parade was long and went down what is known as Jamal Abdul Nasser Street, the longest and most famous street in Benghazi. The slogans rose out of the mourners' throats, the most notable being "The blood of the martyrs will not go in vain." Unfortunately though, when the mourners arrived near one of the dictator's battalions, al-Fadheel, some of the soldiers fired on them, increasing the number of martyrs. It was clear at this point that things would not settle down because once blood is shed, more will follow.

More cities rose against Qaddafi and fell out of his control. The rebels of Bayda moved from the mountains to the neighboring city of Cyrene in the Jebel Akhdar uplands and attacked the battalion of security forces stationed there. The world needed to know our story, so some activists appeared on Al Jazeera and other satellite channels to report on the uprisings around Libya. I remember that the political activist Amer Habeel was the one who announced on Al Jazeera that the city of Derna had been fully liberated from Qaddafi's militias.

In Benghazi, people freed the city, in the process burning everything that belonged to the Qaddafi regime, including police stations, security checkpoints, the Revolutionary Committee's headquarters, the domestic and external security offices, and military intelligence stations. They all fell on Friday, February 17, except for one battalion and the Directorate of Security station, which agents could use as a base for shooting at rebels and running over them with vehicles, raising the number of martyrs. During those days, our daily routine included going to the cemetery to bury martyrs and then going to the courthouse to gather and to follow up on events. On Sunday (February 19), people surrounded the remaining battalion and threw stones at it. Most of the people who attacked it were outraged because the blood of their martyrs was not yet dry, and they were certain that Saadi Qaddafi and Abdullah Senousi were inside.

As they stood unarmed, agents fired at them from the battalion. Finally, the revolutionaries used dynamite to scare the soldiers into not shooting at them. At that time, people thought about only two things: how to avenge their martyrs and defend themselves. But events accelerated quickly, and the battalion fell, with Saadi and Senousi fleeing the city of Benghazi, along with many of the tyrant's agents.

By the sixth day of demonstrations, all of eastern Libya had been liberated, as had some towns in the west, such as Alzentan, Alrajaban, and Gheryan. People walked to the regime's military camps to get weapons and continued westward, full of enthusiasm to support their brothers there. Some stayed in order to do relief and security work. I preferred to do something related to our cause, to be a translator for a number of foreign journalists belonging to French and American publications such as *Newsweek* and the *New York Times*. From the beginning of the revolution, I wanted to deliver our message to the world, regardless of the danger—being murdered by the dictator—that we faced. But at least we finally came to understand that we had not lost our dear martyrs for nothing. Thank God we won and our martyrs did not die in vain.

FIGHTING QADDAFI:
MORE DETERMINATION THAN WEAPONS

Khairi Altarhuni

High school teacher, male, 32, Tripoli

I should say from the outset that I have valid reasons for my opposition to the regime and my support of the revolution in Libya. I am a young Libyan born in Tripoli to an ordinary family, not rich and not poor. I studied mechanical engineering and graduated in 2001. Feeling happy with my degree, I thought that doors would open for me and that a good future awaited. But as I started applying for jobs, I realized that the opposite was true. I applied at many places for jobs in the departments of energy, military industries, and armed forces (at the time they used to recruit college graduates and give them the rank of second lieutenant engineer). Surprisingly, I was never accepted, even though I had excellent grades. Then I discovered the real reason for this irrational and disappointing situation: my family name was on the watch (or black) list and was being scrutinized by state internal security. What had my family done? Three of my relatives were imprisoned in the infamous Abu Salim prison, and two of them had been executed by the Qaddafi regime in the massacre of 1996. I finally found a post in the education sector, whose employees received the lowest salaries in Libya. My monthly salary was only 180 Libyan dinars (the equivalent of about US$360), a salary that, according to the Qu'ranic verse, "neither nourishes nor avails against hunger." In other words, by the twentieth day of the month, I had to borrow money from my brother or my friends.

When the Libyan revolution started to shake the country, I went out on the streets on February 20, 2011. I proudly joined the young people of my neighborhood Arada, which is located between Tajoura and central Tripoli. But we were thrown off guard by the snipers' bullets in reply to our protests. These bullets systemically targeted our heads and chests. Several young people were killed in Arada by these ruthless killers.

One time we started a demonstration after the Friday prayer, moving from the mosque toward the main street, which leads to Martyrs Square, in the heart of the capital. This long street passes through several neighborhoods, and in each district we collected more people, making the demonstration bigger. We shouted words of freedom and chanted slogans against the rule of Muammar al-Qaddafi that I wished we had voiced sooner. But let's remember, we were unable to do so in the past because we lived under a system that pressed on us like a pincer, a system that did not leave any space for freedom or for demanding it. In our first demonstration, we chanted slogans like "There is no God but Allah, and Qaddafi is the enemy of Allah." We marched in the streets, and more people joined us. In fact, there were so many people in the demonstration on both sides of the street that after only two hours, we looked like a human river flowing in one direction. As we arrived in Dhahra, a neighborhood two kilometers away from Martyrs Square, we could not advance any farther because two Toyota Tundras, filled with soldiers, blocked the street. All we did was chant slogans, but the soldiers got down off both trucks and started shooting directly at us. Sadly, those who were at the front of the demonstration fell down immediately while everyone who could see what happened fled the scene. But the soldiers did not stop shooting, even though we were running away from them. The death toll rose because the people at the rear of the demonstration did not know what was going on—because of the congestion caused by the panicked crowds, they could not see what the soldiers were doing. They thought the bullets were being shot into the air so they did not escape immediately, which caused more tragic losses. Many people were killed, and the martyrs were taken away by the regime's security forces. Some of them were found in hospitals with a death certificate stating that they had been killed as a result of "acts of rioting," and some of the bodies still are missing to this day. The regime cleaned the crime scene using fire trucks to wash the blood from the streets; they behaved as if nothing had happened and started retaliating by targeting us in our homes.

We were terrified that some of the battalions would come during the night and attack our houses. They were like dogs who could smell our flesh and attack us in the service of their master. Another harsh reality was the fact that the district where I lived had a number of pro-Qaddafi families who regularly provoked and insulted us. They could detect from the simplest words we uttered if one of us sided with the regime or was anti-Qaddafi. As a result, they treated us very badly and harassed us in every sense of the word. Once, I answered my cell phone and suddenly heard people chanting, "Allah, Muammar, and Libya only." These words celebrating Qaddafi (as the sole ruler of Libya) disturbed me, and I considered them to be against my religion. So I decided not to chant with the unknown caller, pretending, for my safety, that I could not hear. But as soon as I hung up, the person called again. I did not answer, and the same thing happened with the third and fourth call. A few days later, I woke up at midnight, hearing noises. But when I went outside, I realized that a pro-Qaddafi group had thrown pieces of wood and stones at my place, which I took as a threat. I tried to be patient, not knowing what to do except to put my trust in God.

After a few more days, a letter was slipped under my door with this shocking statement: "You all are backward traitors and agents of foreign powers. Muammar Qaddafi will stay in power. If you do not declare where you stand by going out to the street, raising a green flag, and chanting for the King of Kings in Africa (Qaddafi), we will attack your house and arrest you." After reading this, I was actually very afraid, so much so that I could not sleep at night, expecting a raid at any moment by Qaddafi supporters. I would rather be awake at the time of the raid than be asleep. My nights were spent in fear and panic. This terrifying situation lasted for several weeks, but no raid ever took place. So I started to feel a little bit relieved, though not completely. Some of my neighbors, who had received the same letter, had been attacked and their homes were raided. I still remember the family living in the house next to mine; one of their sons was named Ahmad Salem. This twenty-three-year-old young man was arrested at four o'clock in the morning after Qaddafi's forces stormed into his family's house in a raid that took Ahmad and young people from other neighborhoods. After five days—I am not sure if it was May 5 or 6, 2011—a Toyota Tundra came to our neighborhood, and while speeding down the street, a body was thrown out of the vehicle. It was Ahmad, dead with three bullets in his chest. There also were burns all over his body. I was deeply saddened by this tragic event. They killed him only because he was bravely speaking out against the dictator. Fearless against persecution, he used to say, "Death comes only once. We would rather die with dignity than die with humiliation." Ahmad's death and all these ruthless actions increased my determination to oppose the brutal regime.

In early June 2011, the middle and the western mountains of Libya were taken out of Qaddafi's control, and the NATO air strikes targeted Tripoli. We felt it necessary to make some effort to resist the regime in Tripoli in order to ease its pressure on other Libyan regions. But Tripoli itself was completely under siege, with checkpoints at every street. Movement during the night was almost nonexistent. We did not have weapons, but we did have resilience. But what help was determination without weapons? The ousted Qaddafi militia would fire on any group of people, so there would not be any big demonstrations. We needed to do something. So I had a meeting with the young people of my neighborhood, such as Kamal al-Hatami and Naji al-Sayed, and we decided that we needed to start fighting. We wanted to make something to fight with, and everyone had a suggestion about how to make weapons. In the end, we made a gun from metal water pipes, with cartridges provided by Ali al-Niyaji, one of the members of our group. We also made simple bombs using iron bars. We were very careful while buying the materials for these weapons because we did not want to be a source of suspicion. That is why we got the pieces one by one from more than one place. Although the final products were primitive, they provided us with the motivation to continue mobilizing against the regime. Eventually, we were able to get our hands on Kalashnikov (AK-47) rifles, smuggled in by youths in Tripoli from the neighboring areas. I bought mine for three thousand Libyan dinars (US$6,000), all the money I had at that time.

On the night of Saturday, August 20, the time at which Tripoli would be free from Qaddafi's forces, I took my Kalashnikov and joined my friends to participate in the battles. The streets were almost empty after the sunset (*maghrib*) prayer, although we saw a patrol of Qaddafi battalions, ten soldiers. There were only four of us, but we decided to fight them and opened fire. They outnumbered us and were winning. I could hear the whistling sound of their bullets passing close to my body. We were positioned in the streets as we fired but did not know how to defeat those savage people. We were torn between retreating and staying in the hope that another group of revolutionaries would join us. Right in the middle of this critical situation, we suddenly heard voices from a nearby mosque repeating "Allahu akbar" (Allah is the greatest). People in the houses also started to chant "Allahu akbar," which helped us and forced our enemy to escape quickly, driving away. We met up with the people who saved us, and all night they guarded the freed areas against any enemy forces. That night, one-third of Tripoli fell out of Qaddafi's control, including my area, Arada, as well as Tajoura, Alnoufleen, and Fashloum. They all were freed by revolutionaries who were not able to communicate with one another while fighting the more organized Qaddafi battalions. Nonetheless, the revolutionaries operated in the battlefield as if each group knew what to do.

We guarded the free areas until the morning when the regime deployed forces in Tajoura. These special forces had come from Benghazi by sea. Heavy fighting resumed, and some missiles were fired at the houses in Tajoura from the Khamees battalion. But then a resistance battalion, called Bou Atni, took over the Khamees battalion. They were assisted by NATO, whose jet fighters hovered in the dark sky, dropping bombs on targets that posed a threat to civilians, such as Scud missiles, tanks, and armored military vehicles. The NATO forces also targeted the places where Qaddafi's soldiers and mercenaries were stationed. That night was war in every sense of the word. In the morning, the rebels, who came from different areas of Tripoli, were able to enter Tajora. They were equipped with heavy vehicles and weapons, whereas we had only Kalashnikov and rocket-propelled grenades (RPGs), which we got from the regime camps in the suburbs of Tripoli. So we joined the other rebels and shared our weapons with them. We also worked together on the plans and roles for the coming battles, such as advancing to Qaddafi's residence in Bab al-Azizyia. I saw rebels everywhere, and the mosques of Tripoli broadcast "Allah is the greatest, Allah is the greatest, thanks be to Allah."

On August 23 we moved into Bab al-Azizyia; it only took us a few hours to gain control, thanks to the many revolutionaries participating in the attack. When I entered Bab al-Azizyia, I was shocked to see the bodies of Africans dumped on the ground. They and other dead Libyans were dressed in military uniforms; others were in civilian clothes. There also were liquor bottles everywhere. The fall of Bab al-Azizyia symbolized the fall of Tripoli and all of Libya. Even as more areas were freed, two towns remained, Sirte (halfway between Tripoli and Benghazi) and Bani Walid, the last strongholds of Muammar al-Qaddafi. On September 15, I went to Bani Walid and fought for twenty-five days. After I was hit in the shoulder by a sniper's bullet, I went back to my hometown. Even though I was at home, my heart was with my friends who were still fighting Qaddafi's forces. I thank God because they were able to finish the job victoriously. Without the courage of these men and their sacrifices, we would not have achieved freedom, and our revolution would not have succeeded. Without them, we would not have been able to breathe the air of freedom and break the shackles of dictatorship, which defined Arab governments and surprised the world with its brutality. We had a war in Libya, and we fought it before we received our freedom and achieved our victory. Our people sacrificed everything for the sake of our cause. Some lost money, and many paid with their lives. Some lost parts of their bodies while fighting.

During the Libyan revolution I witnessed events and moments that I will never forget, such as seeing innocent people killed before my eyes, the sound of bullets whizzing by, and NATO bombs shelling Qaddafi's camps while I was nearby. My story cannot include all the details or the dates because of the escalating sequence of events. Often, several major events took place on the same day. Thus, I have tried to tell my account of the Libyan revolution with simplicity and objectivity, writing only what I experienced and what still occupies my memory.

THE DARK NIGHT ON THE TRIPOLI FRONT

Abdulmonem Allieby

University student in networking and telecommunications, male, 24, Tripoli

I was born and raised in Tripoli, Libya, but because my father was a dissident, I was forced into exile and eventually settled in the United States. The Libyan revolution was a dream that I and most other Libyans initially saw as impossible, but the spark in Benghazi lit hope inside me for the first time. After a few months of watching the revolution unfold on television, it became the only thing in my life, and I could no longer carry on with basic everyday activities such as work and school. I felt solace only when I found myself in the western mountains of Libya as a member of the Tripoli Revolutionaries Brigade. At the end of August 2011, I had the honor of driving the first car in the convoy that entered Tripoli and raided Qaddafi's Bab al-Azizyia compound. In this account, I would like to share an amazing story, which most of my fellow citizens have not heard and is probably being made public for the first time. It is about an event that took place on the night of August 20, when there was a major uprising in Tripoli. Indeed, if it were not for the grace of God, the event would have been disastrous for the revolution. The main hero of this story is Abdulhakim al-Mishry, a member of the Tripoli Revolutionaries Brigade Media Office. Because I know that he is too humble to tell the story himself, I will narrate the event on his behalf as I saw it.

The place is the Libyan city of Zawyia, which is about forty miles west of the capital city, Tripoli. The time was Saturday night, August 20, 2011. After my brigade came down from the mountain city of Nalut to al-Zawyiah and before we even got a chance to settle into our new building, the capital, Tripoli, decided to revolt. We began receiving news of victories from our revolutionaries in operation rooms inside the city, and we were hysterical from extreme joy and lack of sleep. But our euphoria soon was shattered by the cries of help from our families and fighters inside the city as their ammunition ran out and the Qaddafi regime forces began closing in on them. To our shock and in a purely reactionary manner, our commander ordered all the fighters to pack up their gear, pick up their weapons, and get ready for the battle of Tripoli. I should note here that the official day of the Tripoli operation was supposed to be on August 23, and half the brigade members at the time were new recruits who had not had even basic training.

We were given our weapons and began preparing our vehicles and gear, and a convoy began to form outside the brigade wall. Around three in the morning, we finished our preparations, and a convoy of dozens of cars and hundreds of fighters began moving toward Tripoli. On the way, we were greeted by the families and fighters of Zawyiah with cheers and shouts of "Allahu akbar" (Allah is the greatest), which raised our already high morale. At around four in the morning, our convoy reached the town of al-Maya (twenty miles from Tripoli), which was the farthest point that the western-region revolutionaries had reached. I and my comrade, Abdulhakim al-Mishry, were in the media van at the back of the convoy. We kept moving up until we heard a few shots being fired, which we believed came from enemy snipers. For fear of attracting more sniper fire, our people began to remove the cars' brake lights and turn off their signal lights so as not to make us visible to the enemy. It was a dark night, and I was driving the media van in almost pitch-black darkness. While we were sitting in the van waiting for orders to attack, I saw light come from a car not too far ahead of me, which annoyed me and I said to myself, "Haven't we told these people not use their lights?!"

The light became brighter and began to illuminate its surroundings; only at this point did I realize that it was a fire! I began to worry because we were close to the front line, and the first enemy position was only half a mile from us at the time. The fire got bigger and by then had engulfed the entire inside of the car. As if the situation weren't bad enough, I quickly realized that the burning vehicle was not a civilian car like the others in the convoy but was a truck full of ammunition! At that moment, fear got the better of me, and I expected the worst, which is that the 14.5 millimeter antiaircraft rounds inside the car would begin to cook and explode, causing the rockets and projectiles in the rear bed to explode as well. This is where the disaster would take place: the explosion of the truck and the subsequent explosions of all the vehicles in the middle of the convoy would give away our position. This would be the end of an operation we had long dreamed of and patiently awaited (and a huge downturn for the revolution as a whole, and I'm not exaggerating).

In that moment and in the ensuing chaos and confusion, Abdulhakim jumped out of the van I was driving and ran toward the burning truck to investigate the situation. He then turned around, looked at me, and yelled: "Let's go. Let's go!" I assumed he meant to get away from the area as the ammunition inside the truck had been burning for a few minutes and was on the brink of exploding. I began reversing the van only for him to yell again and tell me to come closer to the burning car. I made a final prayer and accelerated toward the truck thinking that we weren't going to get out of this in one piece. I stopped short of bumping into the burning truck and Abdulhakim jumped in the back of our van and pulled out a fire extinguisher. In a heroic gesture, he ran to the burning truck where he got so close that the flames almost touched his face and he began to put the fire out!

After the fire was extinguished, a few of our convoy fighters found the courage to approach the car and began removing the blazing hot ammunition from the truck. The explosive material was so hot they could not handle it with bare hands. Interestingly, there was no fire extinguisher in our van before coming down to Zawyiah, so I asked Abdulhakim where he had gotten the one he used. He told me that he had found it lying on the floor outside the brigade building in Nalut during our relocation and decided to put it in the van. We still don't know what caused the fire and if it was the result of a cigarette or an electrical short, but what was clear to us is that if it had not been for God's grace and Abdulhakim picking up that extinguisher, we would have been in a mess, for which only God knows the consequences. In Libya during the revolution, I saw countless mistakes made and many accidents resulting from misjudgment or reckless behavior. But Abdulhakim's heroism resonated with me the most. I am positive—and proud to say—that if not for God's watchful eye and the bravery of our men, our revolution would have been gone with the wind.

I would like to conclude with this statement. People sometimes ask me: "Why would someone young like you with a 'bright future' travel out to nowhere and take part in a battle with no end in sight and against a regime unmatched in its madness and brutality?" Most people like me would usually answer by referring to patriotism or duty to one's country. But the reason for my participation in fighting the regime is more than that. Simply put, imagine a person oppressed, beaten, and humiliated for decades and when he finally speaks, he still is strangled. While slowly awaiting death, the oppressor is momentarily disoriented and releases his grip. Knowing that this is absolutely your last and only chance at survival, what would you do? In my case, I fought.

FIGHTING FOR FREEDOM

Ehab Ibrahim al-Khinjari

Battalion of Tripoli Rebels, male, 27, Tripoli

I live in Ghout Alshaal, a residential area located in the capital, Tripoli, and my house is located in what is called Street No. 10. On the night of February 18, 2011, I heard people chanting "With our souls, with our blood, we will sacrifice ourselves for you, Benghazi" and showing support for this Libyan city. At that time, Benghazi was under attack by the regime of the former president, Muammar al-Qaddafi. I went out to the street and started running in a psychological state I have not experienced before. I do not know how to describe that moment. I found about twenty young people who are highly respected in our neighborhood, and for the first time in my life, I joined them in a demonstration. We had never done this before; it was my first time to shout with all my might the word no to the Qaddafi's regime. We started chanting "It is now your turn, dictator Muammar," referring to the Arab dictators who were toppled before Qaddafi. With these words, I felt as if all the fetters with which I had been bound were breaking, and I felt the delightful taste of the word "freedom."

But after half an hour, the police interrupted our euphoria and shot live ammunition at our demonstration. In response, we threw stones at them as more young people joined us. We forced the regime police to flee, but no sooner had they disappeared, riding away in their cars, than the security men came to attack us again, using their plentiful weapons, including 14.5 millimeter antiaircraft artillery. Having no weapons, we resisted them for only a short time before we fled. I went home completely shocked at what happened. It seemed that there was an incredible price for anyone who dared to oppose Qaddafi. At home I told my father about the torment we experienced and described to him the feeling, or rather the meaning, of being free. I was unable to sleep that night, unsure of whether it was because of the extreme joy or the fear still inside me.

The next day, February 19, our street was empty of people; shop owners were clearing their stores of items, a scene indicating that the next days would be tough on Tripoli. At that time, there were many demonstrations in Benghazi. But in Tripoli, which was still under Qaddafi's control, we went out only at night so we would not be caught by the security forces. Our activities included burning old tires in the street and chanting both revolutionary and hopeful slogans. We coordinated with the people of Zawyia, which is about twenty-eight miles west of Tripoli, for them to attack Tripoli, and then we would join them. Our district, Ghout Alshaal, is close to the border of Tripoli, so we wanted them to enter the capital through our area. After sunset, we took to the street as usual, but on this night, February 20, there was a big demonstration: people no longer were afraid of Qaddafi. When we were out on Street No. 10, we heard, but did not believe, the then popular rumor that Libyan leader Colonel Muammar al-Qaddafi had fled the country and escaped to Venezuela after the outbreak of revolution throughout Libya. A confrontation soon started between us and his battalions.

We lost one young man, and three people were wounded. Suddenly, the popular television news channel Al Arabiya, broadcast and confirmed the news that Qaddafi had indeed left the country and gone to Venezuela. This news changed the situation on the ground, for suddenly the pro-Qaddafi forces disappeared and people came out into the streets, some in their cars, yelling and congratulating one another on this good news. I was screaming loudly in the street, "Qaddafi ran away, Qaddafi ran away!" and joined the people who were moving toward Martyrs Square. There, crowds of people came from the area around the square.

After this brief celebration of what appeared later to be false news, a swarm of Qaddafi's militias came out and used their arsenal of weapons to kill with unbelievable ferocity these peaceful people. I couldn't bear to see these people being killed in cold blood, falling in front of me. I fled to Martyrs Square, looking right and left all the way home. Nobody was there because my family had left for my uncle's house. I turned on the television to get some idea of what was going on. I didn't understand what I saw—Qaddafi's son Saif al-Islam appeared on TV threatening people while pointing his finger (in an authoritative and insulting manner). The news was fake!

The next day, February 21, Qaddafi appeared on television, giving a fierce and aggressive speech. He read some parts of the penal code, including the death penalty. After his speech was over, his supporters in the capital took to the streets. Most either were vulnerable people who were trying to stay on the safe side by supporting the dictator or were criminals who had been released from prison on the condition that they support the regime. I became more afraid for my safety because Qaddafi was still in full control of Tripoli. We decided that our operations against the regime had to be selective and carefully conducted. But we continued to write revolutionary statements on the walls and raise the flag of independence, which we had adopted as a replacement for the Libyan flag under Qaddafi's rule.

Qaddafi's obsession with power motivated him to arrest more young people and to kill even more of them. When Benghazi was declared free of his control, I and many other rebels were eager to go there and help advance the freedom of all of Libya. I wanted to keep helping the fighters outside Tripoli, and I decided to go to Benghazi for this purpose. But the roads between the two cities were blocked, and it wasn't possible to get there except by way of Tunisia, passing through Egypt, and then to Benghazi. I did not have enough money for this trip, so I waited for a better chance.

On April 21, the rebels in the Nafusa Mountains, the area in northwestern Libya that was an exception to the Qaddafi-controlled western part of the country, took control of the Wazin Crossing, one of the most important crossings between Tunisia and Libya. This place is close to the city of Nalut, where a battalion, the Battalion of Tripoli Rebels, had been formed. At the end of April, I was assigned to deliver money from Tripoli to the Libyan rebels who were stationed in Tunisia. I delivered the money, and afterward, my dream to join the revolutionaries came true. I crossed the border from Tunisia into Libya, entering the free soil of the Nafusa Mountains, and then went to the city of Alzentan in the western mountains. I fought in fierce battles in Baqoul Zawyia, to the east of Alzentan, and we fought bravely.

Of course, no one denies the great role played by the NATO forces. When the United Nations agreed to allow intervention to save the civilians in Libya, grateful voices were raised in the homes in the liberated areas. NATO's participation was considered a form of victory, and it sent a message to the Libyan people that the world stood with them in their revolution. During the war, NATO chose its targets carefully, and progress was slow at the beginning. (It increased later, hitting the Qaddafi forces hard.) NATO helped save civilian lives because its presence sent the message to Qaddafi's battalion solders that if they hit cities with heavy weapons, NATO would target them.

I joined the Battalion of Tripoli Rebels in Nalut in June because the army division carried the name of my city and my dream was to see it free, a free capital with no dictatorship engineered by Qaddafi, who had displaced many Libyan families. I trained hard with rebels in the battalion, starting in the morning and continuing until sometime in the evening. We then moved to liberate nearby areas, such as Umm Alfar and al-Gazayia. I was almost killed on three occasions in these battles, but I was still motivated to keep fighting. I felt that my soul was a fair price for lifting injustice from my people. We returned to our base in Nalut before moving on to other fronts. We freed the town of Teiji, which is at the foot of the Nafusa Mountains in northwest Libya and is the second largest city in the Nalut region. Teiji was not an easy place to liberate; we battled fiercely and could not get into the town. After we lost two fighters, we went back to our headquarters with tears in our eyes, but we also hugged one another and raised our spirits by saying that the day would come when we would free the city.

In the middle of August, on the fifteenth day of Ramadan, we launched an attack about six o'clock in the morning on the pro-Qaddafi battalions in Teiji, and we finally freed the town. Zawyia, which is about twenty-eight miles west of Tripoli, was our next target, and we joined the forces that freed it, thanks to Allah and to the help of its strong people. On August 21, we headed to Jdaim city, which is between Zawyia and Tripoli, and on that same day we moved on to our final target. During the night we arrived at the outskirts of Tripoli, and we immediately entered the city to start clearing it of fighters of the ousted Qaddafi, moving "house by house and hand span by hand span," as Qaddafi himself planned to do in order to kill his opponents at the beginning of the revolution.

I should mention here that Qaddafi and his regime committed immoral crimes against the Libyan people. In addition to spreading drugs and encouraging prostitution among the youth that followed him, they were responsible for the systematic rape committed by his soldiers in many cities. These soldiers and supporters received orders that they could kill or rape anyone they wanted, and they acted on the orders of their leaders. Worst of all, they raped women in front of their fathers to destroy the dignity and pride of our resilient people. Of course, little information about these crimes is available because the Libyan people consider rape to be a grave shame—you cannot find someone who would say that his daughter had been raped; he would rather conceal such a crime with shame and anger. Other crimes were motivated by the regime's desire to stay in power. Qaddafi spent a lot of money to buy loyalty. His forces arrested the family members of revolutionaries and tortured them to discourage their sons from fighting. They also used the dirtiest means to protect Qaddafi, including using drugs to destroy some poor citizens' minds.

I hope that Libya will be free and more beautiful than before. This country has suffered a great deal at the scourging hands of Muammar Qaddafi and his sons. For forty-two years, he killed, raped, and displaced our people, and we experienced all kinds of torment during his rule. In foreign policy and international relations, he tarnished the image of Libyans in the eyes of the world. After his death, though, Libya can live in freedom, which is what we longed for before and during the revolution. As Libyans, we see Qaddafi's death as the beginning of a decent and free life and the start of mutual interests with the entire world. I see a beautiful and better future waiting for us.

FROM SCHOOL TO THE BATTLEFIELD

Yusef Mohamed Benruwin

Student, male, 20, Benghazi

For my whole life I was raised on the dream of a free Libya. My father, Dr. Mohamed Abdu-Rahaman Benruwin, dedicated his life to that dream. He focused his research on Islamic politics and wrote critiques of Qaddafi's regime and its use of torture against the Libyan people. Blacklisted after attending a protest in Benghazi, which caused the university to temporarily shut down, my father left Libya in 1977 and did not return to the country until November 2011. His passion for Libya permeated my life, and he always told me that his dream was for me to help Libya attain its rightful glory.

When the Libyan revolution began, I felt a sense of pride in the momentum that the Arab Spring had created, but I did not expect things to go the way they did. Since Qaddafi was the first of the Arab leaders to stand violently against the peaceful protest of the people, I fell into a state of panic and concern for the lives of the Libyans confronting him. In the beginning, the U.S. media had not yet reported on the uprisings in the country, so I started a Facebook page called "Libyan Revolution Support" to help raise awareness of the uprising that devolved into bloodshed. Finally, days into the revolution, CNN finally reported on it. "Now the world will be watching," my father said.

Every day I went online or watched TV, trying to keep up with the situation in Libya. Soon after Qaddafi began attacking Benghazi, a few people in Misrata rose up in protest against the violence there. A few of my cousins had been present that day, and they told me that only about one hundred people were protesting. They also told me that Qaddafi loyalists fired live ammunition at them, and on that day the first martyr of Misrata fell. As a result of this injustice, the very next day around ten thousand people in Misrata protested, but this time it was against the regime. We got a call at around three o'clock in the morning from my uncle Abdu-Alaati, and it was difficult to hear him at first, but he finally told us, "I just want you guys to know that Qaddafi is attacking with missiles!" and the line went dead. I had been living with my family and attending college in the United States, but my schoolwork and life were affected. I could not concentrate, and I felt helpless knowing that Misrata was under constant attack. My emotions grew stronger, and I suffered many sleepless nights wondering if I would ever see my family again.

Things got better when a no-fly zone was imposed on Libya. My hope grew, and I began to prepare to travel to Libya. I wanted to stand with my Libyan brothers and sisters against Qaddafi and his troops. Although my father asked me to wait until after I finished the semester to make my trip, his request greatly upset me. Nevertheless, because I wanted to join the jihad against Qaddafi, I wanted to have the full blessings of both my parents, so I waited. On top of my school responsibilities, I began to plan my route to Misrata and my training in Benghazi. Networking with Libyans in the United States, I was able to find one Libyan sister in Dallas whose brother, Mustafa al-Sakoozli, was one of the men who had escaped from prison after an unlawful arrest for alleged charges. I planned to join later my uncle Abdu-Alaati's militia Osoud Alwadi (Lions of the Valley) in Misrata. I found out that one of my aunts had managed to escape from Tripoli to Egypt, so I arranged to meet her on May 17, 2011. Before I departed on my flight out of Laredo, Texas, on May 16, I packed my two bags with clothes, energy drinks, and other things I felt I might need, such as a flashlight, knife, video camera, satellite phone, list of family members' phone numbers, and Qur'an. I kissed my mother, brother, and father at the airport—not knowing if this would be the last time I would see them—and proceeded to my gate.

My trip was long and tiring, but I stayed focused and in tune with my prayers. Once I arrived in Cairo on May 17, I found that there had been some confusion between me and my ride on the time of my arrival so I took a taxi and rented a hotel room for my first night. I was able to meet with my aunt and uncle the next day and contacted my father's cousin, Ahmad Benruwin, who had escaped from Benghazi and knew people moving in and out of Libya and Egypt. I took the next trip out of Egypt and prayed for a safe arrival. The border check was thorough and very time-consuming; they asked everyone questions and for proof of Libyan citizenship. The trip from Cairo to Benghazi took twelve hours, but I was quite impressed with how well organized the rebels kept the border. As soon as I arrived in Benghazi, I stayed with my father's young cousin Mohamed Benruwin. I arranged to meet with Mustafa al-Sakoozli, who was in charge of the fighters, at a military base and began my training. I was taught how to use and fire a Kalashnikov, rocket-propelled grenades (RPGs), and other light weapons that the rebels were using. The training lasted for about three weeks, and then my cousins came to Benghazi to make sure that I would arrive safely in Misrata. Seeing them after ten years was emotional, and I could see in their eyes that they had changed from their experience with the regime. We talked over some tea, during which they told me about the situation in Misrata. I learned that none of my family members had been killed yet and that only a few missiles had landed near my grandfather's house, where my entire family in Misrata had gathered for shelter.

On June 4, I headed for the battlefield in Dafneeyah, a small town north of Misrata, in hopes of reaching Tripoli. All the family on mother's side was in Tripoli, so I hoped to reach them as soon as possible. We traveled to Dafneeyah in trucks that had been armed with heavy antiaircraft guns. I saw that the rebels were set up in a line formation stretching for miles. When we took our places, we made a fire and put down a mat for prayer. We took turns keeping watch with binoculars and spent our off time talking about how worthless Qaddafi was and what each of us would do if we caught him. We used to spend one day and one night at the battlefield and then come back to Misrata for one day and one night. Each time I returned, I stayed with my aunts, uncles, and cousins. My time in Misrata was beautiful. There was a warm feeling in the air, and even though missiles still landed there every day, especially on Fridays, people managed to maintain order and control.

Things got worse in the battlefield when NATO gave us permission to advance on June 11, 2011, and we moved forward as one line and pushed back the remaining Qaddafi troops. On my first advance, we almost reached Zleetin, which is only an hour away from Tripoli. Although we were armed well enough to fight, on several occasions we found ourselves in need of more ammunition. On June 21, I went by sea with my uncle and cousin to the west in search of more ammunition. The trip took longer than expected because one of the boat's engines failed, so it took us thirty-six hours to reach Tobruk, in Libya's western state. As rebels from Misrata, we were given much respect there. But we were in a rush, so we were advised to go to Benghazi, where we had been assured that we could find faster access to ammunition and weapons. We took a taxi and talked with the driver, Basheer al-Faitoori, who insisted on stopping in his home city, Albaidah, claiming that he knew of weapons stored in the mountains. He kindly invited us to stay at his house and fed us very well, and he also invited all his neighbors over for dinner, proudly informing them that he was accompanied by rebels from Misrata. They all came with ammunition that they had found and gladly offered it to us.

On June 23, we traveled to a mountainous area where hundreds of containers of ammunition had been buried at the base of a mountain range and took what had been left. We loaded the back of huge trucks with missiles to send back to Misrata. Later that day, Basheer took us to Qaddafi's house, which had been burned. We found an indoor pool, lion cage, underground pathway from one side of the house to another, and what seemed to be a basketball court. "This is how our wealth has been wasted," said my uncle. The following day, we left by boat for Benghazi in search of more ammunition. Our trip took thirty-six hours, and most of us suffered from seasickness because of the rough surf. When we returned to Misrata, we distributed the ammunition and headed back to the battlefield. Being young and anxious, I was bothered by the special attention from my uncle. I was always held back and just did not feel that I was seen as a rebel, which is what I had gone there to be. So, after a month of being with my uncle and Osoud Alwadi, I joined another militia, al-Marsah, a group of people with whom I had had no relations earlier, but they welcomed me with open arms, and I began my new routine with them. This caused some conflict in my family. I knew that they were worried about me, but I could not pass up this historic moment in Libya to be some guy that just stood in back of the rebels. I wanted to be one of them and to fight against Qaddafi. Al-Marsah was one of the largest militias in our battlefield, and it was definitely a different experience being with them than with Osood al-Waadi.

It was a change of pace with al-Marsah: their weapons were better and heavier, and our second advance on July 13 was a far better experience. Some nights we were exhausted but could not sleep because of missiles being exchanged. We also had to pray carefully, as there had been a few instances of being in the wrong place at the wrong time, and missiles landed near the group that was praying, resulting in some injuries. My best experience with al-Marsah in the war was when I actually felt that any day I could die. When our second and final advance came, we were aware of the mines that Qaddafi's troops had left behind so we proceeded cautiously. We had a bulldozer to help clear the path for us while we kept back a safe distance. During the move, my group found a wall in our path. Without any time to waste, we began to fire and destroy the wall and finished it off with our bare hands. Finally we reached Zleetin and set up camp there.

Unfortunately, my time in Libya ended because I needed to return to the United States to continue my studies. On August 15, I turned in my weapon to my field leader for the last time and said my good-byes to my fellow fighters. I arranged for a boat to take me to Benghazi. When it came time for me to leave, I packed my bags, kissed my grandfather's head, and said good-bye to all my cousins, aunts, and uncles. On my way to Benghazi I felt a sense of pride and confidence in myself knowing that I had completed, to the best of my abilities, my Islamic duties against the dictator of my country. News came while I was in Benghazi that the rebels had reached Tripoli. But I laughed because I knew that it was not my destiny to have been there during that advancement. The entire city of Benghazi was celebrating and gunfire could be heard everywhere and chants of "Allah is great" echoed throughout the city. Although Qaddafi had not been captured yet, it was clear that Libya was now free.

LIVING THROUGH THE LIBYAN UPRISING

Gay Emmaya Tongali

Filipina, registered nurse in a medical surgical unit, Benghazi Medical Center, female, Benghazi

Trying to summarize how I lived my life through the months of the Libyan revolution is challenging. I was hopeful when the New Year started. Plans were outlined; I had goals that needed to be met. I never knew that events would unfold that would drastically change my life. The whole experience was tough, rough, and, frankly, painful.

All right, let me start in mid-February, the seventeenth to be exact, when what started as a simple demonstration turned into an all-out war in Libya. It was a mind-blowing experience that I wouldn't want to go through again. It was downright terrifying, especially at the beginning when we were completely cut off from the outside world. Within a few hours after the protest started, outside phone calls were prohibited, and the Internet was shut down. It seemed that for more than a week, blood continued to flow in the streets of Benghazi while the outside world was ignorant of what was happening in Libya. State television was conveying a different story on the international news networks, showing only those reports supporting the Qaddafi regime when, in truth, unrest was smoldering in the streets. Although the surface of Libya was peaceful, behind the facade, everything was ready to explode! The veil of Libya was slowly being lifted. The history of violence to and abuse of its citizens was slowly being uncovered; the pretense of civility was eroding.

Gunfire, bomb explosions, and burned-out buildings, houses, and cars were everywhere. Police stations, military camps, and proregime properties were the first casualties in the people's quest to gain control of Benghazi. People were taking to the streets en masse to fight for their much coveted freedom. Mostly, it was young men fighting to change their future, refusing to live under the thumb of a ruthless leader, as their ancestors had before them.

I had to decide whether to stay or go back home to Manila. The city I worked in was unsafe; really, the whole country was unsafe. It was pandemonium. Friends and colleagues were opting to go home, too scared to stay. Others gave in to the unrelenting pressure from their anxious families, and still others just went with the flow. It was a good time to go home, anyway. In the meantime, I had to go to work. By the way, I work as a nurse, on call on my days off, and there was no rest. Patients came in bloodied, with bullet holes in their bodies, screaming in pain. Some were barely conscious. Nonetheless, their spirits were strong, and most of them still wanted to go back to the front lines to fight yet again if they could.

For the first time, people carrying guns and knives became a common sight in the hospital. For protection? Maybe. We never knew who was friend or foe then. Benghazi Medical Center's (BMC) surgery ward looked like a market, with relatives swarming in like bees, refusing to leave their injured families alone, scared of retaliation. Security was lost, and hospital protocols were thrown out the window. Just as long as the patients were received and taken care of, that was it. Elective cases were discharged or transferred to other hospitals in order to accommodate those who were injured and in need of immediate medical care and assistance. It was chaos of untold proportions.

But after two weeks, BMC became a ghost town. The staff was gone. Indians, Filipinos, Ukrainians, everyone, had gone home in a massive exodus. By boat, by bus; transportation was limited to these. Flying was not an option because the plane could be shot down at random. Commercial flights were canceled, and the airport was shut down.

For some time I lived in the hospital. But even that did not diminish the threat because the hospital itself was a target. It did not matter that it was supposedly neutral territory. Promises of retribution were being issued by Mr. Qaddafi on state and international television, that Benghazi would be pulverized, reduced to gravel and dust. And that would have been true had NATO not interceded at the eleventh hour.

That was March 19, 2011, a significant date. The day when Qaddafi's minions were at Benghazi's doorstep once again. I was on day duty then. As soon as I left my room, I could feel the difference. I could hear fighter jets roaring in the skies. The whole town was eerily quiet, without any civilians outside. The tension was palpable. The bus driver taking the nurses to the hospital for day duty drove like a maniac; it took only four minutes when the ride would normally take ten. The main road was littered with trucks with antiaircraft machine guns on top of them, parked in strategic areas. Benghazi Medical Center was barricaded by soldiers and military vehicles. The soldiers were ready for battle, if and when it was necessary.

As I walked inside the hospital, I found it empty. There was only one person at the reception desk. Only a handful of Libyan staff members reported for work. It felt like I was moving inside a glass house, totally naked and stripped of any protection. Meanwhile, we could hear gunfire outside, feel vibrations from the bombings, but my colleagues and I still continued to work. I had to stay focused and composed enough to take care of my patients. I felt like I was a moving target. My imagination was my greatest enemy. At one point, I was thinking that a stray bullet might go through the hospital walls and pierce my body; I could imagine my own blood pooling around me, and I wondered whether I would feel the pain or whether I would be too far gone to feel anything. But I had to banish those thoughts right away! There was no need to scare myself unnecessarily when I had patients needing attention. Medications had to be given; new cannulas (or tubes) had to be inserted; patients' tests had to be sent. I had to prepare patients for possible operations. I was trying to be really brave, though deep inside, I was terrified. It was difficult to maintain a calm facade. I just kept praying for safety and protection the whole time. Around ten or eleven in the morning, a plane fell from the skies. I was just glad it missed the hospital and the residential areas. It crashed in the sea, near the hotel where I lived; I had to sleep at the hospital again that night. That day, the battle was won, at least in the city of Benghazi, the bastion of the opposition.

Battles raged in other parts of the country. Cities like Misrata suffered the most. For months the city was shelled, bombed, and isolated. Around May, the opposition was able to gain enough control of the city to transfer patients to Benghazi. It was horrible to see the patients. It was a whole new picture of the horrors that the country was suffering. Their injuries were more massive: bilateral leg amputees, both arms on external fixators, burned bodies, bigger and meaner-looking bullet holes, and patients with chest tubes as well. It was not a pretty sight. The worst part was that more patients were brought in, more than we could accommodate. But they had to be taken care of.

In the middle of all this, personal tragedy struck. My father passed away from a motorcycle accident back home. That was July 31, 2011. I was devastated. This time, there was no question of what I had to do. I decided to go home, without any guarantee of getting back to Libya, since the Philippine government had issued a travel ban.

Fast forward now. I have survived the war, indeed. By God's grace, I did. I witnessed one country's struggle for independence from a tyrannical leader. And they succeeded. Now I am praying for the country to survive the rebuilding, with high hopes that the Libyans will rise from these ashes and claim the victory they so deserve by effecting change among the people and the leaders who will lead this country to progress.

BENGHAZI, MY LOVE

Adel el-Taguri

Child health consultant, male, 48, Libya

As a child in the early 1970s, I remember going out into the streets with my father, as did tens of thousands of enthusiastic Libyans, to salute Qaddafi in the first few years after his 1969 coup. As the years went by, however, things changed. When I entered the university, dozens of small incidents always reminded us of how Qaddafi's revolutionary committees changed the life of thousands of children who grew up in misery. A simple wall journal was confiscated because of a small comment on the value of the scholarship given to a student who had been reprimanded by Qaddafi himself. In student concerts, we were obliged to sing about the life of the greatest leader of all time. We were forced to participate in "pro–great leader" demonstrations. This ended with some students being hanged in front of their classmates and terrorizing them. The cry from the mother of one of those students was in vain when she asked Qaddafi's wife for mercy. The reply was, "You will conceive another son, but there is only one Qaddafi." These words transmitted from the mouth of the poor mother kept ringing in my ears for years. I do not know why.

As the years went by, many attempts were made to stop this brutal regime but to no avail. Qaddafi's strategies were simple and primitive but successful. They were based on spreading terror to prevent a critical mass from going out into the streets to demonstrate against him. This explains his dislike for sports, especially those that could attract thousands of supporters, as sporting events could be a gathering place for the necessary critical mass that could end the life of a tyrant. He was only partially reassured when his sons took over the control of sports in Libya.

With the fall of the Berlin wall and the consequent changes that took place in Eastern Europe, I saw how these people reached the critical mass signaling the end of tyranny, either peacefully or forcefully. When the Arab Spring began, the joke repeated most often was that the Tunisians asked the Libyans to lean forward, as they wanted to speak with the men on the other side of the border, the Egyptians. The joke was a sign of the bitterness that dominated the general feeling in Libya.

A few days before the revolution began on February 15, activists used social media sites to call for a demonstration against the tyranny. Different groups took part in a number of discussions about whether there would be enough momentum to start a revolution in Libya. The question was whether the general consciousness could bring enough people this time to reach a critical mass. These calls were immediately stopped by the secret forces. Another wave of thousands of such calls came through emails, and this time, the place and time of the gathering in each city were precise. In a reckless move, the secret forces imprisoned Mr. Fathi Terbil, a young activist, lawyer, and brother of one of the twelve hundred prisoners in the infamous Abu Salim prison who were killed in cold blood in 1996. They were murdered in just a few hours because they asked for humane treatment in the prison, and the regime negotiated with them using bullets. Mr. Terbil was one of the most active lawyers defending the families of these victims. The regime arrested him on February 15, thinking that he was behind the calls to demonstrate, and this move sparked the beginning of the revolution even before the agreed-on date of February 17.

Mr. Terbil's mother, who had lost her other son in this massacre, gathered the mothers of the other martyrs and demonstrated in front of the security department demanding the release of her activist son. People passing by got out of their cars wondering why the revolution had started early; they all had question marks on their faces, asking, "How did this start without me? Nobody told me." But the pro-Qaddafi people had another plan, again a simple, brutal strategy of terror. The plan was to release, on February 16, as many as possible of the so-called Islamic extremists (mostly from Derna city), as the propaganda machinery of the official Arabic media called them. Then if the revolution started, they would hit that particular city hard at the other end of the green mountain beyond the view of the international community. The plan mandated wiping the city off the map to prevent others in the remaining cities from reaching a critical mass, a strategy that Qaddafi had used before. But as the Qur'an states: "They want to extinguish the light of Allah with their mouths, but Allah refuses except to perfect His light" (9:32). The light of our revolution was shining.

As a pediatrician in a hospital, I did not have a specific role in taking care of the wounded. Those brave young men stood bare chested in front of Qaddafi's heavily armed battalions using arms designed for heavy warfare. These forces protected the military base, the Kateeba, which was the symbol of tyranny in the eastern region, in the center of the city one kilometer from our hospital. I had my own thoughts about the resilience of these youths, who were a good example of the importance of values, for they knew that they would die, but they cared only about the well-being of their society and not themselves. Resilience in our field is a term that denotes a positive spirit in which a person gains an advantage from the difficulties of daily life in order to promote his personal capacities. Some researchers consider it the fourth dimension of health, spiritual well-being, along with the other well-known physical, mental, and social dimensions. In my opinion, these youths who stood bare chested in front of the walls of the security forces' headquarters exemplify active resilience.

Events progressed quickly, as the whole eastern region was liberated in only four days. The region's needs have since changed, especially without any form of state organization. A mixed international delegation came to Benghazi to assess the people's humanitarian and health needs. The delegation reported its findings at the biggest gathering of official health authorities and international and humanitarian organizations in the region: the conference of Arab Ministers of Health, which was held in Beirut on March 9 and 10, 2011. A friend told me that the official statement concluded that Libya did not need any support for at least the next three months. My professional estimation was that this was a big mistake that needed to be corrected before things went wrong. It could harm the nascent revolution. I had to get to the conference in Beirut, even though there were no flights leaving Libya, no foreign embassies for securing visas, and no way to withdraw money from the banks.

I therefore went to Cairo by car (1,200 kilometers from Benghazi) and arrived there 2:00 a.m.—four hours after the beginning of the curfew. Although my flight was a few hours later, I had no place to retrieve my ticket from my email. The mission was not easy. At the conference, I described the crisis in Libya and its broad effect on the health of the population. Most of the delegates were sympathetic, and the official statement that Libya did not need humanitarian aid was reversed. I went back to Cairo the night before the Arab League met, to cover the international intervention through the Security Council. I had contacted a few young leaders of the Egyptian revolution, asking them to demonstrate in front of the Arab League in Cairo, as we knew that five countries probably would vote against the decision. The result was that thousands of Libyan and Egyptian demonstrators prevented even Mr. Amr Moussa himself from entering the building. I realized afterward that I was not alone, that a few other Libyan citizens had taken the same initiative.

That was the beautiful thing about this revolution; everybody tried his best so that it would succeed. Nobody was obliged or ordered to do what he did. The same thing happened afterward. When I arrived in Benghazi, we were surprised to find out that President Barack Obama had announced that the United States would not join international efforts to support the Libyan people in their fight against tyranny, which had managed to survive and make allies of many Western leaders. I had to write a letter to Mr. Obama to convince him of the importance of these efforts, and that despite what happened in

Afghanistan and Iraq, standing aside would be a mistake. Again, I found other people who did the same thing.

News was spreading about the inevitable attack on Benghazi by Qaddafi's battalions, armed with tanks and heavy artillery. These reports were confirmed after Qaddafi, in a speech, referred to Benghazi as his lover, thereby giving the green light for a military operation in the capital. Despite the horrible stories about his forces' criminal behavior in other cities—the cold-blooded killing of civilians, looting, kidnapping, and raping—and despite the threats to obliterate Benghazi, tens of thousands of families decided not to leave. All we did was move from sparsely populated, open, large streets to densely populated, narrow streets that tanks could not enter. Of course, in the first hours of March 19, that did not prevent rockets from falling on Benghazi like heavy rain.

Early intervention by France saved the lives of hundreds of thousands; Benghazi, Derna, and most of the eastern towns gave the revolution space to spread to the rest of the country. We strongly believed that we were going to succeed, as our counterparts in Egypt and Tunisia had, but we had two other strong feelings. The first was the happiness and the enthusiasm for the dawn of a new era in the international scene as we watched the flags of France, the United States, and the United Kingdom hanging in Liberation Square in Benghazi. This was a model for openness and showed that the world had changed and that there was no more hostility and aggression toward us: Libya, and Benghazi in particular, could play an essential role in forgiveness, convergence, and international peace. The other strong feeling was the concern that we were the only country in which the demonstrators would shout: "The people want to build the system and not bring down the system." Qaddafi left us a country without institutions or even a constitution, but with the considerable need for human resources and the fear that we might become like many other countries that threw out their dictator, where killing is routine.

My activities continued. After the defeat of Qaddafi's troops outside Benghazi, we started discovering the evils committed by his troops at the front line, which moved a few kilometers to the west. Some tens of thousands of people were displaced from Ejdabia to the west of Benghazi and were scattered in a triangle of more than 100 square meters in an arid area without food, shelter, water, sanitation, or medical treatment. We arranged relief caravans to those in need. We saw the solidarity of the Libyans at their best. However, in the beginning we did not believe the news that the surviving families told us about the horrors they faced, which included systematic, mass rape in these sparsely populated conservative communities. We realized how vulnerable we were and how unprepared for such widespread disaster. I also managed a national survey for the assessment of health and relief status (LHHNAS), participated in establishing a mental health plan, spread support therapy groups for distressed families and children, and did a dozen small things that would make our country a better place to live for my own and other children.

MY WORK IN REVOLUTIONARY LIBYA

Annabelle Veso Faller

Filipina, registered nurse, female, 29, Benghazi

When I was still in the Philippines, I tried to research the country that was to become my workplace, to at least equip myself with basic knowledge about the very first country I would spend a considerable amount of time in besides my birth country. Unfortunately, I found very little relevant information. I learned that Libya is situated in North Africa and not in the Middle East, as many believe because it is a Muslim country. I also learned that for more than four decades, the country's official ruler was Colonel Muammar al-Qaddafi. I had only seen posted pictures of my intended workplace, the biggest hospital in Benghazi, known as "Alf-O-Methin," or Benghazi Medical Center (BMC).

Of my first fifteen months in Libya, the first day stands out as one of the most interesting in this journey into the unknown. I was a bit apprehensive when I first set foot on Libyan soil, but I was able to overcome this when I arrived at the Garyounis Tourist Village Hotel. I found people in Benghazi courteous and friendly. I noticed that they lived simply. No malls, movies, public transportation (but cell phones always came with unlimited texting and calls). Technology in Libya was underdeveloped; it was not easy for us to call and receive calls outside Libya; it was difficult to buy a SIM card; calls were regulated; and Internet connections sometimes were cut off. But I was gradually able to adjust, thanks to the support of the Filipino Catholic community, with whose members I became close friends and who treated one another as family. I joined and became a representative of the BMC's Filipino Community in Benghazi (FilComBeng).

I consider Benghazi my home away from home. I enjoy a lot here, especially the four seasons, although I love spring the most. I am truly amazed that during spring, even the grass has flowers so beautifully grown. Most of our outings are during this time and throughout the summer. Beaches look so nice with clear blue waters. I am able to enjoy God's wonders here. I did not expect that Libya would have such a history with many places to visit. Moreover, I am able to eat fresh vegetables and fruits that are very affordable, even those that cost more in the Philippines.

It was February 10, 2011, when I heard about the planned silent protest against the regime. I asked some of my Libyan friends about it, but they gave me indirect answers. As I remember, it was February 15 when I received a phone call from a friend telling me to be careful and not go out because some youths were on the streets in strategic locations. The next day at around 5:00 p.m., I saw protesters walking down the streets with their placards. On February 17, I was on night duty. I never thought that the planned silent protest would become an all-out war. Even though I was not feeling well that day, I had to go to my job.

I worked in the operating room (OT) as a scrub/circulating nurse, in addition to being the clinical facilitator. Early that night, although everything there was quiet, the surgeons told us to prepare for emergencies. At 7:30 p.m., we were to go to the cafeteria for our dinner. We first went by the emergency room (ER) to check for any cases, but there were none at that time. At exactly 8:00 p.m., we received a call from the ER for an exploratory laparotomy (ex-lap), gunshot to the lower abdomen. The first patient was brought inside the OT, and after five minutes, another patient was brought inside, and so on and so on until I lost count. There were only four nurses on duty at the time. Normally, two nurses come in every night just for emergency cases because we do all the scheduled surgeries during the day. The three operation theaters were full, with patients for ex-laps, so we called other nurses to come and help us. I circulated between two theaters, and the other theater had no circulating nurse. Doctors and nurses helped each other. Reinforcements arrived only after an hour and a half because there was no bus to fetch them and it took twenty minutes to get here. That evening, we learned that some protesters died in the gunfire. The OR quieted down at 4:30 a.m., and so did Libya, which remained quiet as morning passed. But a doctor predicted that the fighting would resume after the *dhuhr* (afternoon) prayer, and as if his words were from an oracle, his prophecy came true and gunshots rang out again.

Our operations then were performed primarily at night, and we later learned that the BMC's nurse managers had left on the second day. I then acted as the night-shift charge nurse during the war because our regular charge nurse had just resigned, too. We divided ourselves into two teams: day and night. Night duties became more tiring and stressful, since all the cases were brought in at nighttime. But we needed to be up and about to help save the lives of our patients. Every day we were confronted with cases of patients with bullet wounds in different areas. Once we heard news about an airstrike. Everyone was afraid. My colleagues were crying, men and women alike, but I tried to keep myself strong for them (in front of them). But I could not help but cry when I was alone when I was resting when I didn't have any patients. I prayed silently that there wouldn't be any airstrikes because I still wanted to return to my family in the Philippines alive. But I still prepared myself to die. I remembered the time my parents told us about death, that wherever we were, if it was our time, then God would take us without warning, for we had only borrowed the life we had. But indeed, God is so good: He heard me. The OR stabilized a bit at the end of the month, as the war in Benghazi did not last long. Although we continued to receive patients for surgery, they came from outside Benghazi, like from Ajdabiya, Brega, and other neighboring areas.

I stood firm with my prayer when I was in the Philippines: "Let my work in Libya be a part of my mission here on earth." On March 1, the Filipino Repatriation Day, the ship was ready to take us home, but I decided not to leave Libya. Instead I helped my fellow Filipinos go home by helping them to the boat and completing the documents needed for repatriation. I said to myself then that Benghazi is a bit quieter now and that the war here is over, though not in the rest of Libya. I thought then that I would go home only if the situation became worse, confident in the thought that even in the worst situations there is always a way out through God's will. My family wanted me to come home, but I explained the situation to them. I was touched, and tears fell down my cheeks when I heard them say: "OK, we trust your judgment, and we entrust you to the Lord."

On March 3, two weeks after the onset of war, I got a call from Professor Salah el-Taktuk, the head of surgery. He asked me if I could train Libyans to become "first aiders" in case there was another armed "event." Without hesitation, I said yes. I told myself, "I can help patients by myself, but if I train people, then many of us would be able to take care of patients, beyond my own capacity to serve." I believe in the power of numbers, of multiplication, duplication, and leverage. So even when we were so understaffed after the repatriation, I had to set aside time for training. One nurse would have to take care of more than ten patients. I say that because of the situation, there was less quality nursing care available to patients who were war victims.

On March 5, when I met with Prof. Taktuk and Dr. Musa Alqadi, the hospital's executive director and head of the training department, I was introduced to a training committee they had already formed, headed by Dr. Aisha A. Nasef. While preparing for my lectures, I made Power Point presentations for basic nursing procedures when I would suddenly hear bomb explosions and gunfire nearby. It was kind of difficult for me to prepare those lectures, for I was not able to get resource materials, as there were no libraries open and no Internet connection. So I stayed in one room facing the computer and trying to remember everything about performing a certain nursing procedure correctly. March 19 was the target date to start the training. Unfortunately, it did not happen. It was horrible when NATO announced a no-fly zone on March 18. When the announcement ended, I heard gunfire and bomb explosions, but they were only celebrating the news on television. It did not end there.

March 19 was the day of the so-called Benghazi massacre. Everyone was alert. On my way to the BMC early in the morning, I saw people carrying various weapons. Although they were not trained as military personnel or police, they were willing to fight and sacrifice their lives to gain freedom from their tyrant leader. Instead of conducting the training, I worked in the OR because a lot of injured people were brought in for surgery—which was really unexpected because everyone was celebrating the no-fly one news from the night before. It was horrible: I witnessed real war. There were no telecommunications; phone and Internet connections were cut. I was not even able to contact my family in Benghazi. I was so busy in the OR that I put aside my fear of dying. Two days later, Aunt Marty Cañete and Antonette Beldad risked looking for me because we could not communicate after the March 19 massacre.

We agreed that I would go home to Jamahiriya hospital housing so that whatever happened, we would be together. I really understood how other people feared the bullets. I was about to catch a taxi when there was a fight just outside the BMC. Our guards warned me not to go out and to go back inside, but instead I ran to the taxi waiting for me. I crossed the street hearing the gunfire. I saw four corpses in a car that I passed. So, while in the taxi to Jamahiriya, I just prayed that God would spare me and the driver so we would arrive safely at my destination. I told myself, "No one can help to preserve my life at this moment except God." I was shaking, but I tried to be brave. The war continued. I thought it would end after Qaddafi's death, but it did not. Even now (February 2012), I still see protests by various groups, from people expressing their anger, still not getting what they want.

I left the OR and concentrated on the training program that had been postponed, the Healthcare Providers Training and Workshop 2011. I was able to finish training hundreds of participants, mostly medical students. I selected and recommended them to the different departments in the BMC. Some worked in other hospitals inside and outside Benghazi as nurses and nurse aides. I was grateful to them for the kind of dedication they showed in serving their fellow Libyans. June 18 was our "Training Day," the day when we thanked, recognized, and gave each of the participants a certificate. They stayed and worked with us until November 2011.

The effect of war on me was not bad. I became closer to and more trusting of my Creator. I became more mature in other aspects of life. My confidence and my faith became stronger, my friendships grew closer, and I formed new relationships. Through the Libyan war that brought international help and volunteers from around the caring countries of the world, one person, David, said he wanted to share his life with me, for better or for worse. I feel indebted to the people who have provided great help during the crises that we have been through: to Mr. Christian H. Bain, for helping me in the training department and for his friendship; to all FilComBeng officers, advisers, and members for their support of the Filipino community; and to so many others, including my family, for their unending support, prayers, and love and for understanding why I did not come home. I love them and I pray that God blesses us all. And may God bless Libya!

THE DAYS OF MY LIFE

Ezedin Bosedra Abdelkafi

Cardiothoracic surgeon, male, 35, Benghazi

Yes, I am a Libyan, and yes, I did not believe that we would have even an opportunity to say no to Qaddafi's regime, let alone witness and participate in a "revolution." I will describe the three weeks of my work as a doctor during the revolution, particularly from February 15 to March 23, 2011. I will record the hardships we went through, but before that let me try to explain to you how I felt about the Qaddafi era before the revolution. I hated the whole regime, but I personally agreed to his becoming the ruler of Libya and to his son ruling after him, on the condition that they turn Libya into a real country and not just a big farm for Qaddafi's family and loyalists. In fact, however, the latter scenario has been our fate.

A lot of Libyans, including myself, were waiting to see what would happen to our people and our country. On February 15, on my way to the hospital I passed a few protesters in front of the main police department. At first, I thought that they were troops belonging to the Qaddafi regime with the purpose of spotting and arresting potential protesters, who might be anyone wanting to participate in the big day, February 17. That is why I stopped for just a few seconds and then drove away. But in the hospital where I work, we all shared the same positive thoughts about those protesters. The next day, I heard that there were demonstrations in different places around Benghazi, and at that moment, I started to watch the news, especially Al Jazeera, hoping to hear any good word about a possible revolution like the ones in Tunisia and Egypt.

On Thursday, February 17, I couldn't help it. I had to go and see for myself the truly courageous people who are willing to get out and simply protest in hopes of changing our country's future. Because my mother told me that my youngest brother had been out with the protesters, I found myself stepping out of the hospital to drive home and then walking all the way to the midtown square where I heard that some action was taking place. After a long walk I started to see some Qaddafi loyalists, who had been called in from different cities. They were wearing yellow hats (later called the yellow-hat gangs) with sticks in their hands, and a few of them even had guns. I also saw some police along the sides of the roads, just watching.

When I passed through this yellow forest of hostility, I held my head down. I was shaking, but I did not dare to go back for two reasons: first, I didn't want to look suspicious and thus be arrested; second, I wanted to see what these gangs were doing. I reached the square and found a group of young boys standing in front of the gangs. I tried to ask a few of them to find out what was happening, but no one dared answer because everyone was so suspicious of the others. I was left alone with nobody to talk to me, and I stayed like this for about half an hour. Meanwhile, I tried to call my brother, Alaa, with no luck. I remembered that I had to be on duty in a private clinic, so I returned home and then immediately went to work. On my way, I passed another group of young people gathering together, so I knew that whatever we might call it, that thing had just started.

When I arrived at the clinic, I found a lot of work to attend to, but I also had an argument with one of the employees about his fear of what was going to happen and how those young guys don't know what they are doing . . . and so on. Then I went upstairs for about an hour until I received a call from reception saying that there was an urgent case in the ER. I went down and found a very young boy lying on the clinic bed. He was calm but looked pale and in pain. He was accompanied by his parents; his mom was crying, telling us that he was in pain and that his leg was injured. I examined him quickly and found nothing wrong with his legs. I started to reassure his parents that he was fine. But while I was doing a second careful examination, I discovered that he had a hole in his T-shirt. I looked under it and I saw the same hole in his abdomen (an entry point with no exit). At that point, everything went crazy—the family started to scream and cry, the employees gathered, and everyone started to cry, including myself. I tried to do the basics of resuscitating and stabilizing him in order to transfer him to the main trauma hospital. But then his mom started begging us not to send him there because she had heard rumors that police forces were surrounding the hospital to arrest injured people. At that moment I did not know what to do—on one hand, the boy needed urgent medical intervention; on the other hand, I knew that he would be taken by the regime forces if they discovered his injury. Eventually, I told them that he needed medical help that was not available in the clinic and that I would try to contact the main hospital, Benghazi Medical Center (BMC), where I work, and try to arrange the transfer. I called one of my colleagues, and he told me that we could transfer the boy there. Eventually, they operated on him and found multiple injuries to the inner organs. He gradually recovered, and we did not receive more cases that day.

The next morning I went directly to the BMC and joined the others in the main ER, where they told me that they had begun to receive cases yesterday. We received some sporadically, and then they increased for the next five or six days with different types of injuries. Most of them were gunshots, and most of the injured were young boys, though as we treated more patients, both the injured and the injuries varied.

Things went on this way in the hospital until the fall of the Katiba, the headquarters of Qaddafi's forces and his residence in Benghazi. News of our freedom from the Qaddafi regime spread over the eastern part of the country, and other cities in the west followed, but then the number of cities stopped rising. I was very naive to think that soon we would hear in the news that Qaddafi had left the country. It was not too long before I realized that a long journey was ahead of us.

When the Qaddafi forces attacked the civilians in Brega, one of the young doctors in Aljala hospital called me to tell me that they were gathering a team to go in an ambulance to Brega to deal with the causalities. I joined them and even asked them to let me drive the ambulance (being the eldest). We were five surgeons and three anesthetists leaving Benghazi to go to Brega, planning to stay in Brega's hospital to treat the injured people. But we realized that the hospital had only one local nurse because the others had fled the city. In the morning we were told that the Pro-Democracy Fighters (PDF) were making their way to Brega Jadida (or New Brega). We followed them and transferred our base to a new clinic there. We stayed for a few days, and on the third day the war was raging between the PDF and Qaddafi's forces. Among all the hit-and-runs on both sides, two of our ambulance teams found themselves in the disputed city of Ras Lanof, escorted by only three PDF cars. Soon the city was taken by the PDF and not a single Qaddafi soldier was left, except for twenty found executed, probably for refusing to shoot their own countrymen.

The PDF continued their advance, and at that time our medical team had two options: to transfer our base to Ras Lanof, which was the city nearest to the front line, or to stay away from the front line, as we were advised by a few PDF military people (since there was not enough protection in Ras Lanof). We eventually moved to the freed Ras Lanof hospital, and there we saw the nastiest face of the war. For many days we received all kinds of casualties, including gunshots with very large bullets, burns, all kinds of amputations, and martyrs.

In Ras Lanof, the air force fought very fiercely (not like before), and they were regularly bombarding the area, starting at about 8:00 a.m. This hour of the morning became our alarm to get out of bed and run to start our schedule, which included checking on the ambulances. We received more injuries caused by multiple rocket launchers than by air attacks. I remember one time I was supposed to be on an ambulance heading toward the front line when I came across a bunch of PDF members running our way and shouting that there were many injured people ahead of us. When we carefully drove forward, we passed a man beside the paved road. As we stopped, we heard him saying hysterically "I got him! He's injured. I want him to be a prisoner!" But there was only a four-by-four Land Cruiser and no one else with him.

We reached those who had been injured, but after about three-quarters of a mile, we found ourselves in an open area with Qaddafi forces in front of us. Even though we were scared, the ambulance driver acted very quickly and turned the car around before they even started to fire on us, or at least that was what we thought would happen. On our way back, we stopped again for the man who had been shouting and tried to take him with us before they arrived and got him, but he told us that the Land Cruiser turned out to be the property of the Qaddafi forces and that the soldier he was talking about was a soldier he had captured after a fight with four other soldiers, three killed and one wounded. I got out of the ambulance and approached the Land Cruiser to find a soldier lying behind it, injured and bleeding but still alive. I turned around, to call for assistance from the paramedic in the ambulance, when suddenly missiles started pouring from the sky, and the paramedic was injured. The injured soldier died, and the ambulance lost its rear window. All we could do was run away.

The misery continued, and we also continued our work. One day the hospital was hit by air attacks three times, so we decided to evacuate Ras Lanof and go back to Brega Jadida. We stayed there for another two days until we had to retreat again because of the advancing Qaddafi forces. We went back to the city of Ajdabyia, the main city in the area where cases were transferred, and there we met with other medics.

In Ajdabyia, for another two days, the PDF were able to defend the city until the ammunition ran out. On the last day, March 15, three ambulances, including mine, were stationed at the western gate. We stayed until afternoon when it was obvious that the city had fallen, something we never imagined would happen so soon. We made our way back to the main city hospital to join the others and see if we were needed, but we were stunned: there were no medical personnel in the hospital. Everyone had left. Qaddafi forces were attacking the city from the south with all sorts of weapons, so we were facing a situation in which there were few patients in the hospital, but at the same time the Qaddafi forces were surrounding the city preparing to invade it. It was very stressful. Nevertheless, we decided to stay, trying to treat as many people as we could. Right then began the most frightening hours of my life. What actually happened was that Qaddafi's forces did not invade but heavily attacked the city with all kinds of missiles, from the land, sea, and sky. The missiles hit the hospital; the sounds of bombs and missiles were so terrifying that a lot of us were calling home and crying in the ER. I called my friend's mother in Benghazi telling her that I need to get through to Seraj, my friend in the United States, so he could arrange for a call with CNN, as he had previously, to press further for a no-fly zone. I was doing this as if this would save us immediately!

While we were in the hospital, some Qaddafi loyalists came to us trying to take the names of the medics in order to arrest them after the invasion, which is what they had done in al-Zawia. That is why we treated and operated on as many people as we could and immediately got them out of the hospital so they would not be captured as well. We, too, tried to get out as quickly as we could. One of the medical students took us to his house, but unfortunately, later, in October, he was executed with his hands tied, near Sirte.

For the next few days after the Qaddafi forces entered the city, we hid in the medical student's house until we received a call from the hospital saying that we needed to come in. But then the mobile and landline phones were cut off, along with the electricity. It definitely felt like the Middle Ages. We were cooking on wood fires, moving only during the night. We remained like that until the Odessa's Dawn fighters started to attack the Qaddafi fighters in Ajdabyia after they helped Benghazi, forcing the Qaddafi forces to flee and leave the southern area of Ajdabyia. Finally, our beloved Benghazi was freed, and no Qaddafi forces entered the city afterward. Even though they attempted to invade the western side, they were defeated on March 19 and 20, 2011. This moment ended a very long three weeks of "sweet" tiredness mixed with a feeling we never experienced before: being proud to be a Libyan.

BLOOD FOR MY COUNTRY

Aisha A. Nasef

Hematologist, female, 45, Benghazi

On Tuesday, February 15, 2011, my husband and I went to Tripoli to attend a one-day conference on blood banks. We also wanted to apply for a visa to go to France to attend the annual conference of the French Association of Blood Diseases. My brothers strongly opposed our trip because of the possible demonstrations on February 17, which had already been announced by email and on Facebook. They feared that we might get caught up by riots that could lead to all flights being canceled. In fact, I did not take the matter seriously because I thought it was almost impossible to have a demonstration, and even if it were held, I thought, only a few participants would join and face the consequences of arrest and torture. Anyone who demonstrated would expose himself and his family to great torment because I know Qaddafi's savage behavior.

I left my children at home because we planned to stay in the capital for only one day. There, we stayed at the Rixos Hotel, near the zoo, which later became the hideout for the regime's mercenaries. When we went back to our hotel that night, we noticed that people passing the hotel were being inspected with special weapon detectors. Inside the hotel, I was watching television and suddenly saw a blurry scene on Al Jazeera in which people were chanting slogans urging Benghazi to wake up and prepare for the long-awaited day. I was in a state of total disbelief and horror. I thought only of going back to be with my children. They did not go to school the next day because my brother was worried about their safety. We went to the airport and waited for more than seven hours before we could catch our flight.

We returned to Benghazi without knowing how events would develop. On February 17, the revolution began, and in the meantime, my brother had become so sick that he was unable to breathe. His health was getting increasingly worse, so he was taken to the hospital. I was nervous because one of my brothers was very ill and the other was participating in the demonstrations. I did not know which one of them I should worry about more, as they both were in danger.

On Friday, February 18, I went to work, which is a health center where I am the head of the hematology unit. Every employee came to work, and they were willing to do their best to help the patients. Our center turned into a beehive with many doctors, staff, and volunteers from the Red Crescent and the Boy Scouts. We provided blood for the wounded and worked with great energy and happiness as if we had been waiting for this moment and could not believe it had finally come.

The corridor in front of the center was filled with hundreds of men and women of all ages. Both the sick and the healthy wanted to donate blood and insisted that we let them do so even if they were not medically fit. Some of them wept bitterly and protested at not being allowed to donate blood. Businessmen donated large quantities of sweets and drinks for the blood donors. Some of them also brought blankets and sheets and bought drugs from private pharmacies and gave them to the center, and others donated bags containing money without even wanting a receipt. I cannot fully describe this picture because it was incredible. Everyone was working hard and many people were helping us; they were loving and friendly. At the end of the day, we sent the leftover food to participants in the sit-in that took place in front of a nearby courthouse.

As soon as the young people who were shot arrived at the center, the medical staff cheered for them. But we had other revolutionary tasks, such as writing slogans in my office and participating in the first women's march against the regime, on February 22. We also prepared relief convoys to Ajdabiya and Beidhan and participated in the physicians' demonstrations. My colleague Sahar and I wrote a scholarly paper on the number and types of injuries received by our center, which we sent to the Reporting Commission, which sent it to the International Court of Justice. We also participated in the civil society institutions that support democracy, justice, freedom, and equality. It is an indescribable feeling to be free from fear, to be able to express yourself openly against Qaddafi and his regime, in daylight, and in front of everyone! My husband bought our children the materials needed to make many paper flags. They joyfully used them as they participated in the demonstrations and gave some of them away to the demonstrators.

Everyone was in a state of panic on March 18 because Qaddafi threatened to send his military to crush the uprising in Benghazi. Many people left their houses and went east. Men went to the front to fight, and children and women were in crowded convoys seeking safe areas. As soon as the people of Benghazi arrived at the outskirts of the city of Marj (about sixty-two miles from Benghazi), they immediately witnessed a spectacular scene of generosity. They were warmly received by the residents, who gave them food, drinks, and money. Some of their hosts even evacuated their homes and stayed with relatives in order to give their houses to the displaced people! Eventually the military advancement to Benghazi was stopped by our youth and the French forces that attacked it.

I will never forget the devotion shown by my coworkers who did not stop working, even in stressful times. One of them is a lady named Zahra. Her father made her wear her a white robe and badge, that is, her medical attire, and brought her to the center saying to her that if she died, he would always be proud of her. Another lady is named Lubna. Her father used to bring her to work at seven in the morning, telling the people who warned him of how dangerous her work environment was, "Who will take care of the wounded in the center, then?"

Most of the foreign nurses left Benghazi for security reasons, and the city's hospital suffered from the sudden collapse of medical services. Benghazi Medical Center was hit hard by this problem because the majority of their nursing staff were foreigners. Nevertheless, a group of brave nurses from the Philippines stayed with us and supported the Libyans in the darkest circumstances. To remedy the shortage of nurses, my colleague Tahani suggested that we start a program to train Libyans to be nurses. I hesitated at first because I work in diagnostics and had forgotten most of what I learned about nursing. But as I thought about this plan, I realized that it was good and that we needed to start training quickly with what we had.

I started to set up the program and contacted the doctors who were willing to participate in the training according to their specialties. I contacted Dr. Mosa, who was in charge of training in our center, and he was delighted with this plan. He also introduced me to a wonderful Filipina nurse, Annabelle. An American nurse named Christian also joined our training program, adding a pleasant spirit to it.

We began by registering the volunteers, such as the medical students in their final year of medical training. I could not believe the incredible enthusiasm shown by everyone involved in the program. One mother of a female medical student came to the center crying because her daughter had not been added to the program. These interns have helped a lot to maintain services at the center. The young men stayed in the center all the time, going home only to check on their families. Some of them worked and, at the same time, guarded the institutions and the residential areas. The doctors who were residents in the center would go to check the refugee camps in Benghazi and the western region, carrying out medical examinations of the patients in these areas. Some of them also went to the fighting fronts in Braiqa to offer help even during the war.

We also had some relaxing activities, such as singing, reading poetry, and playing music. We enjoyed and admired the satirical comic strips on the walls of Benghazi drawn by Qais Hilali, who expressed our feelings against the regime and as killed for his work. We have discovered the wonderful love we have for our great country. We loved it but not its flag or its national anthem because we associated these with Qaddafi, who made Libya belong to him, not vice versa. We all volunteered to cook for the rebels, to transport supplies, to aid the wounded, and even to clean the streets. When the rebels entered the city, everyone clapped and sang songs of the revolution. Women threw flowers, chocolates, and dates. They kissed the hands of the rebels and thanked them for defending and protecting them. I also saw men kiss the heads of the rebels, and some celebrated their efforts by dancing. My family was moved by these great scenes, and we could not help but cry.

I thank God that I lived to see this moment of freedom and happiness. Perhaps the best writers of any testimonies were the fighters on the fronts or the surgeons in the hospitals and on the battlefield. But all the Libyan people are entitled to write their testimony because they were part of a great symphony played by all of them both inside and outside the country.

4. Yemen

Both Muammar al-Qaddafi and Ali Abdullah Saleh had been military men before they took on civilian roles as "supreme guide" and president, and both turned the army against their rebellious people. Yemen is the poorest state in the Arab world and lacks infrastructural development in almost all the sectors of its economy. This, along with high rates of unemployment and corruption, made the country ready to end Saleh's regime. Saleh had ruled North Yemen from 1978 to 1990 and then, after unification, Yemen since 1990. Even before the Arab Spring, Saleh had been struggling with opposition movements that challenged his rule. Although some of the Yemeni political parties are socialist, the strongest one is Islamist, the Yemeni Congregation for Reform, or Islah, under the leadership of Sadeq al-Ahmar. In 2003, when there was a resurgent call for political and economic reforms, the Joint Meeting Parties (JMP) was established as a conglomerate of five political parties with tribal, Islamist, and socialist-oriented affiliations. By coordinating these parties to oppose Saleh's one-party system and to represent more opposition in the parliament, the JMP gained popular support among many Yemenis. Before the uprisings in Yemen in February 2011, the JMP and Islah were involved in organizing demonstrations known as the Pink revolution, for the color of ribbons and other symbols they wore to identify their peaceful protest movement. Not satisfied with Saleh's promises for reform, students and activists joined a popular movement to oust the president, to achieve the same result as in Tunisia and Egypt. On January 22, 2011, one of the first major demonstrations took place in Sanaa, where the Yemeni authorities arrested the prodemocracy activist and journalist Tawakkol Karman, a member of the Islah Party and later a cowinner of the Nobel Peace Prize in 2011. The University of Sanaa became the hub of the revolution, where students and activists organized demonstrations and sit-ins and also protested Karman's detention, and she was released within two days.

As the demonstrations continued, Yemenis became more aggressive in demanding Saleh's resignation. On February 2, he announced that he would not seek reelection in 2013 and would not hand over the presidency to his son Ahmed, as had been widely speculated. Saleh's actions reflect a common reaction of dictators toward their people; Mubarak tried the same thing, unsuccessfully. The anti-Saleh action continued, and the opposition organized a Day of Rage after his speech. Relying on his army, political party, and tribal support, Saleh remained unmoved by the uprisings, which escalated on the Fridays of February 11 and 18, with thousands of students and protesters marching in the capital, Sanaa, as well as Taiz and Aden. Tents were set up in front of the University of Sanaa, where the largest sit-in ever was held to host Yemenis from all areas, classes, and political affiliations. On February 23, pro-Saleh thugs killed two students and wounded many others in this highly celebrated location. The month of March brought more anger directed against the Yemeni regime, which responded with even more violence. By Friday, March 18, Saleh's forces had killed more than seventy people, fifty-two of whom were killed by snipers on that one day. Two days later, a mass funeral was held to honor the victims, and Yemen's most powerful tribal confederation asked Saleh to end the violence by giving up power peacefully.

In early April, the embattled Saleh gave signs that he might step down, but it seemed that he was looking for an "exit" deal, which was being arranged by the neighboring Saudi Arabia and the Gulf states. After serious defections in the army, led by his former military strongman General Ali Muhsin, Saleh sought allies to facilitate a dialogue between his regime and the opposition. But instead of doing so, the Gulf states wanted him to step down in exchange for guarantees of his safety and protection from trial. Despite the increased pressure on him, Saleh did not accept these terms, even after an attempt was made on his life on Friday, June 3, when his presidential compound was hit by a missile that exploded in the mosque where he was praying. Several bodyguards and aides were killed, and Saleh was flown to Saudi Arabia to receive medical treatment. He returned to Yemen on September 23 amid large uprisings against his determination to stay in power and to prolong the state of constant deadly confrontations between his loyalists and the rebel tribesmen and defected soldiers. The youth revolution, as Yemenis often call it, continued despite these clashes, and the protesters were often targeted with live ammunition by the regime forces. Meanwhile, Saudi Arabia, which has strong ties with many tribes in Yemen, pressed Saleh to take the initiative and save his almost failing country. Finally, King Abdullah of Saudi Arabia and Saleh met in Riyadh, Saudi Arabia, on November 23, and Saleh signed the initiative agreeing that his duties be transferred to the vice president while also securing immunity from prosecution. The new Yemen government had to deal with the army and political divisions, in addition to fighting al-Qaeda, which had long used the country as a safe haven. The U.S. drone attacks against al-Qaeda members, which led to the killing of civilians as well, became a source of anger among many Yemenis. There were some organized protests against what they considered a violation of their sovereignty and a threat to the safety of Yemeni citizens.

WITNESSING THE YEMENI REVOLUTION

Mahmoud Sagheer al-Fasly

Instructor of Arabic, male, 35, Sanaa

I will start with this date: February 3, 2011, which is considered the beginning of the revolution in Yemen. Answering the call of the Joint Meeting Parties (JMP), the largest demonstrations started in the capital, Sanaa, and various other governorates of Yemen. The JMP began preparing for this demonstration about a week earlier, planning to have it in Sanaa, in Tahrir Square downtown. Two days before that date, however—on Tuesday, February 1—President Ali Abdullah Saleh's ruling party set up twelve big tents in the square in order to block the opposition's plan and to control the area. The government also invited its supporters to demonstrate in the same place and on the same day as the opposition. This forced the opposition to move the demonstration to a new location, the University of Sanaa. The timing, nevertheless, was not in their favor, as they had announced the new site only on Wednesday evening, and the demonstrations were supposed to take place on Thursday morning.

I was among those who knew about the change of venue because I saw a news item on the Suhail channel, which is run by the opposition. But I knew many people who wanted to participate in the opposition demonstration but were not aware of the time change. Therefore, on Thursday morning they went to the wrong place, only to find themselves in the middle of the ruling party's demonstration. When I arrived at the new location on Ring Street, in front of the University of Sanaa, I initially was disappointed because there were only a few demonstrators. Ring Street is suitable only for cars, not as a place for people to gather and demonstrate. Nonetheless, people were arriving in large numbers from various sides and entrances to the street, and within an hour it was packed with a crowd of demonstrators much larger than I expected. I could see that people were concentrated in the areas between the University of Science and Technology Building on the north and the al-Jubi Furniture store on the south, but I was told that there were more people whom I could not see, because the street curved.

At this time, the Egyptian revolution had reached its zenith, and many people thought the Yemeni demonstration would be the start of an open sit-in similar to the one in Egypt, even though the opposition was calling only for a demonstration. By two o'clock in the afternoon, all the demonstrations had ended without leading to a sit-in, with the exception of slightly more than ten young people who tried to stay after the demonstration was over. They were quickly dispersed by the security forces as evening approached. Then the talk of the town among the Yemeni people was that they could not organize permanent sit-ins in public parks and squares because of most Yemenis' habit of chewing *khat*. It was believed that they would not be able to give up their sessions of *khat*-chewing, which usually start in the afternoon. Apparently, even the government and the ruling party believed the rumor, and they removed the tents they had erected in Tahrir Square. But after events accelerated in Egypt and Hosni Mubarak gave up power, the ruling party put up the tents again in the square, in an attempt to prevent the opposition or the youth from staging a sit-in. But the morning after Mubarak's fall, people came out and began spontaneously demonstrating at the University of Sanaa. The security forces and supporters of the ruling party responded violently, and this scenario was repeated daily. Then, on Saturday, February 19, one of the demonstrators in Sanaa was martyred at the gate to the university. Some people also were wounded, among whom was Dr. Abdullah al-Shami, a professor of nuclear physics in the university's College of Education. His account is as follows:

> I had a camera, so I started filming what was happening: protesters backing off while security forces and ruling-party supporters advanced until

they approached me. When they saw me using my camera, some of them turned to me and I knew they wanted to attack me. I hid the camera in my pocket and kept my cell phone in my hand. They took my phone and left the camera because they thought I was using my phone only. But they started to beat and kick me, all while swearing. I screamed and told them that I was a professor at the university, but they did not stop until I grabbed one of them and said to him, "For the sake of your honor, please help me and save me from them!" He sympathized with me and told them that I was a professor until they finally stopped beating me. Some of the young men carried me to the university campus.

This is what Dr. Shami told us. He even showed us some of what he had been able to film as well as a clip another person took while the men carried him after the assault.

The next day, Sunday, February 20, the youth set up the first tents in the square in front of the gate to the university and began a sit-in. The faculty at the Yemeni universities were among the first participants in the sit-in. A tent, called the "academics' tent," was set up for them right by the gate. I started my sit-in in this tent on the very first day, taking part in the faculty members' various activities, even though I was not exactly an academic but because I held a master's degree and had a teaching contract at the Center of Arabic and Oriental Studies at the University of Science and Technology. With each new day, the sit-in grew bigger, causing friction and almost daily confrontations with the security agents, who increasingly surrounded people from all sides. Whenever a group of people tried to enter the area or set up new tents, they would be detained by the agents. The youths would gather at a place where something like this happened and try to help one another while the number of security forces increased and usually confronted them using water, tear gas, batons, and, often, live ammunition. Each confrontation ended with injured protesters, and some were killed.

The main difficulty we faced was the spread of rumors about the progovernment forces' preparations to break into the sit-in area. For the young people, these rumors were a source of worry and psychological exhaustion, but they became even more determined. One night, for example, breaking news on al-Suhail television showed militants in civilian clothes moving toward the area to attack the occupants. Such news also spread via text messages and led to a state of alert inside the area: Everyone who had been sleeping was awakened, and the protesters got ready to counter the supposed attack by using clothing and covers as gas masks, as well as other materials, such as Pepsi, vinegar, and onions to counteract the tear gas. News spread that progovernment gunmen intended to storm the place from all directions at once, but nothing happened that night. Nevertheless, the next night the same rumor and reaction were repeated, but nothing happened. On the third night there were rumors about government forces using the streams that ran under the green space to spray tear gas on the sit-in participants, but again, nothing happened. The recurrence of such news made me believe that the purpose of these rumors was to psychologically exhaust the protesters. That is why on the fourth night I joked that we would be attacked by paratroopers landing from the sky! The fourth night was much calmer than the preceding night.

Nobody in the sit-in could sleep during any of those nights, and those who had a job could not participate because they had to sleep in the morning to compensate for the sleepless nights, which is what I did. But despite all these difficulties, the momentum of the sit-in was growing, so the government made another plan to reduce the number of participants. They put up concrete blockades to close the roads leading to us and then blocked the main street where we gathered by building a huge wall to divide the street into two areas: protesters on the north side and security forces and militants on the south. This step led to the massacre on the Friday of Dignity.

On that day, February 18, I completed the Friday prayer in the academics' tent, located near al-Menassa where Justice Street begins. After the prayer, I wanted to return home, but before I got out of the area, I saw thick smoke rising from the southern side of the sit-in area. I stood on the north side, where I heard the preacher of Friday prayer announcing through a loudspeaker, trying to reassure people: "Don't worry; they're trying to scare you by burning tires. Don't get upset. Stay calm." Then we saw a helicopter flying low over the sit-in area, and we started to hear shooting. Then came the massacre: fifty-four martyrs fell and dozens were wounded.

My colleague Abdulla al-Faqih saw the massacre and filmed some of it with his cell phone. He told me that after the prayer, some of the worshippers tried to cross the wall as they were heading home, but the government forces prevented them by setting a fire that blocked them. Then, people gathered and tried to cross the wall and put out the fire. At this point they became targets for the massacre. This was not the only time in which a large number of demonstrators were killed in one day; rather, it was the beginning of more bloody events. At the beginning of April, the youths escalated their protests against the regime by staging a peaceful march: a million people demonstrated by roaming the streets of the capital. Some of the marches succeeded in returning to the sit-in without being attacked. For example, I was in the march on Zubairy Street. We began at four o'clock in the afternoon and crossed Ziraa Street. We came out near the Republican hospital on Zubairy

Street expecting confrontation, so the youths were carrying Pepsi, onions, masks, and headgear, but this demonstration was peaceful. While I was standing on Kentucky Bridge next to the hospital, I saw the wide street full of people. Indeed, there were as many as one million people, perhaps a surprise to the many security forces and government supporters who had lined up on both sides of the street. We waved our hands to greet them as we returned safely from the end of Zubairy Street toward Sixtieth and Rabat Streets and then to the square.

I want to conclude by stating that demonstrations reaching one million people were not always peaceful. During some of them, we were attacked— shootings that left dozens dead and wounded. For example, on Wednesday, April 27, another march was launched at 4:00 p.m. and moved from the square through Sixtieth Street toward the Amran junction and the widest and longest streets in the capital, TV Street, which allowed a full view for everyone to see the real size of this extremely big demonstration. As the demonstrators approached TV Street near Sports City, where some of the ruling-party supporters were stationed, the latter tried to prevent the demonstration from continuing. There was a clash but no shooting or killing, and that is why a large part of the demonstration was able to proceed. During the second half of the demonstration, though, the protesters were heavily attacked by the security forces and gunmen in civilian clothes. The result was fifteen martyrs and dozens of wounded demonstrators.

YEMENI OBSERVATIONS

Joshua Zettel

American student in Yemen, male, 36

I went to Yemen to study Arabic in May 2010. Seven months later, I found myself watching a revolution unfold in a country oppressed for the thirty-three years since the president, Ali Abdullah Saleh, had taken power. Since January 2011, I had been going to these protests on Fridays to listen and watch the prayers and to hear people's opinions on the issue of changing the regime. Being a foreigner and experiencing nothing but American democracy my whole life, I was interested in how a dictator rules his country and what could be done to change that system. It was as if my duty was to observe and talk to as many people as I could, so I started observing the revolution in Yemen from the beginning.

Between the prayers that Yemenis perform five times on Friday, they would chant: "The people want to topple the regime" (in Arabic, Ashab yureed isqat anidham). It was really intense to hear hundreds of men chanting that and then to become silent for prayer. The eloquent imam would have a crackle in his voice that showed how this country had suffered under dictatorship. I would see these men praying with tears in their eyes. After the Friday noon prayers, men and women would gather—separately, of course (because of cultural and religious considerations) —and the men would perform traditional dances in the streets to music blasting out of a boom box. People gathered for lunch inside the tents that had been put up in Change Square. I had observed these peaceful protests for weeks and months and seen how beautiful and strong the will can be of people who have been oppressed for so long. They were happily involved making posters, and all of them were energized to achieve their goal of changing the regime.

On Friday, March 18, I went to the protests and listened to the imam's beautiful sermon and saw Yemenis praying with tears rolling from their determined eyes. Suddenly I heard the sound of an American Huey helicopter that was purportedly given to Ali Abdullah Saleh to fight al-Qaeda in Yemen. I saw it hovering over me and the crowd of these peaceful people praying for change. The helicopter's thumping prompted them to start shouting, "The people want to change the regime." Nonviolent men and women were shouting their demand for change at this helicopter. The helicopter made one round over us and then flew off. I stood there in utter amazement and could not believe what had just happened. I almost felt that this was a sign that something worse was going to happen, wondering how long the government was going to let the peaceful protests of these people continue.

Suddenly, I saw smoke and a gray haze rise in the distance, and that is when I started hearing the bullets ricochet. Magnificent protesters were dispersing the crowds. I stood up on a milk cart to get a better look, only to see thick dark smoke in the distance and people still reacting peacefully. Some of them told me not to worry about the distant gunfire, but I could not help it. Within a matter of moments, I heard ambulances rushing off to the scene, which then brought injured people back to the university's mosque, which had been turned into a hospital during the protests. I saw that they had been shot. In my broken Arabic I asked what was happening, and people told me that mercenaries were shooting from rooftops, killing innocent protesters.

I decided to go into the mosque where the ambulances were bringing the injured men. Inside there was a young man who had been shot right through the head. He had a bullet wound the size of a baseball, and he was obviously dead. The doctors had placed him aside and were starting to attend to the others from the ambulances. I looked toward the entrance of the mosque. There I counted seven ambulances gathered in front of the mosque bringing in injured people, and three motorcycles that also had started bringing in bodies and injured people. On the back of one motorcycle was a dead young man whose friend could not keep from falling over. It was horrendous, but these men were determined to bring him into the mosque. I was so shell-shocked that I really didn't know what to do. I backed off and wondered if I could help with the injured but decided that since I didn't know the language very well and the doctors and volunteers were doing an exceptionally good job on all the injured and dead, my best option was to try to comfort people.

I walked around inside this mosque and counted more than twenty-one dead bodies of young men who had been assassinated and had not fought back with weapons but only with chunks of asphalt. There also were fifty injured, all crammed inside. This was a very small mosque and had probably been built in the 1970s. I soon realized that for hours I had been watching and observing the dead and wounded coming in and that it now was evening, so I decided to leave. Before leaving I asked my Spanish friend, who also was in the mosque, if she wanted to go across the street to drink some coffee and get away from the bodies and violence. We crossed the street and left the dead, who had been placed in rows with Qur'ans on their chests in the Islamic tradition.

We went across the street to gather our thoughts and to see what was happening outside the mosque. A café was open and we went in. The shooting and murdering of innocent, peaceful protesters had not scared people away. The shops and cafés still were open, and people welcomed us, even though there still was smoke rising and the sound of gunfire only five blocks away. People in the café told us not to worry and to drink some coffee and stay calm and that they would look after us. I was amazed by the compassion and calmness of the Yemeni people as their friends were being shot and killed. Inside the café, I watched as more dead and injured revolutionaries passed by me in ambulances and hanging off motorcycles bleeding, making their way to the mosque. The Yemenis inside the cafe told us not to worry. The café owners told us they would protect us. We sat in this cafe and talked and tried to understand why a government would be so brutal as to attack and kill people who had been peacefully gathering for months with no violence. This was disturbing. Probably at least fifty people were killed and more than two hundred were injured that day, according to local and foreign newspapers. We talked about how we had gone to the protests and watched peaceful people uniting for a cause. It

was disgusting to see a brutal dictator in action. As I sipped my tea, surrounded by some of the most hospitable people in the world, I realized that
Yemen deserved much better than this. For a moment, I was able to understand why these people were not fighting with guns and not returning the
bullets. It was because the Yemeni people who want change in Yemen are a lot
stronger than the government; they were practicing nonviolence, in the same
way that Gandhi did, in which "an eye for an eye makes the whole world
blind." These are the real people of Yemen, and they are the ones who have
shown how amazing the human heart can be and how cruel it can be, as well.

We sat inside the café until the gun blasts faded and the ambulances
stopped bringing in dead or injured bodies. I sat there until calm had returned, and soon I heard music again. It was like the sun had come out after a
long dark winter. I heard people saying that they would overcome this horrible situation and that they would be strong until this dictator left. I couldn't
believe how many people had died that day, and now people were in the
streets because they had never left and they were still pressing onward. Some
people in the café kept asking us if we were OK, and they insisted on escorting
us home so we wouldn't get caught up in the violence. So we left the café with
some Yemeni escorts, who were more worried about us than their own lives.
With our many escorts, we walked by the tents that had been set up in Change
Square. We walked for blocks, seeing people sitting peacefully and drifting off
to sleep. None of these people had taken down their tents or fled; they even
shouted "Welcome to Yemen!" as we walked past their tents late in the night.
These strong-willed people kept going forward with the revolution as if nothing had happened. Our escorts soon took us to their cars, and one of them insisted on driving us home, back to our houses beyond the protest in the old
city. And he did, without accepting anything in return for the ride. When he
dropped us off, he told us not to worry about what had happened that day and
that the people of Yemen would be strong and would figure out what was best
for the country. We walked the few blocks to my house, and we reflected on
the day and then went our separate ways. I went home with a very heavy heart
and couldn't sleep that night. The next few days I stayed clear of the protest. I
was busy with school and other things, but I returned the next Friday for
prayer and watched more people gather than had the week before. I watched
and listened as people prayed for the ones who had died. I saw tears in their eyes
and listened as the prayer came to an end. Then some people started dancing
again and chanting, "The people want to change the regime." It was a peaceful
gathering once more. There was no more violence against them that week, and
they pressed on with strength and diligence. People were getting more determined to oust the dictator peacefully.

I stayed in Yemen for two more months after that and watched the protest grow even larger. I would still be in Yemen if I had not been forced out psychologically. I was exposed to unnecessary violence and saw tanks and army vehicles roam the streets; both my family members and the U.S. government wanted me out of Yemen. I had the option of leaving, unlike most Yemenis. In April, I left Yemen, very saddened by what I had seen. I almost felt as if I had abandoned my brothers, but then I thought about March 18 and how they had been more worried about me than their own safety. I thought that maybe this was best because I don't want any Yemenis to lose their life for me. I would prefer that if, sadly, they lost their life, it would be for the betterment of their country.

THE YEMENI DREAM

Reemy Mojahed

Unemployed university graduate, female, Sanaa

I was in my town, which is close to the capital, Sanaa, and I can remember listening to the radio while preparing breakfast when I heard about Mohamed Bouazizi's self-immolation. This news thrust me into a new life and perspective. Like Bouazizi, I also was a college graduate without a job. Belonging to the middle class and studying sociology made me relate to him even more. At that point I felt a mixture of nerve-wracking humiliation and pain. For a moment, I imagined that we were just millions of humiliated people spread on a map of the Arab world. This was the last day that I would feel humiliated and the beginning of long days of pain and wonderful hope. I describe the events here with pain because that is what we know, but the pain now is followed by hope: we have high hopes for the future.

At the time of the events in Tunisia, we in Yemen bid farewell to winter. I left my village in late December to go to Sanaa in search of a job using my new degree from the University of Sanaa. I felt fortunate because in Sanaa I could see the complete picture of the events; in my village we did not have a television! Each time I saw footage of crowds of Tunisians sweeping down the streets while carrying signs and chanting—but also being killed—my whole body shivered, and I cried. They were tears of joy; I felt no humiliation, only hope. This time, I felt proud! The first nights of January were cold, but when we saw the demonstrations in Tunisia, our big dreams kept us warm. I wondered, "How many people have had these dreams before Bouazizi, and how many will have them after him? Have we ever thought or valued words and phrases in our Arabic dictionary like 'people,' 'freedom,' 'overthrow,' 'want,' and 'Allah is great?'" The Tunisian revolution made us find the essence of our lives. Millions of young Arab people like me probably screamed with joy when Leila Sheikhly from Al Jazeera announced that (Tunisia's president, Zine el-Abidine) Ben Ali had fled. We found the meaning of our lives on that day when the earth held millions of dignified, victorious, dreamers and turned them around the sun, showed them to the galaxy and the universe, and expressed pride for those who had a dream. On the following day, which was our Arab Spring day, I went with my friend to the Tunisian embassy. We were surprised to see the army there when we arrived. It was an unforgettable day because it marked our first encounter.

The military has always been the symbol of the government and the regime here in our country—everyone who wears a military uniform is automatically perceived as oppressive and brutal. But my friend and I did not look at them as such; we always saw them as people whose real identity had been stolen. I remember how we went past them and saw familiar faces among the demonstrators. There also were cameramen from several television stations. We were not doing anything, just looking proudly at the Tunisian flag, but I soon began to notice some tension among the security agents around us. I do not recall exactly what happened, but suddenly we heard someone screaming. After we ran to the source of the voice, we realized that some security agents may have assaulted a female journalist and confiscated her camera. But then I also found out that when they arrested Aydarus al-Naqib—a member of the House of Representatives, president of the new Transitional Council, and member of the Yemeni Socialist Party's political bureau—his wife panicked and started screaming and asking the demonstrators for help to get her husband released. Tawakkol Karman, who later became the cowinner of the 2011 Nobel Peace Prize, was with us. After some screaming and fighting, she stood in front of the security vehicle and started to chant the lines of the Tunisian poet Abul-Qasim al-Shabbi (1909–1934): "If the people want, one day, to live [in freedom], then fate will answer their call." Ironically, these lines are known to all Arabs everywhere because, unfortunately for the Arab regimes, the poet's works had already been made part of the educational curriculum.

Both Karman and the security agents began screaming while my friend and I watched silently. They got al-Naqib out, and he went away with his arm around his wife. Karman fought fiercely to reclaim the journalist's camera. Security finally gave in, after a tug-of-war, negotiations, and the intervention of high-ranking military officers—all while hurling insults at us, Karman, and Balkis al-Lahabi, a young political activist. They released the camera without the film that had been in it, and we got closer to one another to protect ourselves!

Another dramatic scene involved a Somali family. The husband was in an area where the security agents were stationed, and his wife and two children were in our area. Either out of bad judgment or stupidity, and with all due respect, the wife was trying to break into the fighting crowd to give her husband a cell phone. The husband and wife ignored the fact that the security agents were involved in a fight over a camera! So when she reached him, one of the soldiers hit the husband's back with his hand and pushed him away while another soldier pushed the wife. I still remember the husband's face, which was filled with confusion. I wished I could say, "Wake up Somalia! We can do what Tunisians have done!" I sadly expected the answer to this call to be, "No, not yet." Nevertheless, when we saw the Egyptians in Tahrir Square, no was no longer adequate as a response. We Arabs are historically, emotionally, and nationally linked to Egypt, and Tahrir Square gave us power. More and more each day, the square became Mecca for us, dreamers with faith in change. Every image of the place gave us a story, a chilling feeling, a tear of pride, and a smile of hope.

On February 3, a group of young dreamers, whom nobody but a few people had ever believed in before, showed perseverance in resisting the regime by arranging a sit-in at the University of Sanaa. We did not join them in the beginning, but we followed what they were doing. Yes, only a few people believed in them, but we all became believers as we saw the fall of Mubarak! "No" was now totally unacceptable as we saw Egyptians go out into the street to celebrate the fall of a symbol of power and oppression; as the security machinery for Mubarak was defeated by the roar of the angry masses; as we saw the pictures of martyrs and the roses that decorated Egypt's gardens and houses; as old and new songs and Facebook postings celebrated such an event. On the night when Mubarak's resignation was announced by the vice president, Omar Suleiman, Yemeni youth went out into the streets. Nevertheless, those in the vicinity of the old university and also in Aden and Taiz were beaten. I went with one of my friends to the university to complete the paperwork for my diploma. As I passed the square in the afternoon, I felt the breeze of freedom, and I later realized that the martyrs had made that breeze. There was a voice on the loudspeaker telling (the president): "Leave, leave." Someone near me was mocking what hundreds of people were saying, but I just smiled.

Then I started to go to the demonstrations, and the first revolutionary task assigned to me by my friend was to prepare leaflets to distribute near the demonstrations. Then on February 16, Mohammed al-Alwani was killed, becoming the first martyr of the Yemeni revolution. When we joined the revolution on that first Friday, the temperature outside was hot during prayer time; nevertheless, we saw tens of thousands bowing and prostrating under the sun while shouting in one voice, full of faith: "People want the overthrow of the regime!" This was a scene that gave me chills, and I was amazed, as were many, by the way that the people in the square treated one another. Even though many came from a tribal background, they were treating everybody with the highest degree of civility. The tribes amazed us with their understanding and acceptance of one another, especially us, women who had joined a coalition of young people and made new friendships.

On April 27, a rainy evening, there was a massive march to the radio building. We were visiting tents in the square to spread awareness of our cause. I remember whispering to those around me: "God save Nasser!" I was referring to a tall and thin young man (twenty-three years old) who used to carry a torn backpack and distribute revolutionary publications and make radical statements for hours. He was run over by a vehicle belonging to the security forces. His face, which had been tanned by the sun, was distorted after the accident. When I was told this bad news, I went with some other revolutionaries to the University of Science and Technology Hospital, and someone told me that Nasser had died. At the sight of bodies in morgues, tears fell like waterfalls from my eyes, and I silently pondered, "How much benefit can a person get from killing another human being?" I thought about the meaning of this young man's death, imagining the dreams and wishes he had left unfulfilled. I could not help but wonder, "What was the last thing he thought about before he left forever? What would be the reaction of Nasser's mother; what would she say?"

I later passed one of the tents and saw the child Omar al-Maqtari, who was martyred in the demonstration in front of the prime minister's office on Wednesday, May 11. I saw his face on a sign bearing his name, and I could not move or hold back my tears. I later wrote a lot about him, preserving his memory. His childish smile will not grow old. For me, he was like a wound I could not heal. Yes indeed, our revolution is not over yet—despite the destruction and pain, we will not go back to life before February. I have a dream that what we are living with, the regime, will come to an end. Just like a million other people, we have a dream that a civil state will be established, justice will prevail, and equality and democracy will shape our country. It is not only a dream; it is a promise to the martyrs in their eternal sleep, to the wounded, the disabled, and the mothers of the dead. Certainly we will honor all of these people, and we will continue the revolution!

THE EMERGING NEW YEMEN

Ameen Jaber Sailaan

MA student, male, 31, Hajja

I grew up in the governorate of Hajja, which is located northwest of Sanaa. The city has been marginalized and neglected by the regime, even though the ruling party claimed victory at all its voting centers in the last parliamentary elections in 2003. The downtown is relatively small—almost everyone knows who does what. Thus, every person is known to be affiliated with a particular political party, whether or not one wants to be. One's appearance, how one behaves, and even the family's title have political significance in such an insulated society. In my early years, I used to watch news of unrest and wars in many countries, and I realized that they all were motivated by chaos, inequality, and exclusion. I realized that these problems were caused by the political regimes, which wear the mask of freedom and justice but do not observe them, and I wondered, "When will it be my country's turn?"

Political awareness or, more precisely, being politically active starts at an early age in my country. You can hardly find a Yemeni child unable to differentiate among the political parties or showing disinterest in joining one of them, or at least being emotionally in favor of a particular party. Nevertheless, this awareness creates a spiral of hatred among children as they adopt political affiliations, even though their country does not support democracy. Instead of cultivating our younger generations in an atmosphere of dialogue among political opponents, which can be taught to children through education and a culture of tolerating differences—as long as there is a commitment to national principles—the tense political situation has become a fertile environment for settling personal clashes and exacting retribution. These latter behaviors do not allow the law to be effectively recognized, because President Ali Saleh's regime plunged the country into the democratic experience without being able to deal with it properly. That is why he said, on more than one occasion, that democracy is totally bad and not having democracy is even worse, which shows, among other things, his rhetorical abilities. Moreover, when he returned to Yemen from Saudi Arabia, where he received medical treatment after a mysterious assassination attempt, he was quoted as saying, "Democracy was a trap." These statements indicate that the Yemeni people spent more than twenty years under the theoretical illusion of having political pluralism and the freedom to form and operate parties.

The exact description of the situation in Yemen is a time bomb, which also defined the country before the outbreak of the revolution. Yemen was like a fire still smoldering under the ashes. The political crisis worsened from one day to the next: economic strangulation created another tragedy experienced by citizens daily, along with shameless foreign interventions in Yemen by the major international powers. All these factors did not leave any room for silence.

In the best-case scenario, the regime's approach to addressing these problems was like putting a Band-Aid on a double bone fracture. It has also been proved that on more than one occasion, the regime was playing a crooked game by fabricating political and security crises in order to achieve two goals: to extort funds by seeking favors from the international community and securing regional support and to create a situation in which opposing factions would fight with one another, thereby allowing the regime to get rid of any power centers that posed an immediate or long-term threat. Here are some examples: first, the six wars that took place in the governorate of Sa'ada in northern Yemen between government forces and fighters of the "Shiite Believing Youth" (known as the Huthis). The regime dragged the First Armored Division into this war in order to weaken the Huthis, thus this major military force in northwestern Yemen played a central role in suppressing the attempted secession in 1994.

The regime wanted to weaken the opposition militarily and morally, using the Republican Guard and the special forces, which are led by President Saleh's son Colonel Ahmed Saleh and are given increasing support. Second, by emphasizing such discriminatory terms as "Northerners" and "Southerners" and increasing the hatred between them, both parties could accuse and exhaust each other. In a deliberate deception, the regime blamed the Islamists, who had been its allies in the 1994 war, and promoted a culture of hatred against them as well, by falsely attributing to them and prominent Muslim scholars decrees declaring that people in the south are not Muslims. But the Islamists and scholars made no such accusations. Third, the regime assassinated influential figures who might form power centers and prevent Colonel Ahmed Saleh from gaining more power. The list of these assassinated figures includes the tribal leader Mujahid Abu Shawarib, whose death was reported as caused by a car malfunction. The regime also attempted to assassinate Sheikh Abdullah al-Ahmar, chief of the powerful Hashid tribe and chairman of the parliament, during an official visit to Senegal. In short, the situation was dire politically and economically, and reform efforts could not flourish under such a regime.

Therefore, there were valid reasons why young Yemeni people, including myself, were motivated to revolt against the regime and join the tsunami that is the Arab Spring. Here are some of these reasons:

1. Violation of the country's sovereignty by the big international powers that have made Yemen the location of their national security operations, sometimes with an excuse and sometimes without one. The president agreed to these violations in order to maintain his family's gains, covering it up in the media by convincing people that his regime was fighting against terrorists in the country. To me, this deception is on the level of treason.

2. The deteriorating political situation, false democracy, and fraudulent elections, which have led to forcing on the Yemeni people those representatives who support the regime instead of work for the people. This situation made meaningless such concepts as freedom, justice, and equality.

3. A policy of exclusion in which almost all qualified people are not allowed to participate in running the country. The regime thinks that these people pose a threat to its existence.

4. The difficult economic situation, which led to the destruction of infrastructure, the proliferation of both huge bribes and commissions, the immigration of educated elites, and the dispersal of more than four million expatriates, some of whom settled illegally in neighboring countries.

I saw with my own eyes the violations of the alleged democracy that the regime claimed to endorse. I saw how the regime forced followers of the ruling party to vote in the presence of someone representing the party and oversaw the ballot box in order to ensure that the vote would go exclusively to President Ali Saleh. As a representative of the opposition candidate in the last parliamentary elections, I used my constitutional right to boycott the elections and abstained from voting because I felt that elections and democracy were staged, metaphorically, like a show. Nevertheless, I found out later that my name had already been used! One of my relatives, who did not boycott the elections, was surprised, too, when he went to exercise his constitutional right and found that someone else had voted using his name as well! The regime also used to bring military and security personnel wearing civilian clothes to the voting centers in areas where the opposition had a chance to win. These personnel were threatened with military punishment and denial of their salary if they refused to pose as civilian voters. Educators and students, as well, were forced to go to festivals in support of the ruling party, under the threat of having their salary denied or reduced or—in the case of teachers—being deported to remote areas. If students refused to participate in these festivals, they were either deliberately dropped from school rolls or harassed and treated with contempt in the classroom.

Since the beginning of the Yemeni revolution, which was launched when tents were set up in Change Square at the University of Sanaa, I joined the other Yemeni expatriates in focusing on this new event. We followed the opposition's activities, some of which were carried out by women activists. The protests became more interesting, especially after the success of the Egyptian revolution. I used to log in to Facebook each day to discuss the new developments. I suggested that the women activists leave the square because Yemeni authorities are armed and that would provoke an inevitable confrontation between the revolutionaries and the regime, an opinion with which many of my friends did not agree. My role was in the revolution's social media, even though Internet services had been cut off in all provinces at the beginning of the revolution and were turned on only later after they were tailored to serve the regime's agenda.

As cyberactivists, using a number of simple strategies, we concentrated on telling the world what was happening in Yemen. Through social networking sites such as Facebook and Twitter, we mobilized moral support for the revolution by identifying and explaining the revolutionaries' causes and demands. We also uploaded videos and documentaries condemning the regime and showing its crimes against peaceful protesters. We sent these materials to many television stations covering our revolution. By distributing leaflets, we also tried to encourage the diverse forces of the revolution to coordinate and overlook their different views, or at least to postpone them until the revolution succeeded. We helped guide public opinion by offering proposals and moderating debates among participants in the Facebook pages dedicated to the Yemeni revolution, such as "Forum of Free Yemeni," "Revolution of the Yemeni People," and "Hajja Youth for Change." In addition to other popular Facebook pages, we also reported on the regime's pages, whose purpose was to distort public opinion about what was happening in Yemen and to present a negative image of the revolutionaries. Some of the pages we identified belonged to the regime's media, such as the "Saba Channel Page." We did all this by creating a page entitled "Virtual Yemeni Army," which has largely succeeded in blocking the regime's pages and its thugs' cyberactivities. Our efforts also included circulating articles and studies useful to the revolution, in addition to distributing on other non-Yemeni pages information and publications about the people's cause. This enabled us to cooperate with the Syrian revolutionary activists, and together we united the demands of the two peoples by arranging the "Friday of Victory for our Sham [Syria] and our Yemen."

As of October 2011, our eight-month-old revolution seemed to have achieved a major goal by roiling the stagnant political waters in Yemen. The revolution has drawn world attention to the demands of a formerly repressed people. But I cannot hide my slight disappointment by the slowdown of events and the stumbling revolutionary work. Yemen must deal with specific local and regional circumstances not found in other Arab Spring countries. For example, we have internal conflicts among the opposition parties, which has divided our efforts. The opposition is made up of different parties united only by their hatred of the regime, with different political agendas and great hostilities toward one another based on opposing ideologies. Moreover, the regime exploited the country's rampant ignorance, which is in fact the outcome of its rule over Yemen for the past thirty-three years. Taking advantage of this ignorance, the regime spread rumors that the revolution is composed of saboteurs who want to destroy the country's security. This has been effective, especially in the rural areas, which is where most Yemenis live. (Some villages have the same lifestyle as they have had since the time of Adam, with no signs of modern civilization. They are connected to the external world only by a government-owned satellite channel.) That is why our young people have suffered a lot, trying to explain our cause to these villagers, even though it should have been very clear. Finally, the family of President Abdullah Saleh has tight control over the most powerful army units, in addition to holding vital leadership positions in the country. Nonetheless, all these factors do not change my belief that the revolution will achieve its objectives after great suffering and that it is only a matter of time before we succeed.

KILLING THE ROSE BUT NOT THE SPRING

Abduljalil Yousef

Teacher, male, 28, Sanaa

I became engaged and interested in the Yemeni revolution on the first day it started, Saturday, January 15, 2011. This is when the Yemeni people displayed their strong opposition to the regime and took to the streets in order to condemn the corruption and Ali Abdullah Saleh's preparations to pass the presidency of Yemen to his son, which had been speculated in recent years. The first demonstration did not last long, as people marched for only two hours and then went home. But a small group of young people who participated and were not affiliated with any political party opted to stay in the square in front of the University of Sanaa.[1] There weren't more than a hundred, and they were expelled by the police after only three hours. The police's rudeness and disrespect only made them more determined and defiant, so they decided to gather again the next day. I did not join them because I thought that things would not evolve into something formidable and that this would not become a full-fledged revolution.

It is true that corruption has affected almost all people in Yemen, and I have personally encountered it more than once in my life. I lost an opportunity to study abroad because a rich person bribed some officials in the Ministry of Higher Education and took my scholarship. I also could not get a license to open a small shop because of the necessity of paying in bribes at least ten times the cost of a license. Even though the area where I live is in the capital, it has electricity only a few hours a day, so I don't have such basic services as a phone and the Internet. Nonetheless, I still was reluctant to participate in the revolution when it started, because I had lost hope and my future appeared no less ambiguous than the future of the country itself. In addition to causing confusion, the regime had indeed killed in us any hope and had replaced it with total despair. It also forced us into submission and to be satisfied with a life of humiliation and indignity.

I felt I was living in a country in which it was natural to pay bribes just to get one's own rights. But it was also taken for granted that people would pay money to get favorable decisions in court cases. We heard that our country was exporting oil but not a single person—not even the oil minister himself— knew the amount that we were selling because the revenues went to the regime's small circle. It became routine for us to wait in long queues in front of gas stations to get the gas we needed. Every part and parcel of life for the average Yemeni was affected by these ills in the city, and even more so in the rural areas. Hunger, disease, poverty, and begging characterized the Yemeni people's lives, thanks to the leadership of President Ali Abdullah Saleh.

The numbers of young people protesting against the regime increased day after day, and by late February 2011, organized opposition parties joined them, marking the real beginning of the Yemeni revolution in the Arab Spring. Until then, I had not joined the revolution because I was preoccupied with some personal matters. But my noninvolvement did not last long, particularly after March 13, which was called the Friday of Dignity. Grave events occurred that day as the regime sent a group of snipers and insurgents to kill peaceful protesters. Even though Yemeni officials promised to protect nonviolent protesters, which is a right for us, innocent people were shot. The hunting and killing of demonstrators began after the snipers burned tires around Change Square to create thick smoke in an attempt to obscure their locations and prevent cameras from photographing them. Their assault started immediately after the Friday prayers and continued for nearly five hours, resulting in the killing of sixty of our finest young Yemenis. Three of them were my closest friends. They all were killed by the regime, which was supposed to protect them. They were guilty of nothing more than wanting freedom and a decent life, abstract notions that we heard about but did not enjoy in Yemen. Despite how bloody these events, they brought us the fresh air of freedom. Despite how dark they were, they brought a glimpse of light. Hope returned to us, thanks to the revolution—we started to hope for a respectful life, for freedom. That is why I decided to join the revolution.

I packed what I needed and joined my friends who were not affiliated with any political party. I found myself in the middle of a peaceful sit-in, located in Change Square in Sanaa, where we all were demanding the departure of the entire Yemini regime. Because I had a laptop and a camera, my friends assigned me to the media committee. My first task was to use my camera to take pictures of the scenes in Change Square, pictures that were to be shared later. As I was wandering in the square, I saw and took pictures of men, women, and children who were waving placards and shouting the famous slogans of the revolution, such as "Leave . . . leave," "The people want to topple the regime," and "Revolution, revolution against the terrified ruler."

Some protesters set up tents and put their belongings inside them, and others gathered around a poet who was reciting what he had composed for the day before reading it at the podium in front of the crowd. Others prepared food. Some of the sit-in participants guarded the entrances to the square, and still others slept next to them, to be awakened when their shift for guard duty started. Finally, some participants were reading and writing or studying for school. For the first time, I felt as if I were in a completely different country, a country whose people loved to work, enjoyed freedom, and said and wrote what they felt without fear or restrictions—it was the country in which I had always dreamed of living in, feeling that I naturally belonged to it and its people.

But, I was about to face a nightmare. I went back to my house to get a cable to transfer the images from my camera to a computer. I took a taxi and was chatting with the driver. As I was talking to him about the sit-in and the demonstrations, he suddenly pulled out a spray can and started to spraying something in my face, which is the last thing I remember from that unfortunate ride. Later, I woke up and found myself in a small dark room in a prison belonging to the national security headquarters—as I was told after I was freed. The room had a small camera attached to its ceiling, and my first interrogator was a huge man who entered the room to blindfold me and tie my hands together before taking me to another room. I could hear his feet walking away, so I just waited there. Suddenly, the voice of another man surprised me with a question directed at me in a sarcastic tone:

"Is the blindfold bothering you?"

I answered him by saying: "It is not a problem. We will endure pain for your sake."

"For our sake?"

"Yes, for the freedom of you, your children, and your families."

Then he asked me: "Do you know why you are here?"

"I'm here because I went out to demand my freedom and my dignity and also to demand your freedom and your dignity. I'm here because I do not want someone like you to have a job that you do not like and that disturbs your conscience, a job you are forced to do only because you are in need."

Apparently offended by what I said, he slapped me in the face while asking: "I do not like my work? I do not like my country?"

I replied: "You are blindfolding me because you do not want me to see you. You are ashamed to slap me while I am looking into your eyes. Deep inside, you know that you are humiliating me, even though I am demonstrating for your freedom. You are keeping me in prison. even though I'm seeking for you to be a free human being. Be honest to God and tell me why are you doing this to us. Are you doing this to protect the person (the president) who deprived you of freedom, who killed your conscience, and who forced you to torture us, your sons? Why are you killing us? Why are you detaining us? Have we broken the law? Have we done anything wrong to you?"

"Shut up," he interrupted, "Which party do you belong to, and who is turning you against the government?"

"I do not belong to any party. It is the government itself that motivated us to go against it."

"The government?"

"Yes, and also the bribery, cronyism, looting, oppression, and corruption engineered by it."

"Shut up! You do not know what we will do with you!"

"What will you do to us? Death comes only once, whether by a bullet in the square or by renal failure in one of your highly esteemed hospitals. We are used to death. We die more than once each day in this country."

Then, the man called a soldier to take me back to jail, but this time to a cell about eleven square feet big. There was no water or mattress and it smelled really bad.

I remained in the cell for approximately twenty hours, at which time a soldier came to me with a sheet of paper he wanted me to sign. It was a commitment not to participate in any more of the sit-ins. I refused to sign it, saying to him: "I will not break the law." As a result, they kept me in detention for an additional ten hours before releasing me without my signature. This awful experience was not as brutal as that faced by some of my friends. A few of them were forced to drink their own urine in prison. Unlike me, some of them were beaten unconscious and remained in prison for many days. Some of them are still there, and sadly, others, with their relatives, died.

On the evening of Tuesday, April 13, I went back to Change Square and saw Salim al-Hazari, a twelve-year-old child, standing on the platform. The last time he could see the square with his eyes was on March 18, which was the Friday of Dignity, when snipers' bullets hit him in the eyes and blinded him. I believed that Salim returned to Change Square to assure those who extinguished the light of his eyes that they were unable to turn off the light of hope in his heart, the heart that desired a new, corruption-free Yemen, a country without ruthless thugs or Ali Abdullah Saleh. I saw how people looked at him with tearful eyes while he looked at them only with his insight. He told the audience what happened on the Friday of Dignity, saluting the rebels in their peaceful struggle and asking them to continue being strong and to honor (with their victory in the revolution) the fallen heroes who died in the squares and sit-ins. Salim demanded, and the masses in the square repeated after him, that the regime that had destroyed his eyes leave the country. He said loudly, directing his words to President Saleh, "Leave . . . leave so that the rest of the Yemeni children can live a decent and safe life." In a touching gesture, he said, "I dedicate my eyes to my country, Yemen, so that its revolution succeeds and sees the light." This moving scene made me compose some poetry:

Greetings
On behalf of all the revolutionary folks
Our men . . .
Our women . . .
Our elders . . .
Our kids . . .
Even the suckling babies
Even in freezing cold
An urgent message
To the terrible winter:
Yes, you can kill the blooming roses
But can you kill the spring?

The peaceful revolution stirred hope and strong emotions among the youth, and many of us in Yemen became very interested in reading, writing, and composing poetry. I personally felt that words raced through my imagination, filling it with poetry whenever I saw one of the impressive scenes of the revolution and its youthful force.

So far, the major achievements of the revolution are what we have felt inside, in addition to some political accomplishments, such as banning hereditary rule and the ruler's ability to hand over power to his own son to rule after him. The revolution showed that Yemenis knew their real enemy, the corrupt regime that showed its brutal face to them. They knew the reality of their president who used the name of the Yemeni people to beg for financial assistance from other countries while looting all the resources and the wealth of his own country.

The president's reaction to the revolution was to further compromise the interests of Yemeni people, by asking for help from abroad and from neighboring countries to remain in power in exchange for allowing them to use the Yemen's airspace as they wished. He stopped the port of Aden's operations so as not to affect the ports of neighboring countries. He also compromised the country's security and stability and did not allow it to use all its resources o eliminate poverty and unemployment. I feel, like so many other Yemenis, that we were deceived. The regime betrayed us, cheated us, and systematically lied to us. Some of us used to believe it and belie the opposition. The regime tricked us into believing that it was the most appropriate form of government for us. Every day during the revolution, we discovered more of the crimes committed by the regime against us and more of the facts that it hid from us for more than thirty years.

Now life is not what it used to be—there is no fear, no despair, no submission or surrender. It seems as if the people of Yemen suddenly were resurrected and saw the truth. It would be impossible to return to the dark past and equally impossible to accept ever again a regime like that of Ali Abdullah Saleh. I can now almost envision the day when I travel with my children in Change Square in Sanaa, telling them proudly about the revolution I lived through with my friends. But I will also tell them sad things like "here is where the regime killed your uncle (name omitted) and here it wounded your uncle (name omitted).

Here we set up the field hospital, where we carried the wounded and dead with our own hands because the regime had blown up the ambulances and destroyed this street. Here we wrote signs and shouted slogans. And here . . . and here . . . and here. I have no doubt that this day will come sooner rather than later, but until then we will continue to recite the slogans of the revolution. We will write, and we will fight for freedom. Freedom is wonderful, and we have inhaled its fresh breath.

THE AROMA OF FREEDOM
AND THE SMELL OF BLOOD

Abdullah Sufian Modhesh

Yemeni educator working in Sanaa, male, 36, Taiz

In the beginning of the Arab Spring, with the first flowers blossoming in Tunisia, I was not so optimistic about the possibility of the same thing happening in Yemen. Although I believed that Yemen needed a regime change more than any other Arab country, I was almost totally desperate about the possibility of that happening by way of peaceful protests. This despair was not because I didn't believe in the potential of Yemeni youth but because I knew that corruption in Yemen, unlike that in Tunisia and other countries, already was institutionalized and woven into the structures of the society through so many mechanisms and under so many guises. It had become a grand narrative through which events, characters, decisions, and values were to be assessed. In other words, corruption ruled the country and shaped relations between people and institutions. I seriously didn't think that people would take to the streets and risk losing their interests with the government. The opposition parties were not very strong, and we didn't have the same level of awareness among the youth as the Tunisians had. So I didn't really see the likelihood of having protests strong enough to force the president to resign. Besides I knew, as did most of the Yemeni youth, that our president would tolerate civil protests, even if they led to civil disobedience, as long as they did not constitute a physical threat to his safety or cause the international community to pressure him to step down. At the same time, I believed that our president and his family had tactics that could help them overcome the situation without provoking the anger of human rights organizations, mainly by getting tribal leaders with strong ties to the president to clash with the protesters. The president's first speeches during the early weeks of the revolution demonstrated exactly that tendency. He kept talking about how Yemen was different and that all the Yemeni people were armed, and so on.

Although I believed that the situation I just described was reason enough for people to realize the problems and take to the streets, I didn't think it would really happen. I remember meeting with an American author, Dr. Isobel Coleman, in Sanaa in mid-January when this came up. She asked whether the Yemeni people were or would be influenced by what the Tunisians were doing and whether I thought there could be a similar revolution in Yemen. I explained that the Yemeni people, culture, societal structure, and leadership all were very different, and so I thought that the possibility of an exact replica of the Tunisian revolution was far from reality. But I told her about the young woman and relentless activist Tawakkol Karman (who later won the Nobel Peace Prize), who at the time was one of very few outspoken activists calling for similar protests and organizing small marches in support of the Tunisian revolution and the fall of the Yemeni regime. I arranged an interview with Karman at her home, and I remember her asking me to join their daily protests at the university gate. I told her that I really admired what she was doing and believed in the cause but that I didn't agree with her oversimplification of the Yemeni situation that, I believed, was not so supportive of a peaceful change of regime. But by the time we left Karman's home, I believed more strongly in the need for a Yemeni revolution and had a little more hope that if we had equally bold activists, we might actually get Yemeni youths to revolt and overthrow the regime. In fact, a week or so later I started hearing about other, equally enthusiastic activists, like the member of parliament Ahmed Saif Hashed and the young female journalist Samiah al-Aghbary. Still, I didn't think these people were powerful enough to overturn a regime that based its stability mainly on a coalition of interests with tribal leaders, army commanders, and religious leaders.

When Tawakkol Karman was arrested late at night in late January, I started to feel that the ground would soon start shaking underneath the president. Unprecedented crowds of people gathered, especially in Taiz, her and my city, demanding her release. It was then that I participated in a march to the public attorney's office with various groups of young people, politicians, and activists. The reason I participated was that I was really moved by the aggression against this peaceful activist, and I started feeling that her detention by the regime was an indicator of its real weakness in in the face of the protests, which meant that it consequently might fall. This made me more interested in participating in events and marches. The biggest factor that I thought then would make me and many other Yemenis take an active part in the revolution was the success of the Egyptian revolution.

In February, the two other activists I admired also were assaulted while participating in a march with dozens of young men and women in support of the Egyptian revolution. I thought then that unless millions of Yemenis took to the streets, this revolution was doomed to failure. I noticed that the Egyptians started going out in small groups and that the numbers kept increasing until millions were out, making it impossible for the world to ignore them or for the regime to silence them. At that time, I had already seen several clashes between protesters and groups of thugs who came to the university gate every day with stones and batons to attack the protesters. So despite my genuine interest to participate, I still saw the efforts to make a Yemeni Tahrir Square as being rather futile. Thugs kept attacking the young people with the help and support of security forces and, as witnesses claim, municipal trucks carrying stones and batons. But after the protesters spent their first night camping out at the university gate, I felt that the snowball had started rolling and that it would not stop until it had taken the regime with it.

My in-laws (all in their twenties), and a nephew put up their tents near the center of the square. I started spending time with them, listening to speeches, discussing with young people the potential success of our revolution, and sometimes taking part in cautious marches near the square. The protesters then did not risk leaving Change Square for fear that groups of thugs or the security forces would take over and they wouldn't be able to come back. Friday prayers were special events, and I would walk to the mosque and listen to a revolutionary sermon that, for the first time ever, would start and end with the national anthem. The anthem was played a few minutes before the sermon and again after the prayers and chants were finished. Although we never felt safe or secure at Change Square, I enjoyed the sense of freedom whenever I was there. As one of my friends put it, "To smell the aroma of freedom, just walk in Change Square." I enjoyed the aroma of freedom many times in February and early March before going to Taiz, where I trained elementary school teachers in reading.

In Taiz I saw a different face of the revolution, a very civil one. I didn't see thugs as often as I did in Sanaa, where they were all over the place. Most of my trainees were against the regime, and at that time they also were on strike. The only reason they attended was because the training was arranged by a very well respected local, nongovernmental organization. Freedom Square in Taiz was even bigger than Change Square in Sanaa, and it was very close to my older brother's house. My brother and his sons would spend hours in the camps, and I occasionally joined them. On March 18, after praying at Freedom Square in Taiz, I heard the news about the Friday of Dignity massacre in Sanaa. I rushed to my brother's home to see Al Jazeera's live coverage of the massacre. Scenes of young people bleeding to death killed every drop of hesitation and skepticism in my heart. I thought even if the revolution failed or, even worse, even if it brought the Islamists to power, I was totally for it and would participate in all events. From then on, I started expressing my anti-Saleh opinions on Facebook, spending hours in Freedom Square and Change Square, and taking part in some big marches in Sanaa. After that massacre, many high-ranking officials defected from the regime, including the commander of the army's First Armored Division, General Ali Mohsen al-Ahmar. Many people felt that this was a big blow to the regime, one that weakened it.

On Wednesday, May 16, I was home with my wife's nephew (Mohammed) who had taken part in all the marches in Sanaa. He wanted to join the march to the prime minister's office led by Tawakkol Karman and Khaled al-Anesi. The two activists at that time were in disagreement with the ad-hoc leaders of Change Square, who were opposing the march for fear of losing lives. Although Mohammed insisted on going, but at my wife's request, I managed to keep him home with me watching the march from the window. Soon there was shooting, and young men started falling right in front of our eyes. Central Security Forces were attacking the protesters with gas and live ammunition. I managed to take some videos of the attacks before a few bullets came through my windows, one passing only about an inch above Mohammed's head into the room. My wife and children were terrified. My six-year-old boy kept talking about how the bullets would come through the windows and kill us all. We all slept in the kitchen because it was farthest from the outside walls. The following morning I took my wife and children to my brother-in-law's house and soon returned to Taiz again for work.

Taiz's peace was destroyed on Sunday, May 29, when security forces and Republican Guards attacked and burned Freedom Square. I was in the square in the afternoon and felt there was something going on. Later in the afternoon and until 3:00 a.m., security forces attacked and burned the protesters' camps. I saw all this from the rooftop of my father-in-law's house and captured most of it on video. The following days were very gloomy for most of the people of Taiz, but Friday of that week was different. I went with my nephews near the square that had been occupied by security forces, only to find it impossible to pray there. Groups of protesters tried to gather in another area nearby, but Republican Guard armored vehicles attacked them and forced them to disperse, shooting one protester in the leg because he refused. It was then that we went back to my brother's home and saw armed civilians shooting at the soldiers and forcing them to leave the area. From then on, the Taiz protests became more symbolic while armed civilians protected the area and engaged in nightly confrontations with the security forces and Republican Guards. The same day we heard about the explosion in the presidential palace. Most of the people I knew were relieved and rejoiced by the news. They felt it was only fair for the president to feel some of the pains experienced by the people of Taiz after the Freedom Square massacre.

My participation in all the events that followed was mainly driven by the feeling that Yemen had reached the point of no return in the revolution. Regardless of the outcome, and even if the Islamists came to power, I believed that the blood of those young people who died dreaming of freedom should never be betrayed even if we shed our own blood on the way to freedom.

Many people are skeptical about the future, and I don't blame them. We have a very complex society in which a revolution can be exploited and taken over by reactionary forces. But since the people have realized their real power, I believe that another dictator will never be likely again to lead our country for thirty-three years. This by itself is a gain worth sacrifice, regardless of who rules, as long as we know that the people can change the regime.

THE TENT AND THE REVOLUTION

Mohammed al-Omari

University of Sanaa graduate, male, 24, Taiz

I don't know exactly where to start; there were so many events that I lived through during the youth revolution in Yemen. Nonetheless, I will give an account of what stands out in my memory as relevant and worth sharing. It all started in February 2011, when we heard about the revolution by the Tunisian people and we doubted that they would achieve success on the ground, particularly to overthrow President Zine el-Abidine Ben Ali. That is why I was greatly amazed when Ben Ali fled Tunisia, thanks to the people's revolt. I wished at the time that those events were taking place in my country; Yemen urgently needed a revolution. But by the time the Egyptian revolution began on Tuesday, January 25, 2011, the germ of a revolution in Yemen already had begun to sprout. That is, we had a minirevolution that did not promise to achieve what it did later. Ours began in the city of Taiz, which is my hometown, and I felt that it would really ignite a full revolution by Yemeni youth. I was attracted to the Egyptian revolution and followed it closely on television when I was in Sanaa. When I knew that Taiz was staging more and more events, but still with no risk to the Yemeni regime, I made a personal pledge to participate in any aspect of the sit-ins in Yemen.

I believed strongly that what we suffered in Yemen was worse than the situations in Egypt and Tunisia, because President Ali Abdullah Saleh had an organized gang ruling the country. His was a very coherent regime composed mainly of his nephews, half siblings, cousins, and sons from his village, Sanhan.

When the Egyptian youths achieved their goal, with the memorable moment of Vice President Omar Suleiman announcing President Hosni Mubarak's resignation, I met Ammar al-Sabri, one of my friends, who is blind, and we congratulated each other on this occasion. Ammar and I were university students in the fourth year at the College of Arts, University of Sanaa, and we prayed that President Saleh would be the next Arab ruler to be overthrown.

During that time, the University of Sanaa had a few small demonstrations at the new campus. As a student at the old campus, I used to go there full of fear for the safety of my friends. There, I saw the brutal violence and barbarous treatment by the ruling party's thugs against my friends and the demonstrators, even using insults and racial slurs. This uncivilized behavior increased my determination to be more than just a bystander or passive participant. That is why I joined a small demonstration on campus, and we received our share of beatings at the hands of the Central Security agents. They assaulted us with sticks, batons, and insults, and some of us were taken to detention centers. Then during the last days of the first-term exams, some antiregime students and demonstrators set up small tents for a sit-in. My friend Ammar and I used to spend some time there from late afternoon to early evening.

Those were the hardest days, for there were many attacks on protesters and our numbers were small, with only a few dozen tents. On the fourteenth day of the sit-ins, Ammar and I decided to join; we arrived with just one blanket and a pillow, which we put on the sidewalk near the *almanassa*, the podium. The sit-in was organized in a well-marked space with authorized barriers to designate its borders. We spent our time reciting slogans, singing some songs celebrating the revolution, and volunteering in the organization committees that were taking care of order and security in Change Square. We did this for eight days and because we did not have a tent of our own, we worked from afternoon till dawn, when we went home for some sleep.

On the ninth day, which was Tuesday, we were having dinner in our spot in front of the Change Square podium, when suddenly, at about 10:30 p.m., we heard shooting coming from the west side of the square. This area had a security barrier erected by the government, or, rather, belonging to the Central Security Forces led by Brigadier General Yahya Mohammed Abdullah Saleh, the president's nephew. Placed on Adl Street, a bit more than three hundred feet from the podium, the barrier was meant to limit the protest's expansion, not to protect the protesters. Some people were injured as a result of the shootings. We took them to the field hospital, which was located in some of the classrooms previously used for teaching the Qur'an in the university's mosque. After half an hour, it was broadcast that one protester, Abdullah al-Jaifi, had died, an announcement that was followed by complete silence in Change Square. Ammar and I went back to our place, praying fervently that the criminals and the gang ruler of our country would be punished for killing this innocent man. Ammar and I went home at dawn but did not sleep. Instead, we searched for a tent that my family used for camping, and we found it. We took it to the square and put it up on the western side, about eighty-two feet away from the podium. Regardless of its small size—only about four feet—we spent the night in it as if we were in a presidential palace. We continued our organizing activities, with even more revolutionary brothers who joined us and shared our cause and love for our country.

Unfortunately, during a stormy night with heavy rain and rough winds, our small, old, tent collapsed on our heads. So the next day Ammar and I sold our Nokia cell phones and used the money to buy a decent six-and-a-half-foot tent. We used the same blanket we'd had since the beginning of our journey in this revolution. In this new tent we used to spend the nights at the sit-in with our colleagues and my brother Ibrahim, may God have mercy on him.[2] We had fun, singing national songs and sometimes trying to think of useful and innovative ideas to develop and protect the sit-in area.

The following month, some young people in a tent next to ours were planning to broaden our protest area for the people coming to perform the Friday prayers. They wanted to extend it from the neighborhood of City Mart to the vicinity of the Iranian Medical Center. On Thursday we helped tell as many revolutionaries as possible about this plan and spread the word to the young people in the tents adjacent to ours. We were able to expand the area the next day, Friday, by carrying our tents and moving to the new area as quickly as possible, taking advantage of the huge number of Friday prayer participants. Although this move forced the stationed Central Security Forces to pull out, they already had planned something awful. The next day, the regime's security forces launched a surprise attack using boiling water and tear gas before we finished the *fajr* (dawn) prayer. The confrontation continued until seven o'clock in the morning, when there was an influx of students, teachers, and some employees in the private sector who did not go to work that day. For the next six days, the security forces tried to recover the space from which we expelled them, but they could not. Instead, they started building a concrete wall to prevent us from expanding further.

On Friday, March 18, which is called the Friday of Dignity, about 800,000 people came from all over the capital to pray in Change Square, even though the regime forces closed the roads leading to the area. When we finished the Friday prayer, I saw heavy black smoke coming out of that concrete wall, and I could hear the sound of bullets everywhere around us. I was close to the wall, and my friend and brother Ibrahim tried to reach it, but when we were about 130 feet away, the intensity of gunfire increased and we could not get to it. Instead, we went to help the volunteer committees, which were transporting the injured and making their way quickly through the crowds in order to move the wounded and the martyrs to the field hospital. During the Friday of Dignity, fifty-seven martyrs fell, and one of them was my colleague on the media committee. Weeks after that Friday, the three of us (me, my friend Ammar, and my brother Ibrahim) bought a large tent, which measured eleven and a half meters. We decided to call it "For you, my homeland."

Yemeni youths stepped up the revolutionary marches, moving to the streets near the square. We held up placards and chanted revolutionary slogans, demanding freedom and President Saleh's departure. I took part in those marches as one of the media documentary officers, which was my assignment after joining the revolution's media committee. I was using my own camera to do my job during those immensely large demonstrations, such as the One Million Man March, which started from Agriculture Street and returned to Change Square after going down Ishreen Street.

There was also the demonstration on June 6, which began at Rabat Street and went down Siteen Street. During this demonstration, we were stopped by the Central Security Forces and the thuggish gunmen who were ironically called the "supporters of the regime and its legitimacy." A lieutenant colonel addressed us and promised that he would let us pass after he asked his commander. He asked us to wait, and we did, as we thought as he was being truthful. While we were waiting, five trucks appeared full of soldiers who immediately got off and took a position as if ready to attack. We still were standing in front of them waiting for lieutenant colonel to keep his promise. Suddenly, they sprayed us with boiling water, tear gas, and live ammunition. We were attacked from all directions in a crazed manner, and all we could do was retreat and use stones to defend ourselves. Because we could not find any stones in the area, we started breaking up some of the sidewalk and throwing pieces at the soldiers. We finally forced them to retreat. but only after they killed six people and wounded dozens more. Hundreds of people were suffering from the tear gas that was used against them. The demonstration continued, and the demonstrators made their way down Zubairy Street and returned to the square. At that point, I was transferred by motorcycle to the field hospital because of an injury to my left leg as well as the suffocating gas. A soldier had hit my leg with his baton. When I went back to the tent, Ammar was already there, suffering from the shortness of breath caused by the gas attack. A lot of similar marches and demonstrations are still vivid in my memory, but space will not allow me to describe more.

Finally, I will state my opinion about the Yemeni revolution several months after it began. In October 2011, I still believe that the revolution had an essential and needed impact on Yemen, and I have never regretted my participation in it. Joining the revolution of Yemen stems from my conviction that the country could not function while being governed by a military dictatorship composed of the same military family. Although President Saleh managed to control the country for longer than any ruler before him—he was in power for thirty-three years—he was not willing to reform the country. That is why he did not have a positive legacy, even though he had the chance and the power to do so. The regime had been working on emptying the memory of the Yemeni people of all the beautiful things they had had in the past. It also wiped from the memory of my and my father's generation anything that was not approved by President Saleh, who made us know him as the only president of Yemen for the last three decades. I do not have the least doubt that the Yemeni revolution was necessary in all regards. It also was the demand of the people who wanted equal citizenship and justice. Most Yemenis want law, not corruption, to prevail in their lives, and they want real and comprehensive development to shape their country. They want Yemen to be a state in which all people truly participate in choosing their own rulers. The Yemeni revolution will be successful, but it will take time, because the situation in Yemen is very complicated—most of the leaders of the army are in favor of and from the Saleh family, and the country's resources have long been in his hands and in the hands of those who have benefited from him.

The revolution carries risks, such as the possibility that the Joint Meeting Parties (JMP) might hijack it and seek narrow-minded partisan interests at the expense of the ambitious young people of Yemen. I also suspect that the neighboring countries will be unhappy with the triumph of our revolution because they are ruled by monarchies that will not like having a democratic state on their border. Moreover, the international community did not support us; it did not consider our revolution with the same high regard as the other revolutions, probably because Yemen is not considered a critically strategic country or maybe because we lack the natural resources that the developed countries need.

Almost one year has passed since the start of the revolution, with very little achieved so far. Some people may think that the youth already might be bored and burned out, which is what President Saleh and his regime counted on from the beginning, but the majority of our young people have proved to be the opposite. They forced Saleh to step down by signing an initiative with which they were not completely satisfied, and so they will continue fighting, regardless of the political compromises that were or will be made.

THE CHALLENGES OF OUR
YEMENI REVOLUTION

Sarah Jamal Ali Ahmed

Sociologist, female, 24, Sanaa

I engaged in civic activism for the first time when I turned fifteen and spent two years working in an Arab-Israeli youth conflict resolution and coexistence network. I got to know so much about the boundaries I had taken for granted. Eventually I chose to become a sociologist in order to understand what my society has to offer me and what I can do improve it. During my four years in college, which was Northwestern University in Chicago, I discovered a whole new world of perspectives and ideologies, and I became a strong believer in two things: social justice and gradual social change. I also worked with different groups and socioeconomic classes in Yemeni society. During my last two years of college, I worked as a social researcher and tried to meet the types of people that Yemeni society has neglected and avoided for centuries. Between breakfasts with unemployed laborers and lunches in ghettos, I got to see how rigid numbers can be. When an Oxfam report states that more than 60 percent of Yemenis live below the poverty line, we turn the page and move to the next number. But when we eat and talk with some of the members of that 60 percent, their daily sorrow becomes ours. Moreover, my sorrow was doubled. Not only are the poor also outcasts, but also more than half of Yemeni society is.

I also had to learn that being a young woman in a conservative society that labels half of its population—women—as tabooed subjects made me more aware of how females are sentenced to metaphorical and sometimes literal death when they are born, without even knowing how or why to value themselves. In my country, every step in a woman's life is decided by men. When I turned twenty-one, I realized that everything in me is not owned by me. My society, my father, and my future husband own everything in me, starting with my name and ending with my body; and in the middle is my education, my career, my clothes, and even what I choose to eat or drink. But eventually I refused to be such a passive victim. In January 2010, I became a social researcher in the Women's Central Prison in Sanaa and also in the local female juvenile home. In addition, I participated in all the initiatives that fought the "early marriage bill." At the same time, I codeveloped several campaigns to fight sexual harassment.

When I close my eyes for a moment to recall the events before January 14, 2011, a strange scene appears in my mind. There is no room for me to go into details or even to mention the clichés that are often used to explain the situation in Yemen, such as the alarming rates of illiteracy, poverty, and the low status of women. Instead, I am more concerned about why a whole generation of young Yemenis had completely adjusted to this.

The majority of young Yemenis were not allowed to form any sort of political identity. Their parents of the 1980s and 1990s generations experienced civil wars, political setbacks, executions, assassinations, and detentions. This appalling history created a passive and submissive climate for Yemeni youth, which forced them to adapt to what their peers in other places around the world would find impossible to tolerate. It also has become clear that most of the people of this generation are children of poor people, even though their parents used to belong to the middle class. This class gradually receded from the ruling minority that controls the country's wealth, leaving most people below the poverty line. All these factors caused most Yemenis to become economically, socially, and culturally marginalized when the infrastructure and the superstructure of Yemeni society collapsed.

I participated in the first protest against Saleh's regime on January 15, 2011, right after Ben Ali left Tunisia. The protest was a response to a Facebook event announced by a group of civic activists and journalists. After that event, I became part of daily protests outside the University of Sanaa campus, where three groups protested simultaneously: the intelligentsia, the university students' committee of the Yemeni Socialist Party, and university students without any particular affiliation. Between mid-January and February 3, all the protests outside the university demanded the end of Saleh's regime. Then on February 3, the opposition Joint Meeting Parties (JMP) called for a demonstration on the "Thursday of Wrath," at which they called for political reform. The JMP encompassed the northern-based, tribal, and Islamist Muslim Brotherhood–oriented Yemeni Congregation for Reform (Islah); the al-Haq Party, a semireligious party; the Unionist Party; and the Popular Forces Union Party, all of which joined together in 2005. The JMP's demands, however, did not meet the demands of the leftist youths, who had begun protesting earlier in January to overthrow the regime, which created a gap between these two groups.

On February 11, the first tent was built in Freedom Square in Taiz, a city midway between north and south Yemen. A week later, Yemeni youth in Sanaa, led by the Students Committee of the Yemeni Socialist Party, put up tents in front of the University of Sanaa, and in the next few weeks, tribes from all over the country joined them in what became Change Square. At the same time, on February 16, a new group appeared in the south, whose voices were different from those calling for separation. These young people in Aden, the capital city of the former southern state, went into the streets waving unification flags and making the same demands as those of the youths in Sanaa and Taiz.

What was interesting is how the right wing in general and the religious parties in particular joined Change Square one month after the protests had started. Also, the official leadership of the left—unlike the leftist students— did not join the square immediately but waited until all the other parties had already participated. In addition, women were important at all times from February to April 2011. Leftist as well as apolitical female students helped put up the tents, guarded the entrances to the sit-in areas, joined marches, and helped in the field hospitals. Most important, they participated in the aware-ness campaigns among the tribes as well as the coalitions that were formed in the square.

My friends and I built what we called the "equality tent." We focused on the tribes that came from very remote areas to camp in Change Square and demand change. We discussed and debated women's rights in Yemen, and their response was amazing. Each day, I was also amazed by the Yemeni women, who outnumbered men in demonstrations and marches. I began to use those women as examples to help the tribesmen understand that women's rights in health care, education, and labor do not affect their social structure or belief system and that giving them such basic rights would only help us as a nation defeat ignorance, poverty, and injustice. The results were very positive for the first few months, but then things changed dramatically when the Islamist par-ties started paying attention to what we were doing. To them, we were the powerful force of change that would help lead Yemen from a male-oriented, patriarchal society to a more gender-equal one. They then began using all sorts of verbal and physical violence against the female activists in the square in order to marginalize them from the political life and consequently, the new state we were trying to build.

Moreover, Saleh's speech on how men and women should not be protest-ing side by side (for religious and moral reasons) was shared by some of the Muslim Brotherhood (Islah) protesters. Using this logic, they beat up female activists, including myself, because we refused to go on separate marches. With the fanatic right-wing ideology that found its way among the poor and the illiterate, women's participation remained significant but not as important as it had been in the square earlier. Nevertheless, it prospered in the other spaces, such as the conferences that represented the revolutions abroad and the media.

By the end of February, more than four hundred coalitions had been formed in Change Square. Liberals, leftists, and apolitical activists formed the Coordinating Council of the Youth Revolution of Change in order to help the revolution's mandates come together under one roof. At the beginning of March, they presented the Declaration of Youth Revolution Demands, which stated the revolution's demands as agreed on in all the Change and Freedom Squares around Yemen. Those demands were announced in a document whose main points I want to put down for the record:

1. The current regime, its figures, and all members of the president's immediate family and his relatives will be peacefully removed from all leadership posts in military and civil institutions.

2. A transitional presidential board will be formed, to be made up of five civilians who are widely recognized for their competence, integrity, and experience. These members must be approved by the revolution's youth leaders and the national powers. Individuals that represent the previous regime should be excluded from the selection. This board will be responsible for issuing all decisions and decrees that will fulfill the demands of the revolution. After serving on the board, members will not be eligible to run for president or prime minister until one electoral cycle has been completed.

3. After overthrowing the regime, the board must declare a six-month transitional period. This period will start with a constitutional decree announcing the expiration of the current constitution and dissolving the parliament, the *shura* council, and the local councils.

4. The transitional presidential board will appoint, within one month, a widely accepted national figure who will form a transitional cabinet of qualified technocrats.

5. A transitional national board will be formed and will include representatives of the youth.

6. The higher judicial council will be restructured to ensure the full separation and impartiality of the judicial authority.

7. The Ministry of Information will be replaced by an independent higher authority that will ensure freedom of expression and the diversification of media and communication outlets.

8. The Ministry of Human Rights will be replaced by an independent higher council for human rights.

9. Corrupt officials will be sought and brought to justice, and public property and money will be reclaimed.

10. All political detainees and missing persons will be released immediately, and all extraordinary courts and private prisons will be abolished.

11. All individuals who caused, assisted, and/or incited the killing and injury of those who participated in peaceful demonstrations will be brought to justice.

12. The Political Security Forces and the National Security Forces will be replaced by a new, dedicated national security agency under the umbrella of the Ministry of Interior. This new national security agency will be responsible for dealing with external threats to Yemen.

13. The Republican Guards will become part of the military forces, and the National Defense Council will be abolished, in order to ensure full impartiality of the army and security forces.

When those demands were announced, the JMP did not react openly. Instead, it restrained its comments in the media, saying only that it was 100 percent behind the decisions made in the revolutionary squares. Meanwhile, marches continued on a weekly basis despite the brutal attacks against the demonstrators, and the sit-in continued to get bigger and bigger every day.

The concept of a peaceful struggle is still new in the Arab world and Yemen, for people have not participated in large numbers in such kinds of uprisings before. In Yemen, there were two examples of these kinds of uprisings before the launch of our revolution: the Peaceful Southern movement, which has been active for quite a while, and the civic activists' protests for human and women's rights in front of the Yemeni cabinet each Tuesday. Nevertheless, those two were still elite oriented and did not include ordinary people. People started learning the concept of a peaceful protest after getting involved in the February revolution and sit-ins. For instance, tribesmen from all over the country who joined Change Square were constantly trying to prove to the rest of the country, the media, and the international community that they had left their weapons behind, which is uncommon in the culture of these people. They showed that they were not willing to avenge their family members who were shot and killed during the protests.

I started a communication network with the Red Cross in order to document the deaths and injuries. I also tried to send all the pictures and videos that I and my friends took to Amnesty International, Human Rights Watch, and international newspapers. In order to maintain the organization and the peaceful approach during the protests, social networks were used to announce the protests' timings and locations. A platform also was built inside the square to announce plans for the marches to the protesters. Even though at the beginning of March, several foreign reporters were asked to leave the country, the protesters managed to build a media tent in each square in the country. Amateur and professional photographers and videographers documented

each day's events and sent their tapes to different international media channels as well as social media and Internet websites. Meanwhile, we endured the
difficult collective punishment that was imposed by the government, such as
the twenty to twenty-two hours a day of no power and no water and the continuously rising prices for basic goods and gas.

The traditional opposition represented in the Joint Meeting Parties continued to refuse to negotiate with the regime (as the youths in the squares demanded) until Friday, March 18. The demonstrations in what was called the
Friday of Dignity, or Karama, witnessed the murder of more than sixty peaceful protesters—two of them were friends of mine—and the injury of more
than three hundred. In less than one hour they were shot during the Friday
prayer by snipers on the roof of a governor's house near Change Square. As a
result of what happened on this day, a huge wave of resignations came from
government officials, diplomats, and national journalists. The turning point
was when General Ali Mohsen al-Ahmar defected with his unit and joined
the square on March 21. Although this powerful general brought with him the
majority of the army, he created a controversy among the square's different
constituents. They were divided between Islah members, who welcomed him
because they were affiliated with him through tribal and ideological ties, and
those who saw in him a real threat to the peacefulness of the revolution. Furthermore, he has an undeniable history as Saleh's relative and as a military
iron fist who in 1994 fought in the south and in Saada in the far north.

As expected, General Ali Mohsen became a burden to the revolution because of the equal armed weight he represented, which simply made him
equivalent to the regime's National Guard. As a result, the fear of a civil war
was Yemenis' biggest nightmare after March 21. We knew very well that the
regime's escalating violence toward the peaceful protesters was one of the
various attempts to drag the army into an armed conflict with the National
Guard. This could have severely damaged the image of the revolution in the
international media. The situation would have been viewed as a fight over
power between cousins instead of a nation's call for freedom, equality, and
social justice. In May, an armed conflict erupted in the al-Hasaba area in Sanaa between the regime and General Ali Mohsen's family, which belongs to
the Hashid tribe. This conflict helped achieve the regime's plan: diverting
the world's attention from the violations against peaceful protesters. On September 18, the regime attacked a peaceful demonstration with rocket-propelled grenades and bombs and fired at General Ali Mohsen's forces, starting
an armed confrontation that lasted for two weeks and resulted in many civilians' lives being lost. Similarly, the regime kept attacking Freedom Square in
Taiz using different degrees of violence, such as shelling and burning the

protesters' camps in order to provoke the tribes there and get them involved in another armed conflict.

We tried to prevent the peaceful revolution from turning into a civil war. A different voice was starting to be heard in the middle of all those challenges: ours. With the help of civic activists, we started to find our way among all that mess in order to maintain the revolution's peaceful approach and steer it away from all the conflicts around it. We tried to highlight the revolution's goals and methods, rejecting the other violent distractions. My friends and I started forming awareness groups to combat the idea of armed conflicts within the camps in Change Square.

During all those events, the traditional opposition, the JMP, agreed to sign the Gulf Co-operation Council (GCC) initiative to resolve the crisis in Yemen, which realized its worth after a series of negotiations between Sanaa and Riyadh, Saudi Arabia. Saleh kept agreeing and then refusing to sign until he ended up changing the GCC's initiative five times, insisting on granting himself full immunity from any sort of legal prosecution. He obtained this immunity, even though he repeated in his speeches for a whole year that his regime did not commit any sort of violations against the protesters!

When the JMP signed the GCC initiative in May and then its detailed plan in November, the youths in the squares felt that the JMP had betrayed them by signing an agreement that saved Saleh from prosecution. But the lack of any other alternatives, the constant threat of a civil war, and General Ali Mohsen's burden on the revolution's shoulders left the square's constituents with no other options than working on what would come after the initiative was activated. They knew that the Gulf countries and the U.S. government had always regarded Saleh as the perfect ally for their interests in Yemen.

After the elections on February 21, 2012, Vice President Abdu Rabu Mansoor Hadi became Yemen's president for the transitional period, which had the option of "one candidate" only. Despite the tension created by the nature of these elections, all the square's constituents, whether for or against them, agreed to look forward to the National Dialogue Conference in order to achieve the following goals:

1. Removing all armed forces from the cities and all the military camps outside the cities.
2. Including all the constituents of Yemen's social and political spectrum, especially women, the Southern movement, and the Huthis, with significant representations in the National Dialogue Conference and the Constitution Writing Committee.

3. Starting preparations to restructure the army according to the United
   Nation convoy's suggestion.

We still feel that our revolution faces various threats. We fear armed conflicts because they can be fatal to any sort of a peaceful struggle. We also fear
ideological conflicts, particularly in the form of religious filtering and lobbying
against any progressive approach. These ideologies might hide behind Kalash-
nikovs and tanks. Recently, a female leftist writer and activist were attacked by
Islah Party members for an article she wrote. Her critics demanded prosecution
and punishment, justifying their point of view by calling it a defense of religion. Such incidents must be seen as reminders to manage the transitional
period wisely, especially when restructuring the army, dealing with armed
civilians, and writing a new constitution that guarantees freedom of faith and
speech as well as gender equality.

NOTES

1. The Yemeni protesters opposed to the regime of President Ali Abdullah
Saleh gave the name Change Square to the area facing the University of Sanaa.

2. Ibrahim was killed by a traffic police officer on September 24, 2011. While
he was in his car with his friends, the officer shot him, even though he had not
broken any traffic laws or argued with them. The case is now in court and the killer
is in prison.

5. Syria

Syrian expatriates created what would be the most visible Facebook page, "Syrian Revolution 2011 against Bashar al-Assad," and they set Tuesday, March 15, to be the start date for revolt. But the timing was not propitious, and nothing unusual happened during the day. Syrians joined the Arab Spring as a response to the events that took place in the southwestern city of Daraa. On March 5, 2011, about fifteen elementary school children wrote antigovernment graffiti that reads in Arabic, "Ijaak al door ya diktoor" (Now it is your turn, Doctor [Bashar al-Assad]), referring to the Syrian president's profession as an ophthalmologist before he was handed power after the death of his father, Hafez, in 2000. The children, who were arrested, had written revolutionary slogans on the walls of their school, slogans that they had heard or seen from the Tunisian and Egyptian revolutions, which were widely reported on Arab and international TV channels.

The treatment of the children in confinement was key to the quick spread of visible protests in Daraa, which sparked the revolution. Before they were freed from prison for writing graffiti, their families were humiliated by the regime's men in Daraa. One of these men was Brigadier General Atif Naguib, the president's cousin, who was later released from his duties without any trial.

The children were harshly beaten, their fingernails were pulled out, and their parents were reportedly told to forget them or to have children other than those in prison. People in Daraa took to the streets, and the Facebook's Syrian Revolution 2011 page started calling for more protests. But when the security forces fired at the peaceful demonstrators, killing several men, even more people became outraged. Other areas of Daraa joined the uprisings, particularly on March 18, called the "Friday of Dignity," denouncing "the thieves of the country." By the end of March, the security forces had shot dead more than twenty protesters, injured hundreds, and arrested dozens. The protests spread to other cities, and the crackdown grew more violent. This was typical of how the Syrian regime responded to any challenges to its dominance. Since assuming the presidency in 1971, Hafez al-Assad controlled Syria by giving the top positions in the army and the state offices to his family members and loyalists, thereby forcing the Ba'th Party on the country. In 1982, after an Islamic uprising in Hama, a city in west-central Syria, Hafez al-Assad sent the military and the air force to shell and bomb the city, killing between ten thousand and twenty-five thousand people.

On March 24, the Syrian regime officially responded to the uprising in Daraa, and this time it was not President Bashar al-Assad, son of Hafez, addressing the people, but his political and media adviser, Buthaina Shabaan. The reforms he announced to pacify the 2011 uprisings in Syria were mainly economic. The government raised state salaries by 1,500 Syrian pounds per month, the equivalent of $32.60. (As the sanctions imposed on the regime began to show results, the value of such a raise in early 2014 was less than $11.) Many of the demonstrators in Syria were killed by snipers. Many people blamed the regime, but government media claimed that armed gangs and infiltrators were responsible for the killings. Using this pretext, the Syrian military was sent to those cities that held overwhelmingly large demonstrations. The regime's hired thugs, called *shabiha*, became major players in creating what seemed to be the out-of-control onslaught of civilian protesters. These *shabiha* were used to beat the organizers and leading figures of demonstrations. As a result, thousands of army soldiers, and some officers, defected and began fighting the regime forces and the *shabiha* in such cities as Homs, Idlib, and Deir al-Zour. By the end of the second year of the uprisings, even most of the suburbs of Damascus had come under the control of the rebels. This now had turned into a brutal conflict between the government forces and Syrian army defectors, who called themselves the Free Syrian Army (FSA).

Some Arab countries, including Saudi Arabia and Qatar, wanted the international community to arm the FSA to help it overthrow the Syrian regime, which received a big blow on July 18, 2012, when the FSA claimed responsibility for bombing the National Security Headquarters in Damascus. Four high-ranking members of the regime defense and security offices were killed, including al-Assad's brother-in-law, who was the deputy defense minister, and the defense minister. Other important figures of al-Assad's inner circle were wounded. But the regime survived, and in 2013, it began to retake some of the opposition's strongholds, such as the strategic city of Qusayr, on the Lebanese border, in June. Al-Assad had the help of Hezbollah, a militia that supported the Syrian regime, which a year earlier had publicly denied any involvement in the events in Syria.

By the third year of the Syrian revolution, with the inclusion of many Islamist groups, the FSA had become more of a loose umbrella organization than an organized army. The leading Islamist brigade, Jabhat al-Nusra, was accused of being connected to al-Qaeda in Iraq and thus was declared by the United States and some European countries as a terrorist organization. The Islamic State of Iraq and the Levant (often abbreviated as ISIS, with Levant standing for Sham in Arabic) is another al-Qaeda–linked group, which was active throughout 2013, particularly in taking over the northeastern city of Raqqa after it fell into rebel hands in early March. ISIS caused a furor across the country for forcing its suspicious agendas on the Syrians, clashing with some FSA units, and operating mainly in already liberated areas. Meanwhile, moderate Islamic rebels in the country began uniting in groups like the Islamic Front or Islamic Army, making the fighting force against the regime appear to be largely Islamic. As the war has dragged on, more Syrians have become radicalized and more radical people have entered the country, eclipsing what once was an exclusively peaceful protest movement seeking democracy and the establishment of civil rule and human rights for all Syrians.

A major turning point in Syria was on August 21, 2013, when chemical weapons were used in the Ghouta suburb of Damascus, killing more than fourteen hundred people. Through social media, images and videos of the victims were seen around the world, initiating an international response against the Syrian regime. The Obama administration reacted aggressively because it had earlier warned the regime not to use its chemical weapons, characterized by President Barack Obama as "crossing a red line." Ten days after the incident, which the United Nations had begun investigating, Obama announced that the United States should take action against al-Assad, stating that he would seek Congress's approval before issuing military orders for such an attack. But on September 9, this crisis came to a conclusion when Russia, after negotiating with the Syrian regime, announced that Syria would turn over all its chemical weapons to be destroyed.

Because the United States remained relatively unengaged with the Syrian opposition after this incident, al-Assad seemed to have avoided the second-largest threat to his rule since the uprisings. He repeatedly announced that he would not resign, offering only dialogue with the disorganized opposition. The opposition refused his offer and the fighting continued. UN-brokered peace talks were held in Geneva, Switzerland, in January and February 2014, with the goal of ending the conflict and installing a transitional government. So far, though, Syria remains in a stalemate, with neither side capable of winning the trust of or defeating the other.

SYRIAN WOMEN'S REVOLUTION: THE NEW WOMEN OF QURAISH

Rustum Mahmoud

Writer and researcher on political affairs, male, 29, Qamishli

"I am shamed by the women of Quraish" is a widely used idiom in our popular culture. It has a sense of defiance: a person engages in an act—despite warnings of its dangers and negative effects—and insists on continuing unless he or she is told to retreat or desist. Here, insistence springs from value-based factors or egoism, which gives primacy to values, the actor, or other utilitarian concepts that may lead to retreat. Historically, the source of this idiom is a folktale about the meeting between Prophet Mohammad and Antara ibn Shaddad, whose courage, generosity, and poetry were praised by the Prophet.[1] According to the tale, Antara asked to become a Muslim in order to be more virtuous, although later, after much reflection, he eventually decided against the idea. He told the surprised Prophet: "I am shamed by the women of Quraish, for they might say that Antara became Muslim for fear of being sent to hell." In the Syrian revolution that began six months ago, many women provided other examples of the impetus behind such irrational enthusiasm as that filling Antara. These are the women that I encountered during my participation in the revolution.

THE WOMEN AT THE MINISTRY OF INTERIOR

The first major demonstration in the Syrian revolution, supporting Syria's political prisoners, took place on March 16, 2011, in al-Marja Square in front of
the Syrian Interior Ministry building. I was walking quickly toward the demonstrators as security agents were trying to drag away one of the young people.
I called to them, though without raising my voice, "Excuse me, guys, excuse
me!" Suddenly I felt a huge pain in my back near my left kidney, pain that
stopped the rest of the phrase in my throat. I turned to see the person who
hurt me, but because I was wearing the traditional Kurdish scarf around my
head, I could only partly see the square and the Ministry of Interior Building.
Even though my friend Mazin Darwish was close to me, his voice sounded as
if coming from afar: "Stop it, stop it, guys!" Then the person who had caused
such stifling pain left me there and headed toward Mazin, but someone else
had already put a stick on Mazin's neck and started dragging him. I was struggling between the men and the pain that almost engulfed me. I moved back
toward a corner that was still sunny on that March morning.

In that moment of horror, I suddenly remembered all my loved ones. I took
a deep breath and plunged my head between my fists. The pain in my kidney
subsided and then suddenly stopped. I heard the screams of a child thrown to
the ground. He was our friend Siba's son. A moment earlier, he had been safe
in his father's arms, but now a woman was harboring him in her bosom. I saw
her as five men came at her from different angles, trying to take the child
from her while she seemed as though she was making another lap from her
soul to protect him. They could not lift Siba's child from the lap of the Syrian
novelist, Samar Yazbek, who was protecting him from any possible harm.

I could not see Samar's golden hair because she bent her head down to
protect the child. (A few months earlier, Samar, the author of *Clay*, *The Smell
of Cinnamon*, and *The Sky Girl*, began following an old Bedouin tradition of
not dyeing her hair or using makeup until the sorrow was gone from her country and people.) I could not see her green eyes because all her senses were directed to the child, who became like her own child. The regime attackers finished their assault without harming him. As I got near Samar and tried to check
on the child, she instinctively pushed me away and rewrapped her hands
around him. I smiled to help her calm down, and she exhaled the remaining
air in her chest, air that she perhaps kept in to help the child breathe if he
needed it.

After the second day of the Syrian demonstrations, there was no news
about Samar. How many other children did she want to put in her lap? How

could she live without doing so? Nobody knows. I remember seeing many women like Samar at different moments in the revolution. The demonstration in Marja Square gave recognition to Syrian women, complementing achievements like those of Sara Mu'ayyid al-'Azm,[2] who gave meaning to Syrian political freedom from French colonialism by socially freeing Syria from a Middle Ages mentality.

THE WOMEN OF MIDAN

Because we came from the south side of Damascus, the security forces prevented us from joining the rest of the demonstrators, who came from the north.[3] It was in the afternoon on Wednesday, July 13, 2011, during what was called the "the Battle of the Intellectuals Demonstration." When we got near the crowd, I saw the Syrian actress Mai Skaf, who screamed loudly, and then a skirmish broke out between the crowd and some of the security agents and the *shabiha*, the armed gangs working for the regime. Eyad Sharbaji, a journalist who became a vocal dissident in Syria, reported what happened in those moments:

> The officers asked us who was representing our group. With my colleagues backing me, I went forward and told him in a clear tone that each of us represented himself or herself. They began to look at us in a challenging way, but we did not care. The officer asked us to leave immediately and disperse because we did not have the license to demonstrate. Before we could answer him, one of the *shabiha* rushed forward. Wearing camouflage pants and a sweater emblazoned with the map of Syria and a picture of the president, he started to talk to us in a challenging and provocative voice: "Did you come to destroy the country?" "We came to express our position," I answered him.
>
> He immediately replied: "Then why are you in front of the Hasan Mosque? All the people here are criminals, and I was attacked last week by these dogs that came out of the mosque." I replied: "It seems to me that you do not pray. Can you tell me why you came to the mosque last week?" When I said this, he shook and sparks flew from his eyes. He was preparing to attack me while the officers kept silent and seemed to endorse him. Then Fadi Zeidan, Sasha Ayoub, and Yam Mashhadi rushed to the officers, arguing, "In what capacity is this person speaking to us?' At this point, one of the officers gestured for the *shabiha* member to back off, and he left. But one of them said defiantly to Mai Skaf while making an

indecent gesture to her: "You signed the milk statement, right? You want milk? Let me give you some." Mai Skaf screamed back at him: "Respect yourself . . . we are Syrians just like you." He said back to her: "You are Syrians while you speak badly about our brave military that is killing those bitches?" We all violently disagreed with what he said and started screaming. And another officer pointed to him to keep silent and he did.

In those moments we—our group of about two hundred young men and women—started to retreat. Those who were nearby crowded around Mai Skaf, but they were violently taken by the security agents. We gathered in the main street in Midan and were about 330 feet away from the security agents and the *shabiha*. From that distance we could hear the cries of those being arrested. What made me feel very hurt and scared was the yellow look in the eyes of the residents watching from their balconies. Most of the women spontaneously put their hands over their mouths in shock. A few seconds later, the men rubbed their foreheads. In those harsh moments, our screams gradually increased: "God, Syria, Freedom, and that's enough. God, Syria, Freedom, and that's enough." I had left the people who came with me to Midan. I caught a glimpse of a nearby girl who was biting the edge of a cloth; you could tell by looking at her that she was overwhelmingly conservative. In great panic, she hesitantly stepped in and out of the crowd. I still do not know what caused her to suddenly relax, but her fear subsided. I saw her raise her hands with us, and then a sob escaped her throat and she began to cheer with us.

Meanwhile, security forces arrived in order to divide us; they slowly advanced while we slowly retreated, but then they began rushing, so we hurried up too. As they got close to us, we started to run. I stumbled as I watched where I was going, as did the girl who was near me. The distance between me and the security agents then was about 150 feet, so I went in one of the buildings on the street. Running upstairs to the highest floor, I heard steps behind me on the stairs and started to repeatedly ring the bell of one door. A voice came from behind the door: "Who is it?" I replied, "Please, Aunt. Please let us in," as the steps behind me got closer. I looked down and saw young people like me climbing up the stairs; the woman opened the door and we all entered her house at once. We then sat in the hallway panting, and the woman gave us water, saying, "May Allah protect and save you," before silently sitting down next to us. There was no chance for any conversation. Suddenly a partly veiled girl came out of one room carrying with her a black cloth. She told her mother, "Your headscarf, Mother!" The mother looked at her daughter, took the cloth from her hand quietly, and set it aside without putting it on!! We stayed for a few minutes in silence, and the woman repeated, "May Allah protect and save you."

I thought, "What do Mai Skaf, the young woman, the older woman, and this country all have in common?" Mai Skaf abandoned her acting career because she considered the acting community to be shameful and hypocritical and not worthy of her presence. She then established an acting institute that has dozens of graduates, artists who are committed to people, not to ideology. The conservative woman did not see anything wrong with joining an audience of young people she did not know. I could not find anything they shared except the spirit of this country and the expected meaning of it.

The Women of the Water Hoses

Since the early days of the revolution, we would gather in the afternoon on Fridays in front of Qasmu Mosque located downtown in the Qamishli governorate, an area in northeast Syria that has a majority Kurdish population. Usually the crowd outside the mosque was bigger than the number of people praying inside. We would begin the demonstration after the Friday prayer was over and walk for about a mile toward the western side of the city, along Aamouda Street, which was originally called Hashim al-Atasi Street. Since the beginning of May, the afternoon sun had become increasingly harsh for the demonstrators, with a temperature reaching more than 122°F. In addition to the sun beating down on the demonstrators' faces, their action raised the temperature, as throughout the slow, three-hour march they did not stop raising their hands, bodies, and voices. This continued even during the month of Ramadan, and many of them fainted while marching the one mile. But from the buildings on both sides of the road, women standing at the windows sprayed the demonstrators with water as they marched between Qasmu Mosque and the Hilalyia neighborhood. The demonstrators walked through the water and the shadows, and the women joined in chanting and raising their hands. The women looked elegant as they smiled at the demonstrators and received greetings in return. Sometimes there was more than one woman at the window and they would fight for the water hose, but the most beautiful moment was when they sprayed the water straight up so it came down lightly and slowly on the bodies of demonstrators!

We all are waiting for the day when the municipal authorities in our country spray us with cold water and peace, because we are exhausted, and so are the "water-hose women."

THE ROAD FROM DAMASCUS
TO A'L-QABOUN

Odai Alzoubi

Philosophy student at the University of East Anglia, male, 30, Damascus

I looked around me as if I were seeing my friend's house for the first time. It is located in the heart of Damascus, where a feeling of claustrophobia had settled in the aftermath of the demonstration that we joined on Wednesday, July 13, 2011. Our plan for the day did not completely succeed: We were supposed to meet at my friend's house at the end of the demonstration, but some of us were arrested, and others escaped and disappeared in the alleys. We went to a café instead. I was trying to recover my calm in my own way: sitting silently and drinking coffee. People differ in how they compose themselves: my friend Rami prefers to remain alone, and Wassfi drinks a glass of whiskey.

My friend Awos insisted that we go to dinner. One of my friend's cousins did not want to go, arguing that two of our friends had been arrested and it was not an appropriate time for dinner. Awos was clear and direct in his response: "The revolution can take a long time, maybe another year. We want to live. Do you want us to sit at home every time someone is arrested? No, after the demonstration is over and after two or three days, or maybe a week, our friends will be released." I myself wanted to go to dinner and to stay with my friends. I had almost been arrested in the demonstration and still was terrified. Each demonstration is scary. Fear does not die. Or maybe I was just a coward. There was a young man among us whom I did not know. My friend offered him some whiskey. "Thanks, but I don't drink alcohol," he replied, because he was a practicing Muslim. After the young man was offered a cup of tea, Awos made a decision that concluded our debate and plan for the night: "We will go to the funeral (in al-Qaboun) and then go have dinner."

I left Damascus in September 2010 to study in the United Kingdom. The revolution began in Daraa on March 15, 2011, and I returned to Damascus in early July for a long stay. I had developed an increasing obsession with following news of the revolution, but visiting and participating were two different matters. I saw that Syria and its people were undergoing a remarkable change. Thousands of Syrians had become activists for freedom. Their keyword is freedom, which means to get rid of the head of the regime, Bashar al-Assad. And this freedom got its meaning on the ground, in the streets where masses of people call it out. Syrians do not need books to explain the meaning of freedom; they are working on it and redefining it with their revolution. I understood the meaning of freedom for the first time when I participated, also for the first time, in a demonstration, chanting: "Long live Syria! Let the regime of Bashar al-Assad fall." I could not help but philosophize about this revolution. In fact, it was something like "I participate in the revolution; therefore I exist."

On Sunday, July 17, my friends and I went to a funeral for a martyr in al-Qaboun, a suburb east of Damascus and about twenty minutes from the capital. It was the first funeral I had attended in my entire life. On the way to al-Qaboun, I remembered my father giving me advice about my possible participation in the revolution:

> Odai, I will not tell you what to do. It is your life and you are free to do whatever you want. But if they arrest you, you will not be able to go to Britain to finish your PhD until the revolution is over. And it is possible, God forbid, that something bad will happen to you. I do not want to think about these bad scenarios. Think about your future.

I was careful, but I had gone to Damascus in order to participate in the Syrian revolution. I wrote several articles when I returned to Britain, using my real name and sharing with others what I experienced and what I know, but there is nothing like taking part in demonstrations. They have a major role in the revolution, and in them I felt like a complete human being. But I was scared to go to the funeral because the Syrian security forces had interrupted several of them and arrested or killed dozens of people. In fact, many Syrians go to these funerals as if they are going to a demonstration. Slogans against the regime and fear of arrest are common elements. I asked myself how the martyr's family would feel if the security forces came to the funeral.

I think about the first time, as a boy, I visited al-Qaboun with my mother. The neighborhood is different now. There are checkpoints on the way, even though we got only a meaningless look from a soldier who did not do any checking. When I arrived in al-Qaboun, I parked my car next to the fence of the Police College. I felt nervous when I heard the famous slogan of people wanting to topple the regime. As soon as I got out of my car, I met more than ten of my friends. People there were chanting "Curse your soul, Hafez, curse your soul!" Some people were carrying their mobile phones and taking pictures, so we smiled at the camera and chanted with them. Two days earlier, on July 15—what the Syrian activists called the Friday of Freedom of Prisoners—dozens of people were killed in Damascus, eight of them from al-Qaboun. There were so many people at the funeral, reportedly about fifty thousand opponents of the regime. Unlike the other suburbs of Damascus, like Douma, al-Qaboun has no clear borders with Damascus, which means that the revolution was at the gate of the capital. A young man hugged me as we arrived at the funeral and welcomed me. "We are not terrorists. Bashar al-Assad and his dogs are the terrorists," he said. The funeral had a tent where the family of the martyr and his relatives received people's condolences in person.

After the Friday of Prisoners of Freedom on July 15, al-Qaboun became one of the centers of the Syrian revolution, and when they lost twelve martyrs, it was a big number in the Damascus area, a number exceeded only in catastrophe-stricken Douma, which was under heavy attack by the regime for its people's dissent. At the time, it seemed that President al-Assad was punishing the Syrian people for organizing a conference in Turkey for the opposition. He wanted everything to be under his watch, as if saying to Syrians: "We will kill your sons and daughters if you do not comply." But as I looked around me, seeing thousands of young people opposed to his regime, I felt I heard them saying, "No, Bashar." I felt proud because we, my friends and thousands of young people we had not met before, were making a new Syria and changing its history. The twelve martyrs were not lost; they will stay with us in our hearts.

Before arriving at the tent, we chanted to show our resistance to the regime: "Hey, we don't prostrate ourselves except to Allah," "Death but not humiliation," "Syria is ours, not for al-Assad's family." Thousands of youths were shouting against the regime. Most of them came to the funeral, even though they did not know the martyrs or their families. At the tent, I asked one person: "Where is the family of the martyr so I can express my condolences to them?" He replied: "My brother, we all are family of the martyr." I could not hold back my tears. What a stupid question! There were feelings of joy for being able to demand freedom, the feelings of anger, sadness, and fear expressed in the eyes and trembling hands. I wondered how people could have and express all these different feelings at the same time. People were afraid of the regime's barbaric reprisals. I still think to this day about those people whom I met in al-Qaboun, some of whom were killed later or were captured and tortured.

In these crowds, I rediscovered myself. Revolution, first and foremost, is a liberating act, and I felt that these people were being liberated from tyranny. The Syrian revolution made me fly with joy. I am liberated. I no longer am just a single number in the population of Syria. Each Syrian has discovered his or her potential. They all have faced death, and their voices have shaken the earth under the feet of their oppressors. Tens of people who chanted "Death but not humiliation" have in fact died and became martyrs. But the journey of freedom was continued by other people who followed them. Everyone demonstrating in the street knew that he or she faced death, detention, or torture. But they have never given up. They are liberated from any authority, and they face the regime with all possible means. They have one of two fates: they either will continue rebelling or will abandon the revolution. If the revolution fails, they will pay the price, which they will pay even before the revolution is over. So they have never hesitated to continue.

Syrians also have become liberated from the collective. Each individual chooses his own road. It is true that before it was fueled by thousands of detainees, missing people, and martyrs, the instigators of the revolution were the children of Daraa. The revolution has a straightforward and simple moral purpose, which is that we will not accept the killing of our brothers who peacefully demonstrate in the streets. What unites us with the rest of the Syrians is our common sense of dignity. Every Syrian citizen is a symbol for each and every one of us. Each martyr is from us and will remain with us. For the revolutionaries, the Syrian citizen has the highest value. But all martyrs have a special value, and their fathers and mothers refuse to abandon them. We will always have hope for a better Syria. In the crowds, I rediscovered myself, asking, "What binds me to these people I do not know?" It is obviously a decision we made together, to oppose the regime. We were shouting, "Long live Syria, let the regime of Bashar al-Assad fall." Whether in Homs, Daraa, or other stricken Syrian cities and towns, these people have the same goal, for which they face live ammunition.

I was thinking how the individual (the president) also lost the collective people. Total loneliness has been the obsession of many intellectuals and thinkers. The Japanese short story writer and novelist Kawabata Yasunari wrote about the feeling of loneliness while one is still surrounded by people. A story in one of his books, *Palm-of-the-Hand Stories*, is about a married woman waiting for her husband. She feels lonely even though she has people around her. I smiled happily at this thought and remembered the lyrics of the famous Lebanese singer Fairouz: "On the crossroad, people are waiting for others. It rains, and they are still waiting for them. But in the fair weather, nobody is waiting for me." The Japanese author and the Lebanese singer demonstrate loneliness, the harsh fate awaiting those who are doomed, those who think they are above the people.

I believe that the Arab Spring has some philosophical dimensions that merit contemplating. In the West, individuality is deeply rooted in the culture, and although it frees the individual from the authority of the group, it probably leaves him or her alone. Here in the East, the individual is still under the authority of the collective. The Arab Spring is the first attempt to form an individualistic concept of the human being. Can Arabs avoid the sin of individuality? I answer myself with a smile and with a yes. Years ago, before my trip to Britain, I was reading Henrik Ibsen and John Stuart Mill. I did not understand then their criticism of twentieth-century individualism. For me, at the time, I thought that we in the Arab world needed a large dose of individuality so we could unleash the possibilities of the Arab individual. After two years in Britain, I learned a lot and felt sorry for those in Europe who live in isolation. It is probably because I am a talkative person and always in need of company, and in Britain I missed the crowds, the noise, and the curious people. In sum, I lost human communication with the collective.

Can the Arab Spring create an innovative vision of the problematic relationship between the individual and the collective? Yes. These individuals do not exhibit an ideology, not even a masked or hidden one. They do not fight in the name of any ideology, either. In other words, they are not leftists, Marxists, or Islamists. The Arab Spring is actually driven by love, not ideology. The people have love for other people, for the collective. They have love and desire for a decent life for themselves and their fellow citizens. No leaders or parties or programs are behind the revolutions of the Arab Spring—only love in the heart of every individual participating in it.

Am I exaggerating? In this historic moment, perhaps there is nothing wrong with overstatement. The world is changing, so let's hope. Day after day, the revolutionaries prove that they will not allow anybody to steal their dreams. From Tunisia to Egypt, the revolution is not over yet. It is continuing. What is important is that the Arab individuals in the street will never return home satisfied with what their leaders tell them. The Arab individual is changing the concept of citizenship. Now every citizen is responsible. It is a historic moment, and these young people in al-Qaboun, Homs, Daraa, and Banias are making the future as well.

When I went to the Ghouta, the agricultural area surrounding Damascus, I saw uprisings in the rural areas. I realized that history is waking up. History seems too unclear for our tyrant—he thinks that he will write the conclusion of these events. He thinks that he is our history. But Syrians will write another history. We always write the beginnings. We have the oldest city and capital, Damascus, and we have the first alphabet in the world. We do not write endings because the future is ours. The future is a beginning, and we are good at beginnings. But our dictator has a history full of endings. Damascus is a beginning, and its tyrant is an ending. There is no sublime beginning for the tyrant, and there is no tragic end for Damascus. We will survive.

After participating in this revolution with my soul and mind, I left Damascus on Monday, August 1, which also was the first day of the month of Ramadan. In the evening I reached Liverpool Street Station in London. The last time I heard the news I felt optimistic, as the revolution had spread to many cities in Syria. Hama and Deir al-Zour joined the revolution and were somehow free from the regime's control. I felt that life was smiling at us and that the regime would not be able to break the will of the Syrians. I knew that the only option for the regime was to send the military to attack civilians. I thought that the regime might not do that for fear of unmanageable defections. But I knew that Syrians would pay a high price if this happened. I was sure that the revolution had successfully passed the first stage and that what we needed was for Aleppo and Damascus to join.

While waiting for the train to Norwich, I felt tired as I tried to collect my thoughts. I was thinking about how to continue my studies and research in addition to helping the revolution all I could. I looked at the TV screen, which usually shows silly ads with sexy girls trying to convince us to eat McDonald's or buy Kia cars. But this time I did not see scantily clad girls or the nymphs, as one my friends calls them. I became anxious as I moved closer to the big screen. I saw images of bombings and artillery damage caused by the Syrian army. There also were dead bodies on the ground. I could not believe what I saw. The Syrian army had stormed into Hama and killed more than a hundred civilians. The number of wounded was unknown. I sat on the ground of the station in humility, helpless, tears pouring from my eyes like a child. People cry when they have no substitute or anything else to do. I was crying in a way that does not represent who I am. I could not believe what was happening and was unable to think. Hama, again! I calmed down for few seconds and listened to the news anchor, who said that nobody expected Hama to be invaded by the military because it had been destroyed in the 1980s. All signs indicated that the regime would try to control Homs and Deir al-Zour and avoid Hama. I burst into tears again. "Oh my God. The regime decided to fight until the end."

A week later, the army entered Deir al-Zour, then the villages of Idlib and Homs. I realized that Syrians needed to prepare for a long and bloody battle. After the storming of Hama, I published my first article using my real name. Then I wrote more articles opposing the rule of the Ba'th Party in my country. My friends did so as well, even before I started. We all believe that part of the revolution is to tell the regime that we are not afraid of its power. If the revolution fails, we will pay the price. There are no compromises or half solutions. The Syrian people know that they are betting on their future. The regime adopted a strategy of sowing fear among people by kidnapping and torturing activists, besieging cities, and intimidating the rebels' families. In short, it followed the strategy of destroying livelihoods and killing people. But the Syrian revolution will have the reverse effect: the greater the regime's oppression is, the greater participation in the revolution will be.

When oppression is intense, there is a need for truth. Wisdom appears in the face of evil and people are reborn. Thousands of ordinary people became heroes in every sense of the word. I learned a great deal of wisdom from them. The revolution taught me to resist with what I have and can do. We are not seeking a war and will not get into a civil war, because of the wisdom of our people on the ground. We may fail, but we do not really care about the results. We are following the light, and in the revolution there is always a clear vision: right is clear and wrong is clear. We know what to do, and this tree of knowledge has been baptized with Syrian blood. I learned not to compromise and to be decisive in standing for what I see as right. It seems to me that an entire generation of Arabs has learned the meaning of action. We will act to become free and will not forget the thousands of martyrs and detainees and missing persons. As part of the Arab Spring, young Arabs have become active agents. We will not be marginalized again.

FREEDOM AND NOTHING ELSE

Hani al-Furati

Teacher, male, 31, Deir al-Zour

The city of Deir al-Zour, just like the entire region around the Euphrates River, is magnificent. But this eastern part of Syria suffers from poverty and unemployment: 40 percent of its young people are in other countries looking for jobs. Most of the people in the towns work in agriculture, and some of them are expatriates living abroad to support their families. Both the educated and the uneducated people in this area seek jobs in the oil-producing states in the Arabian Gulf, even though they come from a place that produces oil and is rich in agricultural and dairy products. The regime made Deir al-Zour a forgotten city, even though it is considered economically viable with its enormous human and natural resources. For the last forty years, the authoritarian regime tried to buy loyalty; it wanted to enslave people and make them subservient. As a result, corruption and the backwardness caused by the regime prevailed in this eastern region of Syria.

The people of Deir al-Zour are generally passionate and emotional. As the city's revolution coordination group, we wanted them to boycott the regime, but they joined the revolution by demonstrating. We worked hard to achieve this goal, which could affect the regime's economic viability, by writing about the benefits of isolating the regime. But many people and even activists did not know about the positive aspects of this strategy. I talked to many people in the city, urging them to boycott: "Why don't we stop using the mobile phones for one hour? Why don't we voluntarily close the stores for an hour? Why don't we boycott the traders of Aleppo, the influential city that did not join the revolution?"

As activists, we continued to try to enlighten our people and encourage them to be more effective. One of our ideas was to have a demonstration *in* the Euphrates River, which passes through the city, close to downtown. We successfully carried out our "water demonstration." I personally participated in this innovative protest by using a boat brought by one of my friends from the family of the martyr Abdel Moneim Alhbashan, who was killed by security agents on Monday, June 6, 2011. We went under the Deir al-Zour Suspension Bridge, which was built in the 1920s when Syria was under the French mandate. We held up a placard that read: "The Orontes River and the Euphrates hug each other," showing our support for the cities of Homs and Hama through which the Orontes passes and where the demonstrations were constantly stifled by the regime.

In September 2011, we were patrolling our neighborhood, al-Rashidyia, and giving food to the youths who joined the revolution. There were some men watching the barriers that we built to prevent the regime thugs and snipers from entering the areas of the demonstrations. We were targeted by security agents, and the bullets directed at me hit a phone booth. My neighbor's son, Zahir Suleiman, was hit in the chest but miraculously survived. The medical committees played a crucial role in the revolution and the people in the streets appreciated their assistance, but the regime was always targeting them. Its security forces arrested a number of my friends who are doctors and treated those injured in the demonstrations. The regime was following all the uprisings, trying to quash them by any means. Once I was walking by a local market and saw some young people smashing the pictures and symbols of the regime. Suddenly they were hit by a barrage of live ammunition. I ran away and hid in one of the market entrances as I watched security agents beat the young people. I also heard them say, "You 'Adnan al-'Arrour dogs want to topple our leader? Allah will fall, but Bashar will not."[4]

The first day of July 2011 was a Friday, and in the tradition of the Syrian revolution, every Friday has a name. This Friday was labeled *irhal* Friday, the "Friday of Get Out." This day had a great impact on me and my friends in the city. We went out from Hamidi Mosque, which is in the heart of Deir al-Zour next to a military security unit and is the place where the governor and some officials used to pray. That is why no demonstration before had been started from this mosque, even though almost all the other mosques had witnessed uprisings. We were proud that we could organize a demonstration from Hamidi Mosque that Friday. We moved our march to Freedom Square and distributed red cards to the participants (the same cards used in soccer matches to indicate that a fouled player has been ejected from the game), indicating our message that the dictator Bashar al-Assad should get out.

On August 19, military security called me at my house and interrogated me. At the end of the call, they asked me to come to their center the next day, threatening me if I even thought about not following their orders. If I did not appear in their office, I was told, they knew how to find me and would bring me there themselves. After this warning, I was worried and feared that they would hurt my family or our house if I did not go, so I went to see them, which was the start of my long detention. They had indicated on the phone that the interrogation would be only one or two hours long and that nothing else would happen to me. After I arrived, they began questioning me, showing some flexibility as I discussed the peacefulness of our activities. The interrogations lasted for two days, one full hour on the first day and seven hours on the second. Some of the questions were, "How much money did you get? Was Nawaf al-Bashir giving you money? Do you know Caesar Hindawi? Why did you write on walls inciting people to riots and revolution? What are the comments you published on Facebook?"[5] I remember replying to the detective's questions with the following statement:

> Sir, in Great Britain a black man was killed unjustly and many people stepped in to protest this act. Why is Syrian blood irresponsibly shed in the streets? As a protester, I did not see any armed protesters in the demonstrations. Why do we have reforms on paper but none in practice? Why isn't the security agent a friend to the citizen, not a monster? We are not against any person who governs Syria, but our peaceful protests were strongly suppressed and the chaos increased. Why is there no serious dialogue initiated by the authorities? Mr. Detective, why do you suppress our demonstrations by using only boiling water and rubber bullets?

Of course, he was annoyed and embarrassed by what I said.

After the interrogation was over, I was transferred to another detention center and saw prisoners of all ages, young and old, from all the Syrian governorates. One day they brought in an eighteen-year-old man who, we later learned, was the only son with nine sisters in his family. His name was Talal al-Nuoman and he lived in Damascus. He came to Deir al-Zour to take a physics exam at his college, and he was an excellent student. After they arrested him, they tortured and beat him and left him for dead. In the military security center, he thought he would die, so he told us his will or "last words," asking us to pass them on to his mother and his family. We started to bang on the door of our jail to ask that they bring a doctor to save his life. All that they eventually gave him were some painkillers; he remained unconscious for three days. To our surprise, his health improved significantly and he did not die. After staying in this center for some time, they transferred me to Damascus to the intelligence center called the Palestine branch. There, I experienced the malice of those infidels who severely beat me and insulted me. They burned my skin with cigarette butts and broke my fingers.

You might ask: Why did we start the protests and the revolution? The answer is two words or terms, which day after day have become the source of love and encouragement for Syrians: the Arab Spring and revolution. Daraa began the revolution, and my city, Deir al-Zour, did not stand by as a mere observer. Rather, we joined the revolution at its inception on March 15. As a result of their hatred for the regime, the people of Deir al-Zour held their first demonstration on March 22. I participated in this demonstration, which started at Mufti Mosque at the city's southern entrance and went down Dalla Street. We were quickly dispersed by the regime's thugs, who were Ba'thists and beneficiaries of the regime, which included the members of two proregime families. They attacked more than thirty protesters with sticks and knives.

Then more demonstrations were held. On Friday, April 1, we had a big demonstration that was coordinated with many activist groups in the city and the villages, including students and media professionals. We held up placards and marched from Uthman ibn Affan Mosque, which was later targeted by the regime's military tanks. Even though we numbered more than four hundred, I was surprised that the number was still so small, which was because the barrier of fear had not been broken yet. The thugs of the Syrian regime tried to take advantage of our demonstration by bringing proregime people to mix in with the demonstration to portray the protests as rallies in support of the regime. They also beat some of my friends, arrested others, and tracked down and followed many of us. Some of my arrested friends were Firas al-Aani, an agricultural engineer, and Mohammed Slaibi, an employee in the health department.

Antiregime groups in Syria called Friday, April 22, "Great Friday," and it was indeed a great day in the city of Deir al-Zour. We had more people participating and many demonstrations in different parts of the city. Demonstrations started after the Friday prayer at several mosques. Downtown, forty thousand protesters reached the statue of Basel al-Assad, the late son of the former president Hafez al-Assad. Despite the presence of security forces and informants, we stood together and chanted peaceful slogans, some of them in support of the cities where the regime had cracked down. Some of these chants were "From Deir al-Zour to Banias: Syrian people will not be humiliated," "O Daraa, we are with you until death," "We are Deirians (from Deir al-Zour) and we do not betray others, but we break the heads of those who challenge us."

But as usual, the security forces attacked us and provoked the assembled protesters, who in return threw stones at them and wounded several of them. I gave some medical assistance to two people wounded by the security agents, who did not use live ammunition against us this time, particularly because the regime had declared the end of emergency law the day before. Some of the young men bravely mounted the statue of Basel al-Assad and burned it after it fell to the ground. Hundreds of young people were arrested after this demonstration because agents had taken pictures of them. They were tortured and humiliated in different security headquarters, and some were threatened with dismissal from their government jobs. I myself was dismissed from my job as a teacher. But we, about thirty of us who were coordinating and organizing the revolution in our city, stood firm to achieve our goal: freedom for our people. More demonstrations followed after the fall of the city's first martyr, Muaaz al-Rakadh, who was killed in early June. His death spurred on the demonstrations, and more people were killed. We had many sit-ins in different areas of the city, such as Freedom Square and the Madlaji neighborhood, and many men and women participated in them.

I want to conclude with an anecdote. When I was arrested, I was in a cell in the basement of the security prison, alone and unable to see the light or know the time, except when I heard the call to prayers coming from nearby mosques. (Sometimes my jailers, even though they were cruel, told me the time.) I looked around and saw the walls of the room covered with writings by the prisoners before me. Some of the writings were sublimations and Qur'anic verses. Reading them in my solitude gave my tired soul a great deal of inner piece. I still remember some of them: "Have no grief, for Allah is with us," which is from the Qur'an, and proverbs like "Patience is the key to happiness." One person wrote, "I have cried for long years for my children and my mother." There were so many phrases and verses from the Qur'an that at first I could not find space to write anything. But when I found a tiny spot, I took a piece of the tin plate on which they gave us food and sharpened it to engrave on the wall my signature: "The coordination of the revolutionary youth of the revolution Deir al-Zour. We will not bow down except to Allah. Freedom, and nothing else."

A STORY FROM HOMS

Mohammed Kadalah

Student, male, west of Homs

At the beginning of the revolution, on February 15, the people, mainly young, answered the call to start the Syrian Day of Anger. In my hometown, about five hundred people gathered in the main street for about an hour, and then it was over. Actually, that gathering was extremely dangerous because we had never before publicly criticized the government. However, nothing bad happened, and we felt that we had done our part to start the Syrian revolution. Even though I was busy at that time, I felt extremely happy that we could challenge our fear and the government as well.

The demonstrations in Syria started after the intelligence forces and the secret police attacked the city of Daraa, in southern Syria, after calls for political and civil reforms. Hundreds were killed at the hands of the intelligence forces, and we decided to express our anger at what had happened. People felt it was cowardly to remain silent while our brothers in Daraa were being mercilessly killed. We are the sort of people who refuse any kind of tyranny and brutality. It was very difficult to think of something like demonstrations, because the government had already started killing all the protesters in Daraa, and we knew that this might happen to us. But in those few days, we decided anyway to demonstrate against the killing in Daraa because we felt that it was our responsibility to stand by our brothers and support them by whatever means possible and to have the courage to challenge the government and its police and intelligence departments. By the way, my hometown, which has a population of only fifty thousand people, has six police and intelligence centers.

Demonstrating was a brand-new strategy because the government had been suppressing any kind of opposition. We had no previous experience with demonstrations, but we wanted to create our own, which brought massive destruction to my hometown. We gathered after one Friday prayer late in March and began our demonstration, calling for freedom, political reform, and a stop to the killing in Daraa. The participants were of all ages, and everyone wanted to speak his or her mind and join in the call for freedom. The people were very enthusiastic and excited that their voices might reduce the regime's brutality against Daraa. The police were shocked that the people of my hometown made that extremely dangerous decision to demonstrate against the government because in Syria, we were not used to demonstrating at all. The head of the police department came to the demonstration and started to talk with the people about why they were demonstrating. He told us, "Please let me know what your demands are, and I will do my best to meet them, and I will call the leadership about them, but please go home and stop demonstrating."

We were surprised by how kind he was, and we hoped that the government would stop the killing in Daraa, although we already knew that the officer would do nothing because he had no power to do so and because he was a hypocrite. After that, we demonstrated every Friday for three weeks, but the killing did not stop; on the contrary, it spread to other cities, mainly Homs. The demonstrations were all we could do to support our people in the other cities. So we started to demonstrate more than once a week and gathered in one main place. At every demonstration, we called for freedom, reform, a stop to the killing, and a better country. We also sang and listened to speeches and poems mourning the martyrs in Homs, Daraa, and other Syrian cities. We were peaceful, which we decided was the best way to express our opinions and calls for freedom. At the end of each demonstration, we prayed to Allah to protect our people and have mercy on us and the martyrs.

Most of the time, these peaceful demonstrations were led by the educated people in my town: a pharmacist, a dentist, university graduates, and students. The demonstrations were going well, with no attacks by the police forces. But the police used to spread rumors that the army and intelligence would attack the town as they did in Daraa and Homs, which meant that a lot of people would be killed. Every time people heard that rumor, most of them, out of fear for their lives, would close their shops and markets and go home. Then it would turn out to be just a rumor. But people's fearful reactions indicate how severe that rumored attack might have been and also how brutal the army had been in Daraa, Homs, Latakia, and other cities.

Then what we expected did happen. On April 27, the police arrested the imam of the town's main mosque because he had participated in the demonstration. In fact, the imam was not only the leader of the prayers in the mosque, but he was also one of the most distinguished people in town, and most people liked and had great respect for him. Everyone was angered by this, so they decided to demonstrate and call for his release. To our surprise, the government had brought in police from the air intelligence forces—one of Syria's most brutal intelligence departments.

They started shooting the protesters with live rounds. The gunfire was quite heavy and lasted for five hours. The protesters ran away, and the demonstration ended, but the firing continued for such a long time because the police wanted to terrorize everyone and send a message: This is what will happen if you continue to demonstrate against the government. I will never forget that day; the firing continued into the night. The police also shot randomly at houses to terrorize residents. My house was shot at and one window was broken, but thanks to Allah, we were in another room. On the second day, the air intelligence forces left town, assuming that we would not demonstrate again, but they were wrong; we began demonstrating again on the same day they left. We had not expected to be targets of the police and their brutality. We had nothing to deserve that attack; we were peaceful and we called to stop the killing and for the regime to fall, but nothing changed and the Syrian forces became more merciless each day. We called for the president to leave, for a democracy in which to choose our future president freely, and for an end to police intervention in civilian life and control of every aspect of our social and political life. We asked that corruption end and that the police and army officers who had killed innocent people be brought to justice, but none of that happened.

Then, in the middle of May, the news spread that the regime had decided to attack the town with tanks and huge numbers of troops; it was no longer a rumor. The troops arrived at the border of my hometown and started attacking us with tank bombs. I was asleep, and a very large explosion woke me up. Everyone was terrified, and most people tried to escape for other towns or to Lebanon, which is close by. The government also blocked the Internet, cell phones, and landline phones. Meanwhile, the army surrounded the town from all sides with tanks and thousands of soldiers. My family decided to stay home, but we could not see the troops and the tanks because they all were still on the outskirts of town. Periodically, the shooting stopped.

Then my neighbor, who is a taxi driver and had already been outside the town, came home in the evening and told us that he had seen more than one hundred tanks surrounding the town from one side only. He added that more tanks were in other parts of the town. We expected the worst and decided to escape immediately and go elsewhere, to a relative's house, which was not far away. The trip there seemed endless. When we left, we were afraid because we had to pass through several checkpoints. At any moment, we could be shot dead—not by a gun but by a tank bomb. The atmosphere was full of fear, danger, and prayers to Allah that we would be able to get out safely. We were stopped at two checkpoints, and fortunately, for some reason, which I still don't know, they allowed us to leave without causing us any trouble. My guess is that those soldiers were, among many others, forced to participate in this attack and that they let us through because they knew that what the army was planning to do was totally wrong.

That night, the soldiers launched the main attack. I could hear the sounds of the bombs and the tanks' heavy shooting. It was a horrible night.

The shooting lasted for more than five hours and stopped at three in the morning. Before that, another cruel thing happened: those who fled to Lebanon had to use a road overlooked by a progovernment village. The villagers started shooting at the fleeing people, and they shot dead a mother and her son. As a result, people tried to avoid using that road or even driving. Instead, they walked through the fields for almost three to four miles till they reached the Lebanese border.

My hometown is surrounded by a number of villages, most of which support the government. The army made use of this fact and attacked my town from those villages. In addition, the army gave Kalashnikov and PKC rifles to those villagers who participated in the attack. We were attacked by the army and our neighboring villagers, who decided to become yet another killing machine.

On the second day of the attack, the army finished surrounding the town and started shooting again, but this time the shooting was from all sides and lasted all day, but with short respites. On that particular day, the many people who had not been able to escape the day before decided to leave on the second day. But by then, the army forces were everywhere. The people who fled had to pass through army checkpoints; they were humiliated, beaten, and insulted by the soldiers before being allowed to leave town. When the army entered our village, they arrested people in their homes and took them to the National Hospital, which had been turned into a military base for the army. People were humiliated in the worst ways one could ever imagine. The army did not even give water to them unless they agreed to "sacrifice their lives for the sake of President Bashar Assad."

Even proregime doctors and nurses helped torture those arrested. The doctors held guns while nurses assaulted the wounded; one of them took her high-heeled shoe and hit one man in his eye, which bled and he went blind. After that, citizens were taken to proregime villages. The people of those villages also tortured the arrested people, stamping on their faces and backs, urinating on them, and insulting their honor by calling their mothers and sisters names. Another man, a lawyer, was arrested when he tried to escape town, and out of hatred, a soldier killed the man by smashing his head with large rock. The man died instantly. What was really painful and shocking to me was that three friends of mine were shot several times. Soldiers arrested them and, because they still were alive, handed them over to the intelligence forces, who executed them mercilessly.

That was the most horrible thing that happened. I used to hear that the army was executing the wounded, and I suspected, and later discovered, that the Syrian army and intelligence forces were much more brutal than anyone could ever imagine and that they would do anything to suppress the revolution. My cousin, who was waiting for his brother outside their house, was shot in his hand and thigh by a sniper, who, fortunately, missed his head.

The army left our town after killing more than twenty people and arresting about a thousand. When people returned from Lebanon and other Syrian cities, they suffered at the hands of the soldiers at the checkpoints, who opened fire randomly in order to terrorize the town's inhabitants. They also conducted raids and arrested innocent civilians. It was a situation from hell. Consequently, people stayed in their homes most of the time in order to avoid being shot.

My family stayed out of town for two weeks, which were the longest days in my whole life. Everything we heard while we were away came from people who had been able to escape. Our town was being bombed by tanks, and many people were arrested. Since my family had escaped to a nearby village, I could hear the sounds of the extremely heavy shooting very clearly, especially at night. On the sixth day, the army left, leaving casualties in their wake. They abandoned several checkpoints, instead arresting people who had demonstrated against the regime or were suspected of having done so. For these reasons, I could not go home for almost two months.

I had to stay in an apartment in the city of Homs for fear that I might be arrested and because I wanted to continue working on my thesis. I even tried to avoid passing by any checkpoints in Homs for fear that I might be arrested. I also usually walked instead of taking buses or taxis because the forces often stopped them and asked the passengers for their IDs. I walked only on streets with no known checkpoints. That was the only way to avoid arrest, especially when I knew that the intelligence forces were looking for anyone from my hometown who had fled to Homs. I was restless and afraid of arrest during those two months because arrest could mean death. I prayed to Allah that I and my family would be safe.

Despite everything that had happened, I joined my friends in Homs and participated in demonstrations there. Although I was afraid of being arrested, my belief in the revolution and my trust in Allah pushed me to continue. Yes I was afraid, but I also believed that it was time for Syria to change into a better, freer, and more democratic place and that I had to help build my new country, which was being born again. Whenever I remember what happened, I just say "Alhamdulillah" (thanks to Allah) because escaping both the town and arrest was like a miracle. But the most impressive and thrilling miracle was that the Syrian revolution has continued despite the killing. Although I was in very dangerous situations that could have cost me my life, I knew that I was not more valuable than the martyrs who gave their lives for the sake of all Syrians.

THE FIRST STEPS TOWARD DEMOCRACY

Bishr Said

Arabic copywriter, male, 35, Damascus

The roots of the Syrian Arab Spring can be traced back to the moment of *tawreeth*, the inheritance of the presidency in Syria, a nightmare that Syrians feared before it happened and that later became both a reality and a torment for all Arabs living in republican states. The citizens of these republics worried that the same fate would befall them. In 2000, the Syrian regime could get away with this unprecedented transition of power to Bashar al-Assad after his father, Hafez, died while in office. In the same year, the Damascus spring began after the young president took control of the country with promises of a new Syria. As a response to Bashar al-Assad's promises of reform, civil society groups and forums emerged in the capital to establish a new democratic era in Syria.

The Damascus spring phenomenon was over by 2001, when the regime shut down these societies and put many of the members in prison. So we Syrians did not see any of these reforms materialize, and the few freedoms that had been given to us upon the arrival of President Bashar al-Assad were abruptly taken away. The regime also took advantage of the U.S. invasion of Iraq in 2003 by enhancing its authority over Syrians. When the Bush administration threatened that Syria might be a target after Iraq, the regime silenced every call for reform during that time on the pretext that the country was resisting foreign intervention in the region.

In 2005, opposition intellectuals released a statement called the "Damascus Declaration for Democratic National Change." This declaration was signed by more than two hundred Syrian activists; some belonged to organized opposition groups and some were independent figures. The Damascus Declaration, which was directed at the regime on behalf of the Syrian people, sought democratic change in the country and demanded political reform. Even though the statement made only modest and legitimate demands, the regime did not respond or even pay attention to them. In 2006, however, the regime took yet another advantage of the Israel's war with Lebanon, exercising more pressure and suppressing any opposition activities. Then in 2008, many of the most prominent opposition leaders in charge of drafting the Damascus Declaration were imprisoned shortly after they held a conference at the house of one of them, in the suburbs of Damascus. The Syrian regime was constantly taking advantage of regional events, using them as opportunities to oppress and control people. In contrast, the regime missed several opportunities for reform, which the opposition had already tried to start.

After the revolution began in Tunisia, the Syrian president was interviewed on January 31, 2011, by the *Wall Street Journal*. He stated that the Arab Spring would not come to Syria and that we needed to be realistic and wait for another generation to bring reform. But I and my fellow activists could not accept waiting another generation for reform; we insisted that it start now. President Bashar al-Assad's statements in this interview incited me to participate in the sit-in that took place in front of the Interior Ministry in Damascus on March 16. I felt that perhaps there was a chance to set the wheels in motion. We counted on the president's prediction in an earlier interview that if reforms were delayed, people would be expected to express their dissatisfaction. The sit-in I was part of was based on a call by a group of human rights activists. They used media communication networks and social networking to announce the event, which also was mentioned in news broadcasts by Al Jazeera. The pressing reason for the sit-in was to submit a letter to the Interior Ministry for the release of political prisoners in Syria.

Security forces cracked down on our sit-in and treated us harshly. I was arrested with six of my friends, two of whom were women; one was five months pregnant. During the arrest, they did not beat us, although many other participants were assaulted. But my friends and I were beaten at the security center where we spent twenty-four hours before they transferred us to a prison. The beating I received in the center did not reach the degree of brutal torture. During their investigation, I was very honest in answering the questions they asked me. I told the security investigator all my demands, including my objection to the lack of freedoms and democracy and the problem of corruption.

The next day, they transferred us to the Justice Palace, a building in downtown Damascus belonging to the judiciary, not the security forces. When we gathered in front of the judge, fourteen men and ten women were detained for the same charges. The judge recited a variety of charges. When my turn came, he told me, "You are accused of harming the sovereignty of the Syrian state." I answered him by saying, "On the contrary, I did what I did to guarantee a better sovereignty for my country. If the state frees the political prisoners of conscience, it will enhance its sovereignty." After the session was over, we ended up being locked in the same prison where the political prisoners, whose freedom we had sought, were detained! We stayed there for two weeks.

In the prison, I was placed a cell with twenty other young men. Some of them were medical school students and others were studying engineering, and they came from different regions of Syria and different backgrounds. Two of them had been only bystanders and were arrested with us even though they had not participated in the sit-in or the demonstration! During this time, we talked with one another in what can be described as a two-week session of political brainstorming and intellectual exchange. We performed our Friday prayers in the prison, which was a chance to meet with all the other prisoners in one place.

Some people who support the regime claim that the revolution is a conspiracy. I do not agree with them. But even if it is a conspiracy or plot against Syria, I believe that the most important player is the regime itself, as its actions have contributed to the success of this alleged conspiracy to devastate the country. There were many solutions for the crisis before it got out of control, and the regime could have avoided much of what happened later. But it did not.

Nonetheless, the revolutionaries themselves have helped tarnish the image of our revolution. Some of them have started breaking such taboos as "Do not criticize the revolution," and some opposition groups accuse others of treason if they do not agree with them. Other groups reject any criticism directed at their practices. Sometimes if someone refuses to call for the regime's downfall of the regime, he or she is immediately accused of betraying the revolution. If someone does not say that we want to hang the president, then he or she is not brave. This happens even on social media: If someone criticizes the revolution on Facebook, some people cannot choose "like" because their other friends are in favor of the revolution. They cannot tolerate criticism, and they consider it a crime unless it is directed against the regime. I think this means that we have replaced an idol, the regime, with a set of idols, the regimes of the revolution, instead of breaking and ceasing to worship any idols.

The Syrian revolution broke through the wall of fear, and as activists, we need to have the courage to lead the revolution, to be in front of the people. But too much courage will leave us out in front with nobody else behind us. I personally can accept all the slogans calling for freedom, democracy, and a civil state, but I cannot accept slogans that insult the president or threaten him with penalty of death because these do not accord with my democratic, civilized goals. Furthermore, I do not chant the insulting slogans if I cannot take responsibility for them if interrogated in the security centers, in front of a judge, or before Allah.

Recently an activist I know was called to one of the branches of state security. The interrogator asked him, "Do you have Internet?" He said, "Yes." "Do you have a Facebook account?" He said, "Yes." Then he asked him about the main reason for his arrest, "Do you participate with activist groups in the revolution?" He said, "Yes." "Do you support the revolution?" He said, "Yes." The interrogator was holding some documents to shove in his face if he denied any of the things he was asked about, but when the activist confirmed all his opposition activities, the documents became worthless. He also was asked, "Do you want to overthrow the regime?" He said, "Yes." "What about the Syrian National Council? He said, "It has problems, but it is the best possible option for the opposition." His interrogation lasted for six hours, but he was allowed to go home because he was truthful when questioned about his role in the revolution. He did not think that they would release him, and he thought his statements would make his release impossible. In fact, he told me that he said what he said because he was ready to die. I do not claim that all people who are arrested will face the same treatment and will be released, but this kind of honesty, regardless of its outcome, is missing today in our revolution.

I refuse to depict the regime as a beast. If you say that these men of the regime are beasts, then you are not looking for a solution; rather, you want to kill the "beast." This person whom some antiregime people wanted to call a beast was in fact a Syrian citizen who went to school with us. We need to deal with one another with honesty. Our slogans at the beginning of the revolution were something like "Death but not humiliation." What I understand from some of the current slogans is that we will have either a civil war or death.

As I have repeatedly said to my friends and family, I am ready to die for democracy, but I am not ready to die to bring death to someone or for someone to become the new ruler of Syria. I believe that if every citizen is honest, our cause will be clear and there will be no confusion about the Syrian revolution. I do not want to kill anybody, and I do not want to persecute anybody. All I want is freedom and democracy for all people. I assume that many Syrian people have been left behind by the revolution, but that is because we have been too far ahead of them. So we need to slow down in this continuing revolution.[6]

A SMALL COMMUNITY OF GREAT SYRIAN REVOLUTIONARIES

Amer Mahdi Doko

Activist and military defector, male, 31, Daraya, a Damascus suburb

The Arab Spring was a big surprise for those who never believed in the will of the people. On the contrary, it came as a dream come true for those who always believed in and worked for change. I was one of those who believed in change. I know deep down inside me that the day will come when we are free. All the suffering from oppression will end. For me, there has always been a small light at the end of the tunnel, even when all my friends started losing hope. I have always believed that we can be what we want to be. I also know that freedom has a price, and I personally have been, and always will be, ready to pay that price for the future of my people and a better future for humankind.

I still remember the day when Sheikh Rashid Ghanoshi of Tunis cried when watching a video of a free Tunisian citizen expressing his happiness that Zine el-Abidine Ben Ali had fled the country (January 14, 2011) and that Tunisia had become free of its dictator. I could not stop listening to his words, so I kept playing that movie clip over again and again.

I also still remember the day (February 11, 2011) when Hosni Mubarak stepped down and the Egyptian people celebrated in Tahrir Square. That moment I cried, and my mother saw my tears of joy. She probably sensed what freedom meant to me and my generation when she saw my tears. I was mesmerized in front of the television and laptop following news feeds with all the updates from television, Facebook, and Twitter. It felt like the whole world was celebrating with our Egyptian brothers. We Syrians have always felt close to Egypt in many ways but probably were a couple of years behind. The question that stayed in the minds of a huge number of Syrians, especially young Syrians, was, Why don't we have something like that? Why can't we get rid of our regime from which we have been suffering oppression and corruption since the 1960s? But neither I nor other Syrians could ignore the fact, which we used to believe, that our regime was more brutal and oppressive than those in other Arab states. I also was not sure how we could even start a revolution that would continue the highly celebrated Arab Spring. All I knew was that we should do something. What happened in Tunisia and Egypt was an opportunity, and we needed to use it to begin our own revolution.

I should mention that these thoughts about change were not new for me. I was part of a group of young, educated, active Syrians from Daraya, a town fifty miles from Damascus. Our group was working on inciting social and even political change in the Darayan community by setting up town-cleaning campaigns and fighting corruption and bribery. We also were raising awareness of current affairs by, for example, organizing a silent rally against the American troops in Iraq in 2003. Of course, all these activities, as useful as they are, are prohibited by the Syrian regime. But my group broke all these taboos, causing a furious reaction from the Mukhabarat, the Syrian regime's brutal security apparatus. That is why most of the group's members, twenty-five of them, were put in prison. Some stayed for two and a half years in the worst conditions imaginable.

The regime wasn't afraid of the activities themselves, they were afraid of the mentality of this Darayan group, as they had never before encountered it during the forty years they ruled Syria. They had never seen such a sincere and pure wish for a change that was engraved in the minds of those young activists. "Do you know why we did this to you?" one high-ranking general in the Mukhabarat asked me on my second day in detention. After having spent a horrible night and being abused in unimaginable ways, I said no. He answered, "Because you were courageous yesterday during our first interrogation session." It turned out that they did not like the way I expressed my opinions and that I was not afraid to show my desire for a change in my country. I was twenty-three years old at the time. That's what they did not like, and that's what made them angry. That's what they have been trying to kill inside us, our pride, spirit, and longing for change and freedom.

When the Arab revolutions started, my friends and I saw the light at the end of the tunnel. In February 2011, those friends, who were more active than I, met with other groups of activists in Syria to coordinate what they might do. All of them were young Syrians looking for change. Each one shared a dream of a free country no longer ruled by the same undemocratic practices that have defined Syria. This was something they had longed for all their lives, and now they had a chance to start achieving it. All these groups wanted to ignite a revolution in Syria, an idea that had seemed impossible a couple of months earlier. Nevertheless, at the time it seemed worth trying, so we began organizing meetings, at which the main subject was how to launch such a revolution. I still remember that meeting (March 2011) when a couple of friends from Douma, the biggest suburb of Damascus, came to Daraya to meet with our group. Knowing that there were other groups throughout Syria just like us, both groups focused on how to gather all the groups in the Damascus suburbs to collaborate and consolidate our efforts. We tried to make sure that when we started a demonstration, it would be so big that the security forces would not be able to arrest or kill all of us. The members of both groups were highly educated Syrians, and we all agreed to

1. Choose a group leader who would be responsible for coordinating the two groups.
2. Choose one person to meet and collaborate with the other groups.
3. Find out whether other groups would join our movement.
4. Create a Facebook page functioning as a "closed group" in order to communicate with one another.

The two groups secretly met several times after that. Avoiding security agents was a big concern for all of us because we were not used to working in secret, but we had to learn how. The final outcome of our meetings with all the groups was the agreement to begin the demonstration on March 18, 2011, after the Friday prayer, from the Grand Mosque in Douma. Some of Daraya group members went to Douma, and some of them started their own demonstration in Daraya, the first ever. As expected, the security forces came with canes and machine guns to both demonstrations and to many other demonstrations around the country. They fired on the crowds and struck some protesters, causing casualties and injuries. But all in all, it was a successful demonstration, despite the cruelty of the attack by the security forces. I personally had the privilege of being there, and I had the great feeling of being able to shout for freedom. Like my fellow Syrians, I had never tasted freedom before. I saw my comrades' eyes glowing with courage and happiness despite the fear of being killed. They knew how brutal this regime was, as they still remembered the Hama massacre (February 2, 1982).

Activists uploaded the first videos of the demonstration to YouTube, and we were able to tell the world that there was a spark of revolution in Syria. We realized, though, that our revolution needed to be organized better. As a result, the groups in each town and city began to emerge and become better organized. These groups were the core of what are now known as the "local coordination committees." I was dazzled by the Syrian talent that emerged after being buried for decades. I had always been proud of my Syrian people, but after the revolution, and for the first time in my life, I felt more than pride.

The following week (Friday, February 25), the plan was to start the demonstrations after Friday prayer, with more people coming out from more than one mosque in Daraya. Each of the activists created his or her own group, and all the groups coordinated to attract more demonstrators. All the participants in the demonstrations gathered in the main street of Daraya and walked to

Shrady Square, which activists now call Freedom Square. We knew that the security forces would come soon to disperse and shoot at us. We knew we were putting our lives in great and immediate danger, but after tasting freedom, we did not care anymore.

I still remember that during one of the demonstrations, while we were gathering at Freedom Square, the security forces came and started shooting at us and using tear gas and guns to break up our peaceful demonstration, creating chaos. The result was three martyrs and around forty wounded. The next day, the whole town mourned the martyrs with sadness and grief. Every time I looked at them, I cried and cried. But this did not break us; instead, it made us more determined to reach our destiny: freedom, and dignity.

In March 2012, I was captured by the Syrian security apparatus, the Mukhabarat, and was taken into detention by the military police, where I faced horrific prison conditions. When they found out that I was postponing my mandatory military service because of my continuing study, they forced me to enlist in the military. After I had spent a week in prison, they gave me a one-day leave and ordered me to go to the Air Defense College in Homs to start my military service. I decided to defect because I did not to be part of such a criminal army. In fact, I considered joining the army as being a despicable service for President al-Assad to kill my own people. So I crossed the border into Jordan. My escape was dangerous, and many people had been shot while crossing the border illegally, but I would rather be shot dead than participate in the killing of my own people.

The revolution kept raising the bar, and the number of hot spots (places where demonstrations were held) noticeably increased around the country, except in some city centers where the security forces had tightened their control. Security forces fought the demonstrators with increasing brutality. The number of martyrs and detainees grew, and no one was able to stop the regime from killing us, nor could anyone in the world stop us from overthrowing this regime and gaining our freedom and dignity. This is our goal, and this is what we are determined to achieve and will achieve, and may God help us in this endeavor.

FROM THE DAMASCUS SPRING TO THE ARAB SPRING: A NONPERSONAL STORY

Radwan Ziadeh

Activist in exile, male, 36, Damascus

When the wave of Arab Spring uprisings brought monumental changes to Tunisia and Egypt, analysts thought Syria would be next. The mass demonstrations that began in Daraa seemed to gather together the country's disparate groups in a call for human dignity. Respect for human rights, equality, and protection from corruption underpinned all the popular revolutions of the Arab Spring, including Syria.

The Syrian revolution had less to do with unemployment than with honor and dignity. An entire people had been brutally oppressed and systematically terrorized by the leaders of their own country, oppression that spanned decades. While the conventional wisdom behind the Syrian leaders' behavior was that dividing and repressing the people would weaken their challenges to the regime, the decades of their abuse actually helped galvanize the revolution. Nonetheless, the legacy of the al-Assad regime still haunts the revolution today.

The Syrian revolution did not spring up overnight. Rather, the resentment of the Syrian people had been building behind the continued humiliation and exclusion by their government. Indeed, there is a history behind the Syrian manifestation of the Arab Spring, and I am honored to have been part of the movement. From the outset, I dedicated myself to documenting human rights violations in Syria. The culture of silence and fear inculcated by the regime had left the Syrian people broken and slow to unite. Indeed, what is the incentive to risk your life in the name of a free Syria when all you know is that the regime is capable of crushing you and your loved ones? The Syrian revolution first broke down the wall of fear that had allowed the regime to remain entrenched, and the Syrian people showed their incredible bravery in the face of a brutal government crackdown. While the numbers in the first Daraa protest represented a new dawn in Syrian political action, the struggle for human rights and dignity already was being waged quietly by a group of dedicated activists.

Before the term "Arab Spring" was coined, I participated in the Damascus spring, a period of increased political discourse, especially calls for reform, that came after the death of Hafez al-Assad in 2000. I founded the Damascus

Center for Human Rights Studies in Syria in 2005, an organization through which I helped document and publicize the government's human rights violations. Through the persistent issuing of reports and statements revealing the al-Assad regime's abuses, I helped chip away at the wall of fear that had kept the Syrian people from rising up to demand their rights.

Of course, my efforts did not go unnoticed by the regime. In typical fashion, the regime sought to terrorize me and my family in order to stop my publicity of the government's corruption. Since 2008, my family—including my mother, brother, sisters, in-laws, nieces, nephews, and so forth—all have been banned from leaving Syria because of my political activities. Because I have stood up for human rights and reform in Syria, my family has been made to live under even greater fear and harassment. Nonetheless, I have remained a leader of the Syrian opposition, relocating my efforts outside the country. Meanwhile, my family has been trapped, and I worry constantly.

My older brother Yassein was arrested in August 2011 because of my activities. Although Yassein is in no way politically involved and is a businessman, security forces arrested him outside the mosque where he had been performing his morning prayers. Yassein had been praying inside Mustafa Mosque in Daraya, southwest of Damascus, while a protest was taking place outside. Security forces moved in to disperse the demonstration, arresting Yassein, who had not been participating but had taken refuge during the crackdown.

After his arrest, my brother was taken to the headquarters of the Syrian Air Force Security. The Air Force Security is notorious among activists for its brutal torture of dissidents, and it was responsible for the deplorable mutilation and murder of thirteen-year-old Hamza al-Khateeb. The security forces, intelligence apparatus, and regime at large have no qualms about torturing and killing political detainees en masse; furthermore, the terror did not stop with the massacres. Just as my brother Yassein was arrested because of my speaking out against the regime's abuses, the security forces also threatened al-Khateeb's parents, saying, "Much of what has happened is because of what your son has done. You know what will happen if we find out that you have spoken to the media."

My family and I experienced similar harassment as the regime tried to exact retribution for my exposures of its human rights abuses. But retribution is not the only goal of this harassment; the main purpose is to perpetuate the culture of fear that plagues an un-free Syria, depriving Syrians of their human rights of freedom of expression and conscience. There is no respect for human rights in Syria, where, as in the rest of the world, a violation of one person's rights is an affront to human dignity in general. The regime has targeted those determined to make the world aware of Bashar al-Assad's crimes and has sought to oppress them by means of torture, murder, and fear. Consequently, after repeatedly receiving threats, in 2007 I left my country. Since I have been living in exile—the pains of which are not difficult to imagine—my family in Syria has received the brunt of the punishment for my activities. Because of my research and human rights documentation, my brother Yassein has been held incommunicado since his arrest in 2011, a man innocent of any crime.

This perpetual wall of fear was broken at the outset of the Syrian revolution in 2011, and many of us have been working to build momentum toward ending the fear, encouraging Syrians to speak out for their rights. But the regime is relentless and is aware that its very existence depends on terrorizing its population into silence. Although the wall of fear has been brought down, the regime is scrambling to rebuild it, and so the legacy of terror continues to plague the Syrian revolution.

The Assad regime has systematically created or deepened the divisions in Syria politically, economically, and socially in order to maintain a divided people incapable of rising up together against his unjust rule. Since the outset of the revolution, I have poured my energy into building a strong Syrian opposition. The Syrian National Council (SNC) has greatly evolved since its foundation and has formulated a sophisticated strategy to guide Syria through a post-Assad transition to democracy. Most significantly, the SNC has worked to overcome the imaginary divisions entrenched by the regime, and the SNC leadership and general membership now include representatives of every political, religious, and ethnic group in Syrian society. Furthermore, it has emphasized transitional justice and respect for human rights, especially accounting for possible attempts to seek retribution against the Alawite community.[7]

While the SNC has been remarkable in its growth and improvement in such a short time and under such daunting conditions, the international community has not responded in kind. Bashar al-Assad has mounted a long, relentless, brutal campaign to restore the wall of fear, slaughtering civilians en masse by shelling neighborhoods like Bab Amr and even carrying out mass executions. The world may never know the true extent of al-Assad's brutal crackdown, as he has not limited himself to terrorizing only Syrian defenders of human rights. Instead, he has likely ordered the assassination of foreign journalists seeking simply to document the crisis for the world to see.

We, the Syrian people, yearn wholeheartedly for a future free Syria, and we hope this revolution will be the turning point in a long history of oppression and fear, toward a future that guarantees human rights for all Syrians. But we are in dire need of action in solidarity from the international community. Now that the Syrian people have finally been successful in breaching the fear barrier, they have been left alone. The current international stalemate is not only frustrating; it is tragic. Every day that international inaction allows the Assad regime to rebuild its wall of fear is another day on which innocent civilians are killed, their families terrorized, and their human dignity defiled. The Syrian revolution holds the key to reform toward a free Syria, in which human rights are championed and the government fulfills its social contract with all its peoples. The Syrian revolution is not political. It is existential. It is about human dignity, justice, and respect—values that when threatened anywhere insult humanity everywhere.

This story is not just my story. It is the story of every Syrian who has lived in terror, who has lost a loved one to an inhumane regime, who feels abandoned as the world watches a people's destruction. Moreover, this is the human story, and history has shown us that justice and humanity, despite the efforts of their enemies along the way, eventually prevail.[8]

BEFORE AND AFTER THE ARAB SPRING: KURDISH STRIFE FOR FREEDOM

Walat Khabat

Kurdish activist and businessman, male, 35, Aleppo

I was a high school student when I became a member of the Kurdish Democratic Party in Syria (PDK-S) in 1994. I chose PDK-S for all that I had learned and seen of the party's long history of struggle and fight to achieve the following:

1. Kurdish political, cultural and societal rights.
2. Overall democracy in Syria.
3. Stronger bonds of brotherhood between Kurds and their fellow Arabs.
4. Women's rights in Syria.
5. The abolishment of all racial discrimination against Kurds in Syria.

The PDK-S's struggle for these objectives has always been peaceful, as we believe in the spirit of democracy and that any political, cultural or societal gain can be obtained only through democracy. The Syrian regime, however, being fascist and totalitarian in a country led by the Ba'th Party, has put all power in the hands of the president. This regime relies strongly on persecuting people, stealing their freedom, denying their most basic rights, and turning them into a lifeless crowd or mob that only does what it is told.

It is tragic that the Kurds are persecuted and suppressed in Syria. The regime took everything from us, even the right to speak our native tongue—the language of our fathers and grandfathers, the language that ties us to our cultural heritage. Our language and culture are deeply ingrained in history, and they define our identity as a nation. We were banned from practicing our cultural traditions and prohibited from celebrating our national and cultural festival days. To save our Kurdish identity, we spoke our language and celebrated our national and cultural festival days in secret. And if the regime discovered us engaging in any of these activities, we would be imprisoned and tortured, and even the organizers of such events were sometimes killed. This depressing situation motivated me to become an active member of the PDK-S advocating the Kurdish language, culture, and rights. My work was recognized by my other party members, and their votes made me a leader of a district where I held two meetings each month for the party members. One was mainly political and intended to strengthen the ties among party members, and the other was educational and cultural, at which the Kurdish language was taught and different literary and artistic talents were recognized and nourished.

I was seventeen when I encountered the regime's brutality firsthand. My membership in the PDK-S party and my political views, which were reported by some of my classmates who were members of the Ba'th Party, brought about my arrest by the intelligence forces. I was arrested and interrogated in a very inhumane, terrifying, painful, and degrading way. I was tortured and asked to become a reporter for the regime and to spy on my classmates and other members of PDK-S. My refusal made them detain me for twenty long and painful days. At the end, probably after they had given up and realized they could not recruit me, I was released after I signed a document stating that I would avoid political and cultural activities. But the pressure at school increased and, becoming unbearable, forced me to drop out. I then worked with my father until I opened an office for business administration while getting more and more involved with PDK-S.

The politics of the Middle East, an area infested with dictatorships, received its first and biggest blow with the demise of Saddam Hussein's regime in Iraq. As a Syrian Kurd, this event boosted my hopes for the long awaited freedom and democracy in Syria. The PDK-S increased its efforts by expanding its membership base and its activities. The goal was to make our people ready for the freedom ahead of us. All our activities were peaceful yet were carried out in complete secrecy. Even so, members of the PDK-S and the other Kurdish parties were still being arrested. Of course, the Syrian regime never thought that the day would come when our struggle, along with the struggle of the rest of the Syrian community and parties, would become as strong as it is now.

On March 12, 2004, the Kurds revolted against the Syrian regime's discriminatory, racial, and persecutory practices. Then, after a soccer match, security agents intentionally shot at Kurdish fans who had come to the stadium to cheer for their local team. The Syrian security and intelligence forces planned this incident to engender animosity between Kurds and Arabs in the area. The Kurds rebelled all over Syria, from Qamishli in the northeast to Afrin in the northwest. The Syrian intelligence and security forces spared no effort in suppressing the protesters and did not hesitate to kill as many as it took to undermine the Kurdish call for equality and their political and cultural rights. Many Kurdish protesters were killed and more were arrested.

I attended the funeral of a Kurdish martyr who had been killed in one of the protests. The funeral turned into a demonstration that condemned the regime's brutal practices. The security forces intervened quickly, shooting at the protesters and arresting them. I was among those arrested. As expected, we endured unbearable torture and humiliation, which concluded with each of us signing a document stating that we would not participate in any protest or antigovernment activities once we were set free. In fact, if it had not been for the massive pressure coming from different public and political figures, we would have stayed in captivity for a long time. After all that I had witnessed during my arrest, I became more and more determined to do everything it would take to achieve freedom and democracy for the Kurds and Syrians. The 2004 uprising and protests thus became a day that Kurds celebrate every year.

The Kurds and their fellow Syrians had to wait seven more years before the advent of the Arab Spring that was launched by a desperate street vendor who set himself on fire. The spark soon spread like wildfire and, soon after, took down the Egyptian regime and Libya's dictator. Now it was Syria's turn to taste freedom. March 15, 2011, signified the onset of the Syrian revolution, when some elementary school students drew on the walls of their schools what they had seen and heard on television about the Tunisian, Egyptian, and Libyan revolutions, simple phrases like "People want to topple the regime." The ruthless security and intelligence forces arrested and inflicted severe torture on them. The children were later returned to their homes with signs of torture and their fingernails pulled out. The security forces wanted to make an example of them. But on the contrary, what those little heroes did broke the fear that the regime had for decades worked on building and strengthening inside every Syrian. Daraa is where all this started, and the revolution gained momentum and soon was in almost every city but Aleppo and Damascus, where the regime's iron fist was tightening its grasp on almost every district, street, alley, and block.

At this point, I made a short visit to the United Stated and witnessed all the freedom, democracy, and plentiful opportunities available for all people to express themselves, their beliefs, and their political views. I wished the same were true in my country. Via the Internet, I kept a close eye on the revolution's development. What I read and saw about the revolution and its objectives made me decide to go home and work side by side with the protesters and members of the PDK-S, putting all the power that my position in the party gave me to support the revolution. The PDK-S declared its support of the peaceful revolution in Syria against the regime and began meeting, cooperating, and strengthening its ties with other parties that shared our position. These efforts culminated with the formulation of the Kurdish National Strife Charter/Agreement in Syria, which consists of the following parties:

1. PDKS
2. The Union of the Kurdish Nation in Syria
3. The Kurdish Democratic Party in Syria
4. Yakity
5. The Kurdish Accordance
6. The Kurdish Future Movement in Syria
7. The Kurdish Reformation Party

These parties declared their support for the revolution and youth movement, in which youth groups were formed and prepared for the noble tasks ahead, through education, sharpened skills, and encouragement to stay the course, as freedom and democracy are closer than ever before. The youth groups consisted of both party and nonparty members. My role was to form new revolutionary groups, organize them, and coordinate the groups of which I was in charge with those in other districts in Aleppo. I also advocated the teachings and objectives of the revolution. All this had to be done through secret communication channels. The revolution grew in the various Syrian cities. But because the regime views Aleppo as its financial backbone, more security forces were pumped into the city, which made it harder for the revolution to grow and gain momentum as it had in other cities. Nevertheless, we were determined to push harder and harder to increase the scale and number of peaceful protests and thus win our city and eventually our freedom from the security and intelligence forces and Assad's thugs.

During August 2011, which also was the month of Ramadan, we planned a protest against the regime in my district, al-Ashrafiya, and we decided on a time and location. But the difference in numbers between us and Assad's thugs prevented us from protesting, so we postponed it. I continued working secretly to gather more people, until Thursday, October 9, the day on which the Syrian Kurdish opposition figure Mishaal al-Tammo was killed by the regime in Qamishli. He was the head of the Kurdish Future Movement Party, a member of the National Syrian Council, and an ally of the Kurdish National Charter/Agreement in Syria. His murder confirmed that the regime had declared war against the Kurdish movement and that we all were possible targets. In retaliation for the cowardly act of murdering Mr. Tammo, we decided to protest on the following Saturday, which we named after him. Although we knew when we protested that we faced arrest or death, that did not stop us from organizing a demonstration in al-Ashrafiya, capturing it on video, and posting it on the Internet. The protest lasted for fifteen minutes, after which we had to flee when the security forces attacked us with knives, swords, and firearms. Unfortunately, a few fellow protesters were captured.

Despite the protest's relatively short duration, we were able to deliver the message to the world that Aleppo was a volcano about to erupt. The protest also drew the regime's attention to the fact that our district was becoming a hot spot. I and the groups I was in charge of participated in a number of other protests in different parts of the city (especially in the Salah al-Deen district, Sayf al-Dawleh, and al-Shaykh Maksoud. Meanwhile, the Kurdish National Charter/Agreement in Syria, the youth and patriotic groups, independent nationalists, and Syrian and Kurdish figures succeeded in forming the Union of Democratic Parties in Syria (also known as Mishaal Tammo's Center). Our position was expressed through a number of views and objectives that also were adopted by these aforementioned parties.

The regime retaliated against the formulation of the new union by increasing the brutality of its crackdown and violent attacks on protests and also by tightening its grip on our life in Aleppo. Our mobility became harder, as did life in general, as more reporters/spies and intelligence forces spread out all over the city. They targeted protest organizers and youth groups, and I knew they were going to find me soon. I consulted with the party leaders, and they recommended that I hide or leave to save my life. In the little time I had left, I managed to get my wife and only child a visa to the United States.

STATE SECURITY AND MY COUNTRY

Hasan Khalil

Refugee, male, 33, Deir al-Zour

It was a winter night when I sat in a café with four friends and heard on the news that Zine el-Abidine Ben Ali, president of Tunisia, had fled to Saudi Arabia on January 14, 2011. It was a strange piece of news! We looked at one another, and all of us were thinking the same thing: "Could it happen in Syria?" But nobody dared to say it out loud. We continued late into the night, and then everybody went home. After a few months, three of us were protesting and could not believe it was really us!

Less than two weeks later, on January 25, the Egyptian revolution started. I was watching television and could not believe the huge numbers of people who were protesting in the streets, with the radiance of bravery on their faces. "Could it happen in Syria?" I thought again. On February 11, Hosni Mubarak delivered his final speech during the eighteen-day revolution, before his newly appointed vice president, Omar Suleiman, announced that the Egyptian president had decided to step down. At that moment, a feeling of relief came over me as I realized that the era of dictators was coming to an end. I smelled the pleasant scent of freedom, but in Egypt, not in Syria.

The revolution in Syria finally began in mid-March 2011, sweeping the country and the capital city of Damascus, but only after a strong start in Daraa. The first demonstration was held in my city, Deir al-Zour, on the first Friday of April, with a few thousand people who then protested each Friday. On Friday, April 22, "Friday the Great," the protesters went to the main square in the city, which is now called Freedom Square, and destroyed the statue of Basel, the son of the former dictator Hafez al-Assad. Around five thousand people participated in this protest before the security intelligence members and the *shabiha*, the regime's special forces and thugs, came and dispersed them. I participated in this protest and in many others on subsequent Fridays. Our numbers started growing, reaching more than 200,000.

One particularly important Friday I will never forget was on June 17, which was called "Saleh al-Ali Friday." Saleh al-Ali (1884–1950) was a prominent Syrian revolutionist and an Alawite notable who opposed the French colonization of Syria in the early twentieth century. We went out into the streets of Deir al-Zour after the Friday prayer. The number of protesters was growing, and by the time we reached Freedom Square, it was like a festival, with protesters' voices reaching the sky. We demanded that the regime step down, and our chants were loud and clear enough to deliver this message of freedom. There was a celebratory and historic atmosphere, and we felt the pleasure of freedom, especially because the thugs, *shabiha*, and intelligence forces were absent. We spent around three hours in the square, and even women and children participated.

As we reached the main street, marching toward the sports stadium, some people followed the protesters, handing out bottles of water and juice. I saw one person, who was angry at the crowds and their chants, throw bags of rubbish on the protesters' heads! They shouted back at him and continued on their way. But the man came back and threw big stones from his house on the third floor of the building, hurting some protesters and cars passing by. The protesters got angry and wanted to go up and fight with the regime supporter, but the protest coordinators prevented them, saying that we had to remain peaceful, even if we got hurt. We passed the al-Hajjanah military unit's headquarters. On one of its doors were photos of the former dictator Hafez al-Assad and his son Bashar.

When one of the protesters went up to the door and tried to take off the photos, bullets showered the place like rain! We ran and tried to hide in the side streets. I could not identify the source of the attack. It was like a war, and a group of women protesters got scared and hid in a small street among the trees. Apparently, the soldiers inside the military unit had started to fire at us, but they were shooting mainly into the sky. With the bullets spraying in all directions, some of the protesters were injured. The shooting lasted for about an hour and a half, and I barely managed to get home, using side streets. After about forty-five minutes, I passed al-Nour hospital and saw a group of young men carrying an injured person there. While I waited outside for a few minutes, a young man came out shouting: "Allah akbar [great]. He is a martyr of freedom!" I got close to the car, where I saw a man lying with blood on his head. I realized that he was the protester who tried to take off the photo of the dictator! The people gathered around the hospital and began shouting against the president and the Ba'th Party. An atmosphere of anger and anguish came over us, and one of the protesters shouted, "Until when should we wait? Until when? We have suffered enough from this regime!"

I went back home and heard the news that another three martyrs had fallen on that bloody Friday. My family was scared to death when I joined that protest, and they were relieved when they finally saw me entering the house. My sister shouted at me and said that my mother fainted when she heard the shooting around the city. I was lucky enough to get home safely after that protest. I was thinking of all those protesters and the martyrs, wondering how many people would die before we got our highly priced freedom. I thought about the black days when we suffered greatly from the regime and its intelligence forces, the evil forces that shaped our lives with misery, poverty, and fear.

I remembered how they forced us to join the Ba'th Party during secondary school. We did not have a choice: We either became members or were investigated by the security and intelligence forces about our political views. They would prevent those who did not join the party from exercising their human rights and the opportunity to find employment. Others were punished and put in prison.

For several years, I worked outside the country and frequently traveled to Europe and other Arab countries on business. A few months before the revolution, I had to face the regime's thuggish security forces without having done anything against the regime. One of the intelligence members came to my house around nine o'clock in the evening. He said that I had to go to the intelligence center the next day for an investigation. My family and I were shocked, and some of my family tried to discourage me from going, but I did not have a choice, as they would have caught me any place I went. Luckily, I made phone calls to some influential persons who know people in the government and the intelligence center, and they supported me and told me not to worry, that it would be only a routine investigation.

I could not sleep that night, and the following day I said good-bye to my family as if I were going to my death. I could hardly hide my tension and fears, but I nevertheless tried to calm down my mother and family. I reached the intelligence center around nine o'clock in the morning. The officer at the door told me to leave everything with him: keys, watch, glasses, and mobile, which was switched off. He said I had to wait for the investigator, and then he put me in a cell! When I went in, I said to myself, "This is the end." The underground cell was twenty-two-by thirty-two square feet, and the bathroom was inside. It was dirty enough to make you scared to sit on the floor, which was full of dirt and dead cockroaches. I sat down on a piece of paper and started counting the minutes, which were like years. One hour, two hours, passed and still the investigator did not come. Suddenly, a big man opened the small iron window attached to the door and gave me a spiteful look. This man was the one responsible for torturing people. I got up and walked slowly toward him and asked him: "May I make a phone call?" Then he looked at me with a dirty smile and said, "Do you think you are at the Sheraton?!"

Another few hours passed, and I wondered why I had come back to my country, Syria. It is a strange feeling when you blame yourself for coming home. My work and business were outside Syria, but I still loved my country, family, and the place where I was born. That is why I always felt the need to come back. Around one in the afternoon, the investigator came and the big man took me from my cell to the investigation room. I could not reveal to the investigator that I was against the regime because that would be the end of me. He started asking me about my life, work, travels, relatives, and so on. I stood in a small spot, and on the walls I could see the tools of torture spread all around the room. It was obvious that they did not have anything against me. They were just expecting that I would collapse and ask forgiveness for doing something against them, which they did not know. This is a mind game they play with many other people.

After an hour of investigation they returned me to the cell, telling me that they would check my name with all the intelligence centers to see if I had committed any crimes or violations. I stayed calm and did not show that I was nervous or tense. After a few hours, they released me. Later, I found out that the people I had called had connections in the intelligence center and that they intervened to ensure my release. Back at home, my family was happy that I had not been hurt and received me like a soldier returning from war.

I endured many other difficulties and pain at other intelligence centers, which I cannot describe here, for security reasons. The questions I always ask myself are, Will the revolution succeed under these circumstances, after more than a year of killing and destruction? While the world and the United Nations keep silent in the face of the Syrian regime's tyranny and arrogance, is it still possible? History has proved that no tyrant can resist forever the will of the people and the winds of change. We have nothing to do but to continue our revolution. We must keep praying for success even if the entire world has closed its eyes to the continuing crimes of our tyrannical regime.

NOTES

1. Antara ibn Shaddad is a semi-epical character in Arabic folklore symbolizing bravery and heroism.

2. Sara Mu'ayyid al-'Azm was the wife of the Syrian politician 'Abd al-Rahman Shahbandar (1879–1940) and a former minister of foreign affairs (May–July 1920). She played a social and cultural role in Damascus during 1930s. It is widely believed that she was the first Syrian Muslim woman to take off her veil in public.

3. On July 13, a number of Syrian intellectuals organized a demonstration to reject the security solution adopted by the authorities in their crackdown of large-scale protests. The demonstration took place in the neighborhood of Midan in

the center of Damascus. These protests were violently suppressed, and dozens of Syrian intellectuals were arrested.

4. 'Adnan al-'Arrour is a Syrian cleric exiled in Saudi Arabia. He gives advice on his television shows to the Syrian people, providing them with moral and religious support for the revolution. Not many activists in Syria agree with his confrontational way of supporting their cause, which could be perceived as sectarian.

5. Nawaf al-Bashir is a Syrian dissident and tribal chief from Deir al-Zour. He was kidnapped by the security forces and spent a few months in prison before leaving Syria for Turkey at the end of 2011.

6. Bisher Said promotes political reform and democracy in Syria by nonviolent means. He is the son of the prominent Muslim intellectual and nonviolent activist Jawdat Said. Born in 1931 in the Syrian town Bir Ajam, his father was among the Syrian reform-oriented figures who signed the Damascus Spring Declaration in 2005.

7. Alawites make up about 10 percent of the Syrian population. The president and top officials in the regime belong to this community.

8. Professor Radwan Ziadeh is a leading Syrian opposition activist. He now is a senior fellow at the U.S Institute of Peace in Washington, DC, and a fellow at the Institute for Social Policy and Understanding (ISPU) in Washington, DC.

BIBLIOGRAPHY

Ajami, Fouad. *The Arab Predicament: Arab Political Thought and Practice Since 1967.* Cambridge: Cambridge University Press, 1981.

Anderson, Benedict. *Imagined Communities: Reflections on the Origin and Spread of Nationalism.* London: Verso, 1991.

Barakat, Halim Isber. *The Arab World: Society, Culture, and State.* Berkeley: University of California Press, 1993.

Black, Ian. Introduction to *The Arab Spring: Rebellion, Revolution, and a New World Order,* by Toby Manhire. London: Guardian Books, 2012.

Borger, Julian. "Tunisian President Vows to Punish Rioters After Worst Unrest in a Decade." *Guardian,* December 29, 2010. Available at http://www.guardian.co.uk /world/2010/dec/29/tunisian-president-vows-punish-rioters (accessed February 28, 2012).

Ghonim, Wael. *Revolution 2.0: A Memoir.* Boston: Houghton Mifflin Harcourt, 2012.

International Labour Office. "Youth Unemployment in the Arab World." April 5, 2011. Available at http://www.ilo.org/global/about-the-ilo/press-and-media-centre /insight/WCMS_154078/lang--en/index.htm (accessed April 23, 2012).

Jamal, Amaney A., and Mark A. Tessler. "Attitudes in the Arab World." *Journal of Democracy* 19, no. 1 (2008): 97–110.

Kassab, Elizabeth Suzanne. *Contemporary Arab Thought: Cultural Critique in Comparative Perspective*. New York: Columbia University Press, 2009.

Lewis, Bernard. *Islam and the West*. New York: Oxford University Press, 1993.

Naguib, Nefissa. "Basic Ethnography at the Barricades." *International Journal of Middle East Studies* 43, no. 3 (2011): 383.

Sadiki, Larbi. *Rethinking Arab Democratization: Elections Without Democracy*. Oxford: Oxford University Press, 2009.

Said, Edward. *Orientalism*. New York: Vintage Books, 1979.

Saqqar, Wajih al-. "The Demands of Revolutionaries Unanswered." *Al-Ahram*, January 25, 2012.

Selim, Samah. "Literature and Revolution." *International Journal of Middle East Studies* 43, no. 3 (2011): 385–86.

Shakry, Omnia, el-. "Imagining 'the Political' Otherwise." *International Journal of Middle East Studies* 43, no. 3 (2011): 384–85.

Tignor, Robert L. "Can a New Generation Bring About Regime Change?" *International Journal of Middle East Studies* 43, no. 3 (2011): 384.

CPSIA information can be obtained
at www.ICGtesting.com
Printed in the USA
LVHW041715290820
664471LV00008B/1007

9 780231 163194